Attention-Deficit/ Hyperactivity Disorder

A Clinical Guide to
Diagnosis and Treatment for
Health and Mental Health Professionals,
Second Edition

Larry B. Silver, M.D.
Clinical Professor of Psychiatry
Georgetown University School of Medicine
Washington, DC

Washington, DC
London, England

Copyright © 1999 American Psychiatric Press, Inc.
ALL RIGHTS RESERVED
Manufactured in the United States of America on acid-free paper
02 01 00 99   4 3 2 1
Second Edition

American Psychiatric Press, Inc.
1400 K Street, N.W., Washington, DC   20005
www.appi.org

Library of Congress Cataloging-in-Publication Data
Silver, Larry B.
    Attention-deficit hyperactivity disorder : a clinical guide to
diagnosis and treatment for health and mental health professionals /
by Larry B. Silver. — 2nd ed.
        p.   cm.
    Includes bibliographical references and index.
    ISBN 0-88048-940-5
    1. Attention-deficit hyperactivity disorder—Diagnosis.
    2. Attention-deficit hyperactivity disorder—Treatment.   I. Title.
        [DNLM: 1. Attention Deficit Disorder with Hyperactivity—
diagnosis.   2. Attention Deficit Disorder with Hyperactivity—
therapy.   WS 350.8.A8S587a 1999]
RJ506.H9S545   1999
616.85'89—dc21
DNLM/DLC
for Library of Congress   98-27809
                                                              CIP

British Library Cataloguing in Publication Data
A CIP record is available from the British Library.

Contents

Part 6 **Conclusions**

About the Author

Larry B. Silver, M.D., a child and adolescent psychiatrist, is in private practice in the Washington, DC, area. He is Clinical Professor of Psychiatry at Georgetown University School of Medicine. Prior to his current activities, he was the Acting Director and Deputy Director of the National Institute of Mental Health. Before that, he was Professor of Psychiatry, Professor of Pediatrics, and Chief of Child and Adolescent Psychiatry at the Robert Wood Johnson School of Medicine.

Part 1

Introduction and Overview

Chapter 1

Introduction: Attention-Deficit/ Hyperactivity Disorder

With the major breakthroughs in medicine, a new morbidity pattern—emotional, behavioral, and academic problems—is found in individuals seen by health professionals. Mental health professionals have always been concerned with these areas of difficulty; however, the number of children and adolescents referred to these professionals for these reasons has increased. As I discuss later in this chapter, 3%–6% of school-aged children have attention-deficit/hyperactivity disorder (ADHD). This figure might apply to children seen by pediatricians and other family physicians, but for mental health professionals who see children and adolescents, 30%–50% of the patients they examine might be individuals referred to them for possible ADHD. Therefore, understanding the diagnosis and treatment of ADHD is essential.

School is the lifework of children and adolescents. Thus, anything that interferes with mastery and success in school will cause stress for the student and for his or her family. ADHD can be one reason for academic and school difficulties. ADHD can also lead to emotional or behavior problems, difficulty with peer relationships, and family stress. Unrecognized and untreated, this disorder will interfere greatly with all aspects of the individual's life.

The presenting problems often are emotional or behavioral difficulties at school, with peers, and in the family. These difficulties must be assessed and treated, but in the process, possible causes should be sought. If the presenting problems are secondary to ADHD, treatment interventions might not be successful until the ADHD is addressed. In Chapter 2, I discuss a continuum of neurologically based disorders believed to be comorbid with ADHD. The clinician must consider each of these disorders and must clarify whether the emotional or behavior problems are primary or secondary to ADHD or to another neurologically based disorder. "Blowing away the smoke" without "putting out the fire" will not provide adequate treatment for these disorders.

| Is ADHD the "Disease of the 1990s"?

Discussions of ADHD seem to be everywhere. We read about it in newspapers and magazines. We hear about it on television. Parents and teachers frequently suggest that a child has ADHD. As a professional, you might feel that the number of individuals referred to you for possible ADHD, and the number of individuals you diagnose as having this disorder, have multiplied significantly in the past 10 years. Is there an epidemic? Is ADHD the "disease of the 1990s"?

No. ADHD has been in the medical literature for more than 100 years. It has been part of the official classification system since 1968. I gave my first patient medication for this disorder in 1965. What has changed is the effort expended to educate parents and teachers. What is new is an increased awareness of ADHD.

In the mid-1980s, a major effort was made to educate parents and classroom teachers about ADHD. The concern of parents was that too many children with ADHD were not being identified properly and that too many physicians were unaware of this possible diagnosis. Parent organizations, such as Children and Adults With Attention Deficit Disorder (CHADD), formed throughout the United States. An increasing number of books on ADHD were written for the general public. The electronic and print media were encouraged to present specials on ADHD. As a result, parents and classroom teachers became more aware of the disorder, they began to recognize the behaviors suggestive of ADHD, and they began to seek help.

The increase in the number of children and adolescents given the diagnosis of ADHD is a direct result of this educational effort and the new level of awareness within schools, among parents, and among health and mental health professionals. Similarly, the impact of the media and of many popular books has led to an increasing number of adults being given the diagnosis of ADHD. Until the mid-1980s, we thought that children with ADHD outgrew this disorder by puberty. This is not true. As I discuss later in this chapter, ADHD continues into adulthood in up to 50% of those individuals who have it earlier in life.

Are we overdiagnosing ADHD? Are we overtreating it? I discuss these questions later in this chapter.

One of the earliest references to what would now be called ADHD was a nursery rhyme written in 1863 by Heinrich Hoffmann. It is about a boy who was restless, fidgety, hyperactive, and a behavior problem to his family:

"Phil, stop acting like a worm,
The table is no place to squirm."
Thus speaks the father to his son,
severely says it, not in fun.
Mother frowns and looks around
although she doesn't make a sound.
But, Phillip will not take advise,
he'll have his way at any price.

He turns,
and churns,
he wiggles
and jiggles
Here and there on the chair,
"Phil, these twists I cannot bear."

In Chapter 3, I review the history of the diagnostic labels used in the United States to describe these children and adults. Although the name for the problem has changed over time, the descriptions have remained consistent. These individuals show one or more of three sets of behaviors: hyperactivity, inattention/distractibility, and/or impulsivity. I explain each of these terms in detail in Chapter 5.

Several neurologically based disorders are frequently found in individuals who have ADHD. Learning disabilities are the most common disorders. Between 30% and 40% of children or adolescents with ADHD also have a learning disability. Other related difficulties include anxiety disorders, depression, anger regulation problems, obsessive-compulsive disorder, and tic disorders. I discuss these relationships in Chapter 2. These disorders are covered in greater detail in Chapter 8.

| What Is the Prevalence of ADHD?

Because of the changing criteria for establishing the diagnosis of ADHD and the absence of a formal blood, urine, brain imaging, or other test to establish the diagnosis, no firm data are available on the disorder's prevalence. Studies on the prevalence of ADHD have been conducted in various populations. The patient sample used is critical because of variations in different settings. Within a general pediatric practice setting, at least 10% of behavior problems seen are the result of ADHD. Within the practice setting of child and adolescent psychiatrists, up to 50% of children seen with behavior problems have ADHD.

Studies conducted in the United States and in other countries, especially in New Zealand and Germany, suggest that 3%–6% of the school-aged population has ADHD. This statistic is the one most accepted at this time. These studies were conducted across a geographically, racially, and socioeconomically diverse population.

Surveys show that ADHD is more common among boys. In clinic-referred samples of patients, the ratio of boys to girls with ADHD has been reported to be from 2:1 to 10:1. However, among nonreferred children (i.e., from community surveys rather than clinical surveys), the ratio is closer to 3:1. The higher ratio of boys to girls seen in clinical surveys probably reflects referral bias. Boys are more likely than girls to express their frustration by being aggressive or antisocial. These behaviors are the most disruptive and, thus, result in a referral for clinical services.

Previous data suggest that girls are underidentified. Despite having attentional problems similar to those of boys with ADHD, girls with ADHD are less intrusive, and they show fewer aggressive symptoms; thus, they are less likely to come to the attention of their teachers or other professionals. The group of students most often not recognized, referred, or given the diagnosis of ADHD may be girls who are only distractible.

Life History of Individuals With ADHD

Between 40% and 50% of children with ADHD seem to have fewer problems than do others, or their ADHD behaviors disappear after puberty. In these children, maturation of the frontal cortex may either directly correct the ADHD or enable the children to compensate better for the problems. Although no firm data exist, 50% of adolescents will continue to have ADHD into adulthood.

Why Is ADHD So Controversial?

Is there controversy? Within the professional and research communities, little controversy appears to exist. Within the public press, however, there appears to be much controversy. Within the scientific community, various aspects of ADHD have generated controversy over the past 30 or more years. One area of debate relates to establishing the diagnosis. No hard, biological measures are available to make the diagnosis. We cannot use laboratory or radiological studies to confirm a diagnosis. The diagnosis, like that of other mental disorders, involves obtaining a history and conducting behavioral assessments. Debate over what criteria would lead to the diagnosis of ADHD has resulted in general agreement at this time. I discuss these diagnostic criteria in Chapter 6.

Current debate over ADHD within the research and medical communities has been minimal and mostly concerned with subtle details in the diagnostic process and the treatment program. By contrast, highly inflammatory public relations campaigns and pitched legal battles have been waged, particularly by groups, such as the Church of Scientology, that seek to label as a myth the whole idea of ADHD as an illness and to brand the use of stimulants in children as a form of mind control. These efforts are seen as sensational by the news media and have been reported widely in both the electronic and the print media, creating anxiety and confusion among the general public.

Legitimate concerns raised by scientific studies must be separated from abstract, distorted, or incorrect information from other sources. The source of controversial statements should be noted. For example, were the statements made in a scientific article, in the newspaper, or on a television show? Was the information on the Internet? Remember that anyone can have a Web page and can put anything he or she wants on this page, without the material being edited or reviewed.

Are We Overdiagnosing ADHD?

Studies conducted by the American Medical Association and by the Centers for Disease Control and Prevention show that we are not overdiagnosing ADHD. Some parents might have a "war story" about a physician who diagnoses ADHD in every patient he or she sees, but national surveys do not support this view.

More individuals are given the diagnosis of ADHD today than in the past, but there are several reasons for this increase. First, as noted earlier, a major effort was started about 15 years ago to educate parents and teachers. Thus, more children and adolescents were referred for evaluation. Second, more professionals learned how to diagnose ADHD accurately, by using established criteria. Third, we now know that ADHD can continue into adulthood, and more adults are now being given the diagnosis of ADHD.

Are We Overprescribing Ritalin?

Despite the information sometimes reported by the news media, formal studies show that we are not overprescribing methylphenidate (Ritalin). More individuals of all ages are being given the diagnosis of ADHD.

Also, children who take Ritalin are more likely to continue to use this medication over a longer period of their lifetime than used to be the case. A new population is now using Ritalin—adults with ADHD. In addition, Ritalin has become the treatment of choice for narcolepsy.

A related question might be, Is there an increase in the misuse or abuse of Ritalin among adolescents? The Drug Enforcement Administration has published reports of thefts of Ritalin, street sales, drug rings, illegal importation from outside of the United States, and illegal sales by health professionals. However, reports of Ritalin abuse by patients with ADHD or their family members rarely have been reported. According to a recent review by the American Medical Association (Goldman et al. 1998), little evidence suggests that Ritalin abuse or diversion is a major problem, particularly among individuals with ADHD.

Important Clinical Concepts Relating to ADHD

In this book, I stress several clinical concepts I believe are important when working with an individual who has ADHD.

- ADHD is a *life disability*. Hyperactivity, distractibility, and/or impulsivity are not just school problems. They are life problems. These behaviors interfere with the student's availability for classroom learning and with his or her use of proper behaviors. They also interfere with family life, peer interactions, and successful participation in sports and other activities. The concept of ADHD being a life disability is important when treatment is considered. If the clinician treats the ADHD during school hours and months only, the individual might do well in school but continue to have behavior problems at home and with friends. Summers may be a disaster.
- ADHD is a *lifetime disability* for about half of the children with this disorder. Thus, treatment interventions must be considered for each phase of the individual's life.
- As I discuss in Chapter 4, a familial pattern exists. For about 50% of individuals with this disorder, other family members will have the same disorder. Parents or another sibling might have ADHD. If so, these family members also will need help.

- The possibility that a child or adolescent with ADHD might have a learning disability is so high (30%–40%) that this disability must be considered whenever ADHD is diagnosed. Often, the underlying learning problems are noticed after ADHD is treated. ADHD and learning disabilities are related disorders, but they are not the same disorders. A learning disability affects the student's ability to process and use information, thus interfering with his or her *ability to learn.* ADHD results in behaviors that make it difficult for the student to sit, attend, or reflect, thus interfering with the student's *availability to learn.*
- ADHD is a complex problem. Clinicians must be aware of the individual in his or her total world when treatment is planned and carried out. Any related neurologically based disorders or secondary emotional or family problems must be treated. I discuss these treatment aspects in Chapter 12.

Reference

Goldman LS, Genel M, Bezman RJ, et al: Diagnosis and treatment of attention-deficit/hyperactivity disorder in children and adolescents. JAMA 279:1100–1107, 1998

Chapter 2

The Continuum of Neurologically Based Disorders

Attention-deficit/hyperactivity disorder (ADHD) is a neurologically based disorder. As I explain later in this book (see Chapter 4), ADHD is a result of a neurochemical deficiency in specific areas of the brain. Other neurologically based disorders relating to brain function might coexist with ADHD. As in other fields of medicine, clinicians should be aware of this possible comorbidity.

Children, adolescents, and adults with ADHD may have one or more of these related disorders, which also must be recognized, diagnosed, and treated. In this book, I focus primarily on ADHD; however, I also discuss these comorbid disorders.

I find it helpful to have an overview or road map for understanding these related disorders. There is a reason that an individual may have more than one of these problems. Parents occasionally say to me that no one seems to know what is wrong with their child. Every professional they see offers a different label or diagnosis. Often, the problem is that the child has more than one neurologically based disorder, and each professional might have focused on only one of them.

Neurological Concepts Relating These Disorders

Let me share my understanding of the probable causes of these related disorders. In many children, something affects the brain early in development, often during the first months in utero. When this happens, it is unlikely that only one area of the brain is involved. Several areas might be affected. To make it easier to study these individuals, professionals separate the possible problem areas and label them. So, depending on which areas of the brain are involved, these individuals will have different disorders.

In at least 50% of individuals with neurological disorders, the developmental effect is the result of the genetic code. The problems run in the family because the genetic code tells the brain to wire itself differently. We do not have a full explanation for the other 50%. I discuss some of the possibilities in Chapter 4.

Before I get to specific details, let me review another concept needed to understand this pattern of comorbid disorders. The brain is immature at birth. It grows constantly by having new neurons activated and put into operation. These maturation spurts take place throughout childhood, adolescence, and early adulthood. Each maturational spurt is like someone going to a computer store and buying a software package. The purchaser installs the software on his or her computer, and suddenly the computer can do things it could not do before. So, too, with each activation of new neurons in the brain, the brain can do things it could not do before. As each new area begins to operate, one of two things can happen. If the new area of the brain is wired normally, the individual suddenly will be able to do things that were difficult before. On the other hand, if the new area is wired differently, the individual will encounter new problems as this previously silent area of the brain begins to work.

This is why some children struggle and struggle, then suddenly master things that were difficult before. It is great to be the professional working with the child at that time: he or she gets the credit for it. I am sure you have heard the story before: Mary struggled with reading for several years; finally, she was assigned Mrs. Jones as a teacher, and within a month she was reading. This activation of new areas is also the reason that some children improve in one area only to have another area of difficulty surface. For these children, the new area of the brain is wired differently as well.

Faulty Wiring in the Cortex

The cortex is complex and has many functions. For this discussion, I focus on four basic functions: language skills, motor skills, cognitive skills, and organizational skills. Any or all of these areas might be wired differently.

If the area of the brain that is wired differently relates to language functioning, the child will have a problem with language, called a *language disability*. The first clue to this disability often is a delay in language development. For example, the child is not speaking by age 2, or by age 2½ or 3 years the child is using only a few words. Some children may show little improvement by age 4 years. If a speech and language therapist works with this child, it might be possible to speed up the child's development of language. There is a sigh of relief. Then, by age 4 or 5 years, another problem becomes clear. This child may have difficulty processing and understanding what is being said (called a *receptive language disability*) or might have difficulty organizing thoughts, finding the right words, and speaking in a fluid and clear way (called an *expressive language disability*). More help is needed.

As this child enters the early elementary grades, another problem might become apparent. The first task in reading is language based. The child must recognize units of sound (called *phonemes*) and connect these sounds to the correct units of symbol (called *graphemes*). The English language has 44 phonemes—each letter has a sound, vowels have two sounds (a short and a long sound), and certain letter combinations (e.g., sh, th, ch) have their own sounds—and 36 graphemes (A through Z and zero through nine). To learn to read, the child must "break this code" by learning what sounds go with what symbols and by sounding out words. Many children with a delay in language development, and later with receptive or expressive language problems, have problems learning to read in first grade. Spelling is the reverse process. The child must start with the language in his or her brain and connect it with the right symbols by writing on the page. Thus, many children with reading problems also have problems with spelling.

Some children have a delay in language, receive help, improve, and never have another problem. Others might improve but show up later with receptive or expressive language problems. With help, these problems improve and the child has no further problems. But some children then progress into reading problems. It just depends on whether the next area of brain activation is also wired differently.

If the area of the brain that is wired differently relates to the use of muscles, we see what is called a *motor disability*. For some children, the primary problems relate to the ability to coordinate and use teams of large muscles or gross motor skills. These children have difficulty running, jumping, skipping, or climbing. Others might have difficulty coordinating and using teams of small muscles or fine motor skills. They have difficulty learning to button a shirt, zip up their coat, tie their shoes, color within the lines, use scissors, eat with utensils, and, later, use a pencil or pen to form letters and write. Still others might have a broader pattern of motor problems called *sensory integration disorder*.

I explain sensory integration disorder in more detail in Chapter 7. Briefly, in addition to gross and fine motor planning difficulties, children with this disorder might have difficulty interpreting information coming from nerve endings in the skin. They might be very sensitive to touch or misread temperature or pain. They also might have difficulty processing information from the vestibular system, information needed to know where the body is in relation to space and gravity. They have difficulty with movement or position in space. The specific problems present depend on the areas of the brain involved.

If the area of the brain that is wired differently relates to the processing of information for learning or cognitive functioning, the child is said to have a *learning disability*. In some ways, this division of the cortex is artificial. If a child has a learning disability, more than one area of the brain is involved. I discuss learning disabilities in great detail in Chapter 7.

The most recent development of the cortex, primarily the frontal cortex, is the sophisticated area of the brain that acts like the chief executive officer in a company. This area carries out what are called *executive functions*. It orchestrates behaviors. This area assesses a task or problem, decides how to tackle or solve the task, orchestrates the necessary activities or functions, continually makes midcourse changes or corrections, and eventually reaches a successful conclusion. If this area of the brain is affected, the child will have difficulty with organization, planning, and task completion.

Faulty Wiring in the Area of Vigilance

A problem with wiring might extend beyond the cortex. The *area of vigilance,* an area of the brain found in animals, primitive humans, and modern humans, is the part of the brain that allows us to be hunters. This area makes it possible for an animal (or human) to sit very still so that it does not scare away its prey, to track its prey and not to be distracted by any background activity, and to strike just at the right time. Picture, for example, a frog sitting on a lily pad, watching a fly. Not a muscle moves, or the fly will go away. The frog's eyes track the fly without losing sight. And, just at the right moment, the tongue comes out and catches the fly. Some children have problems with the wiring of this area of the brain. As a result, they might be hyperactive, distractible, or impulsive. We call this disorder ADHD.

You can see why some children have a learning disability, whereas others might have a language disability or a sensory integration disorder. Still others might have ADHD. Many children might have one, two, three, or all four of these problems. These children do not have multiple disorders. They have multiple examples of the initial underlying problem that resulted in areas of the brain being wired differently.

Faulty Wiring in the Area for Modulation

With the dramatic new imaging methods available for studying the brain, other problem areas are being identified. For example, the *area for modulation* facilitates maintenance of an emotional equilibrium. This area maintains an emotional balance, avoiding extremes. It modulates many functions. If a specific area is involved, the child will have a problem with modulation of a specific function. Because this problem has been present since birth, the specific modulating problem has also been there since birth. For this reason, children often have a chronic and pervasive history of difficulties.

Some children have problems modulating anxiety. They have a history since early life of being high-strung or anxious. Over the years, the focus of the anxiety may change, but the central theme is a high anxiety level. These children might be afraid to go to sleep alone at night. Later they might be afraid of being in part of the house alone or of robbers or of bees or of something else. As these children move into adolescence or adulthood, they might develop a full-blown anxiety disorder. Some of them might have so much difficulty regulating anxiety that their anxiety level gets too high and triggers a fight-or-flight sympathetic response, called a *panic disorder*. Individuals with this disorder will break out into a sweat, their hearts will pound, and they will feel weak.

Another regulation problem relates to a child's ability to modulate anger. These children have been more irritable and angry since early childhood. They have always had tantrums. As they get older, they show a specific form of difficulty regulating anger called *intermittent explosive disorder*. When they get angry they don't just have a tantrum or pout or slam doors. Children, adolescents, or adults with this disorder have a very short fuse. Sometimes they explode so fast that you do not know for sure what caused the explosion. Once they exceed their threshold, they "lose it." They yell, scream, curse, hit, throw, and threaten. They act in an irrational way and cannot be reasoned with. Sometimes they seem paranoid, saying people are trying to hurt them. The episode may last from a few minutes to 15 minutes or more. Then, the episode ends almost as abruptly as it started. After the episode is over, the person may be tired and want to rest or sleep. He or she usually does not want to discuss what happened and seems confused about his or her behavior. Later he or she might feel remorse about the outburst. These are the "Dr. Jekyll and Mr. Hyde" children.

Some children may have difficulty modulating their moods. They seem to have been unhappy or sad most of their lives. They are moody or depressed some or all of the time. Some will go on to develop a depressive disorder. A few, in adolescence, may show difficulty modulating not just the down side of their mood (depression) but also the up side (mania). This behavior might evolve into a bipolar disorder.

Another pattern of difficulty with modulation relates to the ability to regulate thoughts and behaviors. Some individuals will have difficulty controlling their thoughts and experience the need to think a thought or thought pattern over and over (obsessive behavior). Others might have difficulty regulating behaviors. They feel they must do certain things or they will get too anxious. They know "it is silly," but they cannot stop. They might need to touch things a certain way or number of times. They might need to check and recheck things (e.g., if the front door is locked or the stove is off). They might need to engage in certain patterns or rituals. These individuals have an obsessive-compulsive disorder.

Some individuals have a problem with modulation that may or may not be part of this pattern of comorbid disorders. This problem is seen as comorbid with ADHD and relates to difficulty regulating certain motor functions. Individuals may experience clusters of muscles contracting, causing what are called *motor tics*. Others may experience the need to say certain sounds or words, called *oral tics*. These individuals have a tic disorder or a specific form of this problem, called Tourette's disorder.

The Continuum of Neurologically Based Disorders

Our brain is a beautifully functioning, fascinating part of our body. It has many functions. If something affects the brain early in development, areas of the brain will develop differently. Depending on the areas of the brain involved, different problem areas will arise. We have a name for each problem.

Understanding this possible continuum of disorders helps us to understand the full clinical picture seen with individuals who have ADHD. Children, adolescents, or adults with ADHD often have one or more of these disorders. The more disorders an individual has, the more likely that he or she will have others. For example, it is not uncommon for a child to have both learning disabilities and ADHD. This same child might have a tic disorder or obsessive-compulsive disorder, be overly anxious, have trouble regulating anger, and so on.

Statistics on the other neurologically based disorders seen in children and adolescents with ADHD remind us of the concept of comorbidity. Of all youths with ADHD, 30%–40% will also have a learning disability. For this reason, I cover learning disabilities in this book in greater detail than the other disorders. The likelihood that a child or adolescent with

ADHD might have a language, motor, or learning problem is so great that the possibility must be explored.

Of all youths with tic disorders or obsessive-compulsive disorder, 50% will also have ADHD. We do not yet have the data on the reverse—how many children or adolescents with ADHD have a tic disorder or obsessive-compulsive disorder. The suspicion is that the results, once known, will be greater than expected in the general population.

The primary focus of this book is ADHD. To give a more complete clinical picture of ADHD, I discuss each of the related disorders mentioned here. Clinicians must assess the total individual, recognizing not just the ADHD but any related disorders present.

Chapter 3

History of Attention Disorders Including Attention-Deficit/ Hyperactivity Disorder

B etween 10% and 20% of the average school-aged population will have difficulty with academic work. These difficulties have a variety of causes. Some children have mental retardation—that is, they have below-normal intellectual capacities; therefore, they will always function academically below normal. Some children have emotional problems that interfere with either their ability to learn or their availability to learn (i.e., their disruptive behavior often leads to their removal from class). Some children have average or above-average intelligence but have academic difficulties because of the way their brain processes information. Although these children may have problems with vision, hearing, or both, their learning problems are not caused by these impairments. Children with learning disabilities fall into this group. Finally, some children have difficulty sitting still, maintaining their attention on the task at hand, and thinking through their answers before they respond to questions. These children have attention-deficit/hyperactivity disorder (ADHD).

As I discussed in Chapter 2, children and adolescents with ADHD may have one or more of a group of associated neurologically based disorders. Between 30% and 40% of students with ADHD will have learning disabilities. In addition, some students may have a motor tic disorder or Tourette's disorder. Others may have an anxiety disorder, obsessive-compulsive disorder, anger control problems, or depression. Some students may have two, three, or more of these difficulties.

Most individuals with ADHD develop emotional, social, and family problems because of the difficulties they get into and the frustrations and failures they experience. These emotional, social, and family problems are referred to as "secondary" to emphasize that they are the consequence and not the cause of the academic disability.

The most frequent pattern seen is

1. Learning disabilities
2. ADHD
3. Secondary emotional, social, and family problems

I discuss each of these difficulties in separate chapters of this book. Before doing so, I review the evolution of knowledge that led to the term ADHD and explain the many labels used for this disorder.

The Evolving Concepts of This Disorder

Over the past 50 years, our understanding of ADHD has expanded significantly. With new knowledge came new concepts and diagnostic terms. Some professionals still use old terms or terms they learned during training. A frequently asked question, for example, is whether ADD is the same as ADHD.

Before the 1940s in the United States, if a child had difficulty learning, he or she was considered to have mental retardation, to exhibit emotional disturbances, or to be socially and culturally disadvantaged. In the early 1940s, a fourth group was identified, children who had difficulty learning because of a presumed problem with their nervous system. Early researchers noted that these children had the same learning problems as individuals who were known to have brain damage, for example, after brain trauma or surgery. Because these children looked normal, researchers concluded that the children also had brain damage, but that the damage was minimal. The term *minimal brain damage* was introduced.

Observations and testing revealed no evidence of brain damage in most of these children. Research information indicated that the cause of the problem lay in how the brain functioned—that is, the problem was physiological and not structural. All of the brain mechanisms were present and operable, but some of the wiring was hooked up differently and, thus, did not work in the normal way. Scientists created a term to suggest this concept of faulty functioning. The prefix *dys,* which means difficulty with, was incorporated, and the term *minimal brain dysfunction,* or MBD, came into use. The literature on MBD described these children as having 1) learning difficulties, presumed to be the result of a dysfunctional nervous system; 2) problems with hyperactivity and distractibility; and 3) emotional and family problems considered to be a consequence of the first two sets of problems.

From the 1950s through the present, professionals from a number of disciplines studied MBD intensively. Because each discipline trains its specialists and subspecialists differently and uses a different vocabulary, each investigator described what he or she found somewhat differently. Only now have we been able to see what the whole elephant looks like.

History of Learning Disabilities

Special education professionals (educators who work specifically with children with academic problems) studied the learning problems noted under the concept of MBD. Initially, they used labels that had been used for many years in schools of education to describe the primary presenting problems. Thus, children who had trouble with reading because of language-based problems had *dyslexia* and were called *dyslexic.* Children with writing problems had *dysgraphia* and were called *dysgraphic.* Trouble with arithmetic was called *dyscalculia.* Other special educators found these terms too general and not helpful. These professionals began to look for the underlying learning difficulties or disabilities that explained the academic skill difficulties. The term *learning disability* was finally selected and has become the primary term used today.

If the student has difficulty receiving, processing, and expressing language, the term *language disability* is used. Speech and language therapists would use terms such as *receptive language disability, central language disability,* or *expressive language disability.* Special education professionals might call the same problems *auditory processing, pragmatic language,* or *demand language disabilities.*

A special education professional might refer to a child's difficulty with motor planning activities as a *fine motor* or *gross motor problem.* Occupational therapists might refer to these problems as *motor dyspraxia* or might identify other problems and refer to the total clinical picture as *sensory integration disorder.*

History of Attention-Deficit/Hyperactivity Disorder

Other professionals studied those children who were described under MBD as hyperactive and distractible. The first official term for these children, established in 1968 in the medical classification system, was *hyperkinetic reaction of childhood,* and with it came the concept of the *hyperactive child.* The description noted overactivity, restlessness, distractibility, and a short attention span. In 1980, the term was changed officially to *attention deficit disorder,* or ADD, to emphasize that distractibility with a short attention span was the primary clinical issue and that hyperactivity or impulsivity also might be present. Two subtypes were used: ADD with hyperactivity and ADD without hyperactivity. A child needed to have only one of the three behaviors (hyperactivity, distractibility, or impulsivity) to receive this diagnosis.

In 1987, the official classification for these children changed to ADHD to reflect that although distractibility is the primary issue, hyperactivity is also an important factor of the disorder. Again, children could have any of the three problems and be given the diagnosis of ADHD. They did not have to be hyperactive.

In 1994, the official classification changed again, although the same term, ADHD, was used. The term *inattention* was substituted for *distractibility* in the description of the disorder. Three subtypes of the disorder were established: 1) individuals who are hyperactive, inattentive, and impulsive—called *mixed type;* 2) individuals who are primarily inattentive—called *inattentive type;* and 3) individuals who are primarily hyperactive and impulsive—called *hyperactive-impulsive type.* Despite these changes, many professionals and parents like to use the term ADD for children who are only inattentive (distractible) and ADHD for children who are also hyperactive. However, the only term that can be used on official reports or other records is ADHD.

These changes in names over the years do not reflect ambivalence on the part of the professionals who develop these classifications and guidelines. They reflect the rapidly expanding knowledge of this disorder.

History of Emotional, Social, and Family Problems

Mental health professionals studied the emotional, social, and family problems described under MBD. These professionals also clarified an important issue. For the individual with a learning disability, the emotional, social, and family problems were not the cause of the academic difficulties. Rather, these problems were the consequence of the academic difficulties and the resulting frustrations and failures experienced. I reiterate this important concept throughout this book.

Where Are We Today?

The term MBD is no longer used. In its place, the different components are identified and labeled individually with current terms. The treatment plan would address each of the individual problems. Thus, a child who used to be labeled as having MBD would today be identified as having learning disabilities; ADHD; and/or secondary emotional, social, and family problems.

Attentional Disorders

A child or adolescent might have difficulty maintaining attention for a variety of reasons. ADHD is but one cause. Thus, understanding attentional disorders is important. Later in this book I discuss in more detail how ADHD is diagnosed. For now, I explain the concept of attentional disorders.

Professionals studying attentional disorders identify three broad tasks involved with attention. Attentional problems might relate to any of these three tasks:

1. The ability to seek out what one wants to attend to and focus on it
2. Once focused, the ability to maintain this attention
3. Once the activity is complete, the ability to stop attending and move on to something else

The most common cause of difficulties with the first task, seeking out and focusing, is avoidance. For example, a child or adolescent knows he or she has homework to do but keeps procrastinating or putting off the task. He or she might say, "I just want to watch one more TV show," or "I'll do it soon. I promise." Or, he or she might start to do the homework, then get up to get a drink, later to get a snack, later to call a friend, later to take a break. Remember what it is like when you have several tasks to do. Somehow, the one you least want to do keeps being bumped to the bottom of the list. Avoidance is best understood by looking at what is being avoided. Perhaps the student does not know how to do the homework or believes it will be too hard. Perhaps he or she has a learning disability. Avoidance is not ADHD.

The second task is the ability to sustain one's attention once the assignment is initiated. Children and adolescents who are anxious, worried, or depressed might have difficulty maintaining attention. If the environment is too noisy or stimulating (e.g., doing homework at the kitchen table while dinner is being prepared or trying to work in a too-noisy classroom), the student will have difficulty concentrating. If the work is too hard or not understood, the student's attention might wander. If the student has difficulty screening out unimportant stimuli from what is being focused on, sustaining attention will be hard. Only the last of these examples might be ADHD.

The third task, breaking away from the activity and moving one's attention to another task, might be a result of the current activity being more fun than the expected next chore. For example, a child is watching television and is told to turn off the television because it is time to go to bed. The child will not want to do so. Or, a child is playing a computer game and is told to turn off the computer and start his or her homework.

None of these examples involves ADHD. Some neurological disorders result in difficulty stopping one task to start another; this difficulty is called *perseveration*. A child or adolescent with obsessive-compulsive disorder may have difficulty stopping one task to move onto another until the necessary thoughts or behaviors are completed.

Thus, by looking at the full scope of attentional problems, we can see that ADHD is but one of the possible causes for these problems. Individuals who have ADHD have difficulty maintaining attention once they attempt to focus. This difficulty is the result of a problem with blocking out unimportant stimuli that then compete for attention. In Chapter 5, I describe the different forms of inattention found with ADHD.

Clinical Concepts

Diagnosis and treatment of ADHD requires understanding the four basic clinical concepts discussed in this chapter:

1. This child or adolescent does not have mental retardation, nor is he or she primarily displaying an emotional disorder.
2. This child or adolescent is at risk to have a group of clinical difficulties. The most common pattern is learning disabilities; ADHD; and secondary emotional, social, and family problems.
3. Between 40% and 50% of children with ADHD will improve or no longer have ADHD after puberty. However, the other 50%–60% will continue to have ADHD throughout adolescence and adulthood.
4. The clinician must assess the total individual to clarify what difficulties in addition to ADHD he or she might have because of the complex possibilities of related disorders.

Chapter 4

Etiology of Attention-Deficit/ Hyperactivity Disorder

The etiology of attention-deficit/hyperactivity disorder (ADHD), or of the related neurologically based disorders I discussed in Chapter 2, has not been determined. Research findings suggest that for most individuals, something affected or influenced the brain during development, probably early in the first 3 months in utero. The consistent finding of a familial pattern among 50% of individuals who have ADHD suggests that the genetic code tells the brain to wire itself differently. When a family history of ADHD or learning disabilities is present, it is easier to assume the cause. For the other 50% of individuals, we have leads on what might cause the faulty wiring, but no firm answers are available. We will have to wait for more research.

We do know that the brain is wired differently in ADHD. Research on ADHD has shown the cause to be related to a neurochemical deficit related to a specific neurotransmitter in specific areas of the brain. I discuss the details of this neurotransmitter deficit later in this chapter.

Familial-Pattern Attention-Deficit/ Hyperactivity Disorder

Genetic Patterns

Studies suggest that as many as 50% of children and adolescents with ADHD inherited this pattern of brain functioning. The genetic code results in the brain wiring itself differently in specific areas. The disability runs in families, with siblings, parents, and extended relatives having a similar problem. This 50% statistic also applies to learning disabilities.

Family studies, twin studies, and adoptee–foster home studies support the importance of a genetic factor. Parents or children who have relatives with ADHD or a learning disability are at increased risk for these disabilities. For example, if one of a pair of identical twins has ADHD or a learning disability, the other twin is much more likely to have these problems than is another sibling. The likelihood of a fraternal twin having ADHD is no greater than for any other sibling. The familial pattern appears to be clear; however, the specific genetic markers, pathways, or processes are not known, although researchers are getting closer to identifying them.

Current understanding suggests that if the genetic code instructs the brain to wire itself differently in the areas of the cortex, the individual will have a learning disability. If the genetic code instructs specific cells to develop without the ability to produce the normal amount of the required neurotransmitter, the individual will have ADHD. In many individuals, both areas are involved.

A related area of genetic study might someday help us understand another possible cause of ADHD. Our genetic process takes place through specific units of function, the *chromosomes*. Each chromosome is composed of specific units, or *genomes*. Each genome has a specific task in instructing the body to develop. Research has identified genomes related to specific functions and genome defects that result in specific diseases.

Each genome is made up of a specific number of amino acids. These amino acids are arranged in a unique way. One possibility is that something might influence a genome, causing one or two amino acids to shift position on the chain, changing the specific pattern of the genome. This shift might result in faulty development for the area controlled by that genome. Someday, researchers might discover that some forms of nonfamilial ADHD are the result of such an accidental shift.

Adoption

The incidence of adoption among children and adolescents who have ADHD is five times higher than would be expected from the national norms for adoption. The same incidence has been found among children with learning disabilities.

One could speculate about the parents of children placed for adoption or about the possible risk factors that were experienced by these children while in utero and during delivery. The incidence may be higher among children who were adopted from Third World countries and from poverty areas within these countries. Often mothers in these areas receive minimal or no prenatal care and may have been malnourished. The children are often malnourished during the weeks or months before adoption. Proper brain development requires the intake of appropriate foods, especially protein, during fetal life and during the early months of life.

The reason for the high incidence of these disabilities among adopted children is unknown. Remember that the statistics cited refer to the number of children with ADHD who were adopted. This is not the same as looking at how many children who have been adopted have ADHD. Researchers suspect that the incidence of ADHD among these children would be similar to that in the general population. Parents should not be discouraged from adopting children; however, they might try to learn as much as possible about the birth parents, the mother's pregnancy, and the baby's life between delivery and placement.

Nonfamilial-Pattern Attention-Deficit/ Hyperactivity Disorder

Chemical Systems of the Brain

Neurotransmitters. The brain is composed of trillions of nerve cells, each of which communicates with other specific cells. This communication must take place in such a way that only one other cell, the right cell, is stimulated. Each cell produces minute amounts of a specific chemical that passes across a microscopic space (called a *synapse*) and stimulates the next, correct cell. These chemicals that transmit messages from one nerve cell to another are called *neurotransmitters*. How do they work? Each nerve cell releases a neurotransmitter with a specific structure. The neurotransmitter crosses the synapse, passing over thousands of cells. The cell targeted to be stimulated has a specific site on its surface, called a *receptor site*. When the neurotransmitter passes over this specific cell, it connects with the receptor site, and the new cell is stimulated. After the neurotransmitter matches with its specific receptor site, stimulating the other cell, another chemical process occurs that neutralizes or breaks down the neurotransmitter.

The brain produces many different types of neurotransmitters. We know of about 50. There may be as many as 200. This new knowledge of the neurochemistry of the brain has resulted in a rapid expansion of knowledge of brain function and dysfunction. ADHD is the result of a deficiency of a specific neurotransmitter in a specific area of the brain. Certain types of depression are the result of a deficiency of another specific neurotransmitter in another area of the brain (norepinephrine). No data suggest that a neurotransmitter factor might be the cause of learning disabilities.

Neuroendocrines. Knowledge is expanding about other chemical activities related to the developing brain. These chemicals control brain and behavioral interactions. New research at the molecular level on the genetic process of transmitting messages from the heredity-carrying gene to the developing brain offers much promise. Specific chemical messages, called *neuroendocrines*, travel to the brain throughout fetal development. Each neuroendocrine binds with a particular cell or cell group that has the correct receptor site for the specific message. This binding results in growth of these cells. Each day, different sites are stimulated to grow in a precisely orchestrated, complex process, slowly weaving together the networks of nerves that make up the human brain.

Could these genetic messengers be affected or influenced, resulting in a brain that functions differently? Could this explain ADHD or learning disabilities? Might certain drugs or other chemicals interfere with the biochemical messenger process, resulting in the absence of brain growth for that particular unit of time when that messenger should have been active? And would such a block during a brief time affect other brain growth that should link later with this area of nongrowth? Research in molecular genetics and cellular biology offers the promise of such answers. With these answers lies hope not just for understanding the disorders but for preventing and possibly treating them.

One set of studies was of enough concern that the information resulted in prevention efforts even before all of the facts were known. These studies found that 80% of pregnant women in the United States took over-the-counter or prescription medications during pregnancy or at the time of delivery. It was not known which of these medications crossed through the placenta into the fetus nor what effect these chemicals might have had on the chemically driven genetic process described earlier in this chapter. Further, after delivery, some of the medications used at the time of delivery could not pass from the infant back to the mother to be metabolized by her liver. Thus, they remained in the infant's blood for a longer period of time until the immature liver could metabolize them. Could these medications explain the more subtle changes found in the brains or other organ systems of children with ADHD? The answer is not available. However, as a preventive effort, pregnant women are advised to take no medications during pregnancy, prescription or over-the-counter, and there is an increasing effort to use no medications at delivery, encouraging women to use more natural childbirth methods.

Another area of research supports the possibility of a chemical blockage of specific neuroendocrines as an explanation for the faulty wiring present in children with ADHD. Before explaining this research, I need to explain in more detail how the brain develops. As the initial cells of the developing brain begin to evolve, new cells multiply and then migrate out to new sites in the brain. These cells migrate out beyond where they will be in the ultimately developed brain. More cells are produced than will exist in the fully developed brain. Once these cells reach their temporary position in the developing brain, they send out nerve endings toward the area of the brain to which they are to connect. If a nerve ending establishes a connection, the cell survives. If a nerve ending does not establish a proper connection, the cell does not survive. Once this process is finished and the proper number of cells is present, these cells migrate back toward their expected place in the cortex. Once they reach their ultimate location, the migration stops. The proper number of cells, each connected to the correct area of the brain, is then in place.

Microscopic studies of the brains of individuals with learning disabilities show a consistent pattern that may show how an event can affect the brain's normal growth pattern. In these studies, the previously described process was interrupted. Areas of the brain were found where cells had migrated out to their first position but had not migrated back to their proper site in the brain. In addition, all of the cells that did not form a connection did not disappear. Too many cells were present, and some had nerve endings that did not connect with other cells. Clear microscopic evidence indicated faulty wiring.

One line of thought is that the genetic code does not orchestrate the neuroendocrine system correctly, resulting in the dysfunctional pattern. Another line of thought is that a chemical present in the developing fetus temporarily interferes with or blocks this process, resulting in a disruption and a dysfunctional pattern. This possibility is linked to the discussion of medications taken during pregnancy or at delivery.

Fetal Development

Events or experiences while in utero, at the time of delivery, or soon after delivery can affect the developing brain. Socioenvironmental factors also can have a negative effect. Examples include poor nutrition; the absence of prenatal care; and the presence of metabolic or toxic factors, infections, or stress. Each factor can result in difficulties during pregnancy, premature delivery, and low birth weight. Studies show a relationship between low birth weight and prematurity and later academic difficulties or later hyperactivity and inattention. But the pattern is not consistent. For example, some children who were born prematurely or at low birth weight do not develop learning disabilities.

Two major national collaborative projects are studying these factors, one in the United States and one in England. Children have been followed up since their mothers learned they were pregnant and volunteered for the study. Multiple studies have been conducted during certain age periods, and extensive observational information has accumulated. These children are now approaching adulthood.

Studies conducted at age 7 years (second grade) and at age 10 years (fifth grade) identified those children who were having academic difficulties for any reason or who showed evidence of hyperactivity, inattention, and/or impulsivity. Through a study of the data on each child, efforts were made to find statistical patterns or correlations with specific factors.

It must be noted that these data are suggestive at best and that factors such as socioeconomic status were not considered. However, the data obtained at both age periods found a suggestive correlation with the following factors: maternal cigarette smoking during pregnancy, convulsions during pregnancy, low fetal heart rate during the second stage of labor, lower placental weight, more breech presentations, and more of a specific type of inflammation called *chorionitis.* Also noted was a history of the mother drinking alcohol during the pregnancy. In these cases, two or three drinks a day were consumed, far less than the amount associated with a more serious disorder called *fetal alcohol syndrome.*

Although no firm association exists between these factors and problems found in children, preventive efforts are in effect. Women are told not to smoke or drink during pregnancy. Proper nutrition throughout pregnancy is stressed. For reasons discussed earlier, mothers are told not to use over-the-counter or prescription medication during pregnancy or at the time of delivery unless it is essential and directed by the physician. Although the final results are not in, these preventive efforts seem more than appropriate.

Metabolites and Toxins

Metabolites are chemicals seen naturally within the body. *Toxins* are chemicals present in the body that are not there naturally. Metabolites include glucose, specific hormones, electrolytes, and other chemicals. Each metabolite has a normal range of expected levels. If the level is too high or too low, difficulties can result. No specific studies have related ADHD to either high or low levels of these metabolites; however, all of the evidence is not in.

The presence of toxins in the blood and brain while in utero, during the early months of life, and for some, throughout childhood, can result in brain dysfunction or brain damage. The toxin most studied is lead.

Depending on the amount of lead present, the stage of development during which it is present, and the amount of time it is present, the result could be mental retardation, ADHD, learning disabilities, or milder forms of academic difficulty. Many other toxins are being studied.

Substance Abuse

Studies of substance abuse during pregnancy are distressing. As many as 50% of the babies of mothers who use crack cocaine during pregnancy show evidence of learning disabilities, ADHD, and impulse problems as they grow up. Data on other drug use during pregnancy are not as complete, but the pattern appears to be the same. Studies show that the problem is not just with a mother who uses drugs or alcohol during pregnancy. Evidence indicates that if the father is using drugs or alcohol at the time of conception, the genetic patterns of the sperm might be affected, resulting in difficulties with the fetus and with the baby after birth.

Problems at Delivery

Many studies have examined whether complications during delivery have any effect later in a child's life. The long-term effect of factors such as a long labor, the use of forceps, the baby's position, and the presence of fetal distress is unclear. No direct correlations exist.

Fetal distress noted at delivery (e.g., low Apgar scores) that persist over minutes and a bilirubin level that persists above the accepted safe level are factors that seem to suggest a higher likelihood of ADHD and learning disabilities later in life. However, here, too, no direct correlation exists.

Factors in Childhood

Infections such as encephalitis can result in changes in the brain, resulting in ADHD or learning disabilities. Trauma can result in structural changes and academic difficulties.

Fascinating findings from brain research offer another view, both of brain development and of the potential for brain dysfunction. The key to much of this developmental research is that the electrical and chemical activity of the brain cells changes the physical structure of the brain.

At birth, a baby's brain contains 100 billion nerve cells (*neurons*), about as many neurons as there are stars in the Milky Way. Also in place are a trillion cells that protect and nourish the neurons, called *glial cells*. Although the brain contains virtually all of the neurons it will ever have, the pattern of wiring between them has not stabilized. Researchers suggest that the brain lays out circuits that are its best guess about what is required for every function, including vision and language. Then, neural activity—no longer spontaneous but driven by a flood of sensory experiences—has to take this rough blueprint and progressively refine it.

During the first year of life, the brain undergoes a series of extraordinary changes. Starting shortly after birth, a baby's brain produces trillions more connections between neurons than it can possibly use. Then, through a process that involves competition, the brain eliminates connections or synapses that are seldom or never used. The excess synapses in a child's brain undergo a pruning, starting around age 10 years or earlier, leaving behind a mind with patterns of emotion and thought that are, for better or worse, unique.

A child's brain that is deprived of a stimulating environment suffers. Children who do not play much or are rarely touched develop brains 20%–30% smaller than normal for their age. Rich and stimulating experiences result in many more synapses per neuron.

Experts now agree that a baby does not come into the world as a genetically preprogrammed automaton or a blank slate at the mercy of the environment but arrives as something much more interesting. Nature is the dominating factor during this phase of development, but nurture plays a vital supportive role.

To relate this research to topics discussed earlier in this chapter, changes in the environment of the womb—whether caused by maternal malnutrition, drug abuse, or a viral infection—can destroy the clockwork precision of the neural assembly line. Also, the instructions programmed into the genes can affect this developmental process.

This research clarifies that the genes control the unfolding of the brain; however, as soon as the neurons make their connections and begin to fire, what they do begins to matter more and more. Experience becomes critical. A wealth of new knowledge exists on the importance of this experience on the developing brain. Wires that are stimulated persist; wires that are not used disappear.

For example, when a baby is born, he or she can see, hear, smell, and respond to touch, but only dimly. Over the first few months of life, the brain's higher centers explode with new connections. By age 2 years, a child's brain contains twice as many synapses and consumes twice as much energy as the brain of a normal adult. Experience influences this wiring process. Each time a baby experiences something (like a sound, touch, or sight), tiny bursts of energy shoot through the brain, weaving neurons into integral circuits. Decreased experience or the lack of experience can result in a brain that is less developed, or worse.

Where all of this research will lead us is mind-boggling. Certainly, it raises not only questions about child rearing but also questions about the critical role of day care centers. How it might clarify issues relating to ADHD or learning disabilities is not known.

We do see one possible clinical problem that might best be explained by this new developmental knowledge. A higher percentage of children with language disabilities have a history of frequent ear infections over months or years of early childhood. Until the infections are treated, the child's hearing might be impaired. Is it possible that reduced hearing during certain critical periods of early development influenced the brain's ability to develop the sites needed to distinguish the subtle differences in sound we discussed earlier, the phonemes? Might this effect on development have resulted in the language problems? We do not yet know the answers to these questions.

Other Possible Factors

To date, studies have not shown a consistent relationship between ADHD and variables such as birth order, number of siblings, number of family moves, family income, mother's age, mother's educational level, or father's educational level.

Cultural factors may be involved. Cultural and bilingual factors might influence the quality of education received or the level of academic accomplishment reached. However, these difficulties related to cultural, bilingual, or socioeconomic factors are not the result of processing problems. No underlying neurological dysfunctions result in difficulties processing and using information.

Etiology and the Clinical Picture of ADHD

Future research will probably show that more than one form of ADHD exists. Currently we subdivide this disorder into three groups, as described in DSM-IV (American Psychiatric Association 1994). However, future research on brain function will likely clarify that several forms of ADHD exist, based on specific biological factors. This information might help us understand why some individuals respond to one medication and not to another or why some individuals experience side effects with one medication and not with another. We might someday understand why some medications improve expressive language or handwriting and others do not, or why some medications decrease hyperactivity and inattention but not impulsivity, whereas another medication might help impulsivity and not hyperactivity or inattention.

The areas of the brain that appear to be involved in ADHD include the frontal cortex, the limbic system, the basal ganglia, and the reticular activating system. These systems operate in a closed circuitry. The suspected neurotransmitter is thought to be norepinephrine; however, it might be one of the precursors, dopa or dopamine. Any deficiency of either of these neurotransmitters at any site within this complex system of the brain might result in hyperactivity, inattention, and/or impulsivity.

Someday we might find that a deficiency at a specific dopamine receptor site in the limbic system produces the same clinical picture as a deficiency at a specific dopa receptor site in the ascending reticular activating system or a deficiency of norepinephrine in the locus coeruleus.

When biological markers can be used to clarify the form of ADHD present, we will be able to develop medications to address the specific biological difficulty. Until then, we remain at a state of the art and not a state of the science. But that art is more than adequate to help individuals with ADHD.

| Summary

We know a lot about ADHD, but in some ways, we also know very little. We understand many possible causes of ADHD, but we do not have a definite answer regarding the actual cause. Until we do, we cannot speak in terms of prevention or cure, only in terms of hope for preventive efforts and better treatments.

ADHD appears to be the result of a neurotransmitter deficiency in a specific area of the brain. The cause of this deficiency is not fully understood. We cannot correct the nerve cells involved and cause them to start to produce more of this neurotransmitter. But, as I discuss in Chapter 15, medications are available that increase the level of this neurotransmitter in this area of the brain and thus decrease the level of hyperactivity, inattention, and/or impulsivity.

| Reference

American Psychiatric Association: Diagnostic and Statistical Manual of Mental Disorders, 4th Edition. Washington, DC, American Psychiatric Association, 1994

Part 2

Diagnosis

Chapter 5

Clinical Findings Suggestive of Attention-Deficit/ Hyperactivity Disorder

As I discuss further in Chapter 6, the official definition of attention-deficit/hyperactivity disorder (ADHD) describes the essential features of the disorder as a persistent pattern of inattention and/or hyperactivity-impulsivity that is more frequent and severe than is typically observed in individuals at a comparable level of development. These problems have to be chronic; that is, they must have existed before age 7 years. They must also be pervasive, occurring in two or more settings (e.g., home, school, or work).

Individuals with ADHD usually show some difficulties in each of these areas but to varying degrees. Some children and adolescents will exhibit one, two, or all three of these behaviors; however, they need not have all three behaviors. A child can be relaxed, even hypoactive, and have ADHD if he or she shows inattention or distractibility. Because some clinicians still believe that the child or adolescent must be hyperactive for this diagnosis to apply, too many of these individuals are not accurately diagnosed.

If the individual being evaluated is hyperactive, inattentive/distractible, and/or impulsive, and if these behaviors have been present over most of the individual's life, the possibility of ADHD should be considered.

| Clinical Behaviors

Hyperactivity

Hyperactivity may be a misnomer. We do not necessarily mean children who run around in circles or up and down the hall. Such children exist. However, for the most part, we are talking about fidgety, squirmy behaviors. In the 1960s, the focus was on hyperactivity. Physicians were taught, "If you went out to your waiting room and it was in shambles, you knew you had a hyperactive child." We now understand that most children with ADHD who are hyperactive are not this out-of-control. They are more likely to be fidgety or restless. If you look, you will see that some part of their body is in motion, often purposeless motion. Their fingers are tapping or they are playing with a pencil. They may be sitting, but their legs are swinging or they are twisting or squirming in the chair. Teachers report that these children sometimes sit with one knee on the floor or they rock their chair. You may hear from parents that these children have never sat through a whole meal without getting up and moving around. Some children appear to be verbally hyperactive, talking constantly.

As children move toward adolescence, the more obvious high activity level may be less apparent; however, they remain fidgety, especially with their hands. They might stand or pace when they are doing their homework. Individuals whose ADHD continues into adulthood seem to work at controlling their activity level by selecting careers that allow for movement. They might avoid jobs that require sitting at a desk all day. But you might see them sitting in a chair, both feet on the ground and their knees moving up or down. Or their legs might be crossed and one leg will be swinging.

Inattention

Before the most recent change in the diagnostic criteria, the term *distractibility* was used. The term is similar to its substitute, *inattention.*

Individuals with ADHD will be inattentive because they are distracted. As a result, they have a short attention span and have difficulty staying on task. For children and early adolescents, the most frequent problem is with their ability to block out unimportant stimuli in their environment. These individuals are distracted by auditory and visual stimuli. Individuals who are auditorily distracted will hear and respond to sounds that most others would hear and tune out. For example, teachers report that if someone in the back of the room is tapping a pencil or whispering or if someone is walking in the halls, others will ignore it, whereas the child with ADHD must turn and listen. If someone is talking in another room or a basketball is being dribbled on the playground, this child looks up and notices. At home, he or she might react to minor sounds like a floorboard creaking, the dog's tail wagging, traffic outside, or someone on the telephone.

Individuals who are visually distracted might pay attention to a picture, a poster, or a design on a rug rather than to what one should be focused on. Some parents report that they leave their child in the morning to get dressed, but when they return the child is playing with a toy. The child saw the toy and became distracted from the task of dressing. Or a child is sent upstairs to do something but does not return. On the way, he or she saw something, began to play with it, saw something else, and began to use that. Outside, this child will notice birds flying, clouds going by, or trees moving and not stay focused on the appropriate activity.

By later adolescence or adulthood, another form of inattention or distractibility might be noticed. Some individuals have difficulty blocking out their internal thoughts in order to focus on what they should be attending to. In general, two types of internal distractibility exist. Some individuals complain that their mind *drifts*. They daydream all the time. They may be engaged in conversation and suddenly realize that their mind wandered and they were not paying attention. They are not avoiding something stressful because this drifting occurs all the time, even when relaxed and with friends. Other individuals complain that their mind *jumps*. They describe having many thoughts at one time and not being able to block out the unwanted thoughts. They are trying to listen or do something and are thinking of two or three other things at the same time. Sometimes they make a comment related to one of the other internal thoughts and people wonder why they changed the subject. Some adults describe being in the middle of doing something when another thought occurs to them, and they drop what they were doing and move on to something else. Then another thought occurs, and they jump to another activity. The lives of these individuals are full of unfinished activities.

Some children and adolescents with auditory or visual distractibility appear to be able to attend to certain tasks for long periods. Parents question whether the individual is really distractible if he or she can spend hours watching television or playing a video game. These tasks are usually ones that are enjoyable. In order to attend, the child or adolescent learns to *hyperfocus*. These individuals often appear to be in a trance. You cannot reach them unless you touch them, shake them, or stand between them and the activity on which they are focused. Some adolescents with auditory distractibility seem to study best with music playing in the background. Parents will wonder how their child could be distractible if he or she does homework with music playing. Many of these adolescents will tell you that the music is like white noise, blocking out all the small sounds that distract them (e.g., people talking or the telephone ringing).

Young children with auditory and visual distractibility might experience *sensory overload* when in a busy, noisy place (e.g., at a shopping mall, a birthday party, or the circus). They become irritable, upset, and complain about the noise. They may cover their ears and want to leave.

Impulsivity

Individuals with impulsivity appear not to be able to reflect before they talk or act. Because they cannot delay action long enough to recall past experience and consequences, they do not learn from experience. In class, they may call out without raising a hand or may blurt out something or interrupt the teacher while he or she is working with another student. At home, these children or adolescents might interrupt parents when they are on the phone or talking to someone else. Older individuals may say something before thinking and hurt someone's feelings.

Actions may be impulsive as well. Children may get upset and push or hit. They may want something and grab for it. These children act quickly and may run into the street or away from a parent while in a busy shopping center. Adolescents may use poor judgment in their actions. Adults might buy something without thinking whether they can afford it, or they might quit a job before having another. Some individuals are described as being risk takers or having no fear. Some may drive without thinking of their next move, resulting in more accidents than their peers. All may be seen as having poor judgment.

| Observing and Collecting Clinical Information

The clinical office is often the least effective place to observe hyperactivity, distractibility, and/or impulsivity. Thus, other data are needed. Most physicians see a child for 5–7 minutes. This child may have learned to be very alert in the office or run the risk of being stuck, gagged, or poked as part of a further examination. Thus, he or she may be quiet and very attentive. If the office is that of a general psychiatrist, child and adolescent psychiatrist, or other mental health professional, the room is likely to be quiet and the child will have one-to-one interaction with the professional. If hyperactivity, distractibility, and impulsivity are not seen in the clinician's office, this professional should not conclude that the behaviors do not exist.

The best source of observational data is from real-life situations. Professionals must learn from parents, teachers, tutors, activity leaders, and other adults who interact with the child or adolescent and who can describe what he or she is like in structured and unstructured situations. These individuals can describe the child's behaviors at school, in the home, and with friends, including whether the behaviors exist all the time or only during certain activities or tasks. It is most important that these observations be obtained.

It is usually not realistic for the health or mental health clinician to visit the school or observe the child at play. It becomes critical, then, that parents be a primary source of developmental and current history. Clinicians can obtain behavioral descriptions from teachers and may give rating scales and other informational forms to parents or teachers to complete. These data are helpful. I discuss these instruments and other methods of collecting behavioral data in Chapter 6.

Differential Diagnostic Thinking

The most common cause of hyperactivity, distractibility, and/or impulsivity among children, adolescents, and adults is anxiety. When someone is anxious, he or she cannot sit still or pay attention, and he or she may become irritable and snap at people. The second most common cause of these behaviors for any age group is depression. As with adults, children who are depressed might be restless and unable to stay focused. The third most common cause of these behaviors is a learning disability. Here, the child or adolescent may not finish classwork, have difficulty doing homework, or appear not to be listening because of the underlying learning disability and not because of ADHD. The least frequent of the common causes of hyperactivity, distractibility, and/or impulsivity in any age group is ADHD.

Thus, the cause of the presenting problems must be determined. Not all children and adolescents with one or more of the three behaviors discussed here have ADHD. A teacher might report that a child cannot sit still or stay focused in class. This observation is important, but it does not lead to the diagnosis of ADHD. The described behaviors might be the result of anxiety, depression, a learning disability, or pinworms.

In Chapter 6, I discuss how ADHD is diagnosed. The critical issue to understand is that not all individuals with one or more of these behaviors has ADHD.

Summary

The clinician evaluating an individual for ADHD must understand the criteria for establishing this diagnosis in order to decrease the number of individuals who are given an incorrect diagnosis of ADHD or whose diagnosis of ADHD is overlooked. The presenting behaviors must have a chronic and pervasive history. As I discuss in Chapter 6, after clinical data are collected, this clinical history will establish whether the hyperactivity, distractibility, and impulsivity are a result of anxiety, depression, a learning disability, or ADHD.

Chapter 6

Establishing the Diagnosis

N o formal tests are available to establish the diagnosis of attention-deficit/hyperactivity disorder (ADHD). No physical, laboratory, or neurological findings are associated with the disorder. However, excellent psychological tests, rating scales, and computer-based tests are available. I discuss some of these tests later in this chapter. The data collected from these assessment instruments might clarify that a child or adolescent is hyperactive, distractible, or impulsive. However, none of these evaluations will clarify the reason that this individual has one or more of these behaviors. The clinical problem in establishing a diagnosis is that hyperactive, distractible, and impulsive behaviors in children, adolescents, and adults can have many causes. The reason for the behaviors must be clarified before the disorder can be diagnosed.

The clinical history is the only current means to finalize the proper diagnosis. Information obtained from the individual; from parents, teachers, and others; and from previous records leads to the diagnosis.

Official Diagnostic Criteria for Attention-Deficit/Hyperactivity Disorder

The official guidelines used by health and mental health professionals to diagnose ADHD are found in DSM-IV (American Psychiatric Association 1994). Some parents become upset that ADHD is classified as a mental disorder. It may help to explain to these parents how this classification resulted. One of the goals of the World Health Organization (WHO), which consists of representatives from each of the United Nations's member nations, is to have a common definition of all medical disorders with specific criteria for diagnosing each disorder. In this way, there can be uniformity in diagnosing diseases around the world; thus, uniform data on diseases can be collected. These guidelines are developed and finalized by committees of representatives from around the world. Once agreed upon, each member nation must follow these guidelines. About every 10 years, WHO publishes an updated set of guidelines called the *International Classification of Diseases*. The current edition is ICD-10. After a disease appears in ICD, each nation must modify its own classification system to conform with ICD. In the United States, the American Medical Association is given this task. The edition of the ICD modified for the United States is called the *International Classification of Diseases—Clinically Modified for ICD-CM*. The American Medical Association assigns different parts of the diagnostic system to the appropriate specialty organization to prepare this publication. WHO determines which disorders are classified as mental disorders. In the United States, the American Medical Association assigns the American Psychiatric Association to update the existing guidelines for these disorders to conform with the new guidelines from the ICD. These changes are published in the current version of DSM. DSM-IV reflects ICD-9-CM.

In the past, much of our approach to working with mental disorders was based on our understanding of the mind. Knowledge of the brain was not yet available. With the major explosion over the past 20–30 years of knowledge of the brain and of the mind-brain relationship, many mental disorders once thought of as psychologically based are now understood to be neurologically based with possible psychological consequences. ADHD is one of these disorders. In DSM-IV, ADHD is diagnosed in five major steps, each with specific criteria (Table 6–1).

DSM-IV notes three subtypes of ADHD. The clinician should identify the individual as having one of the following:

1. Attention-deficit/hyperactivity disorder, combined type: to be used if both Criteria A1 and A2 (see Table 6–1) are met for the past 6 months

Table 6–1. DSM-IV diagnostic criteria for attention-deficit/hyperactivity disorder

A. Either (1) or (2):

   (1) six (or more) of the following symptoms of **inattention** have persisted for at least 6 months to a degree that is maladaptive and inconsistent with developmental level:

   Inattention

   (a) often fails to give close attention to details or makes careless mistakes in schoolwork, work, or other activities
   (b) often has difficulty sustaining attention in tasks or play activities
   (c) often does not seem to listen when spoken to directly
   (d) often does not follow through on instructions and fails to finish schoolwork, chores, or duties in the workplace (not due to oppositional behavior or failure to understand instructions)
   (e) often has difficulty organizing tasks and activities
   (f) often avoids, dislikes, or is reluctant to engage in tasks that require sustained mental effort (such as schoolwork or homework)
   (g) often loses things necessary for tasks or activities (e.g., toys, school assignments, pencils, books, or tools)
   (h) is often easily distracted by extraneous stimuli
   (i) is often forgetful in daily activities

   (2) six (or more) of the following symptoms of **hyperactivity-impulsivity** have persisted for at least 6 months to a degree that is maladaptive and inconsistent with developmental level:

   Hyperactivity

   (a) often fidgets with hands or feet or squirms in seat
   (b) often leaves seat in classroom or in other situations in which remaining seated is expected
   (c) often runs about or climbs excessively in situations in which it is inappropriate (in adolescents or adults, may be limited to subjective feelings of restlessness)
   (d) often has difficulty playing or engaging in leisure activities quietly
   (e) is often "on the go" or often acts as if "driven by a motor"
   (f) often talks excessively

(continued)

Table 6–1. DSM-IV diagnostic criteria for attention-deficit/hyperactivity disorder *(continued)*

Impulsivity

    (g) often blurts out answers before questions have been completed
    (h) often has difficulty awaiting turn
    (i) often interrupts or intrudes on others (e.g., butts into conversations or games)

B. Some hyperactive-impulsive or inattentive symptoms that caused impairment were present before age 7 years.

C. Some impairment from the symptoms is present in two or more settings (e.g., at school [or work] and at home).

D. There must be clear evidence of clinically significant impairment in social, academic, or occupational functioning.

E. The symptoms do not occur exclusively during the course of a pervasive developmental disorder, schizophrenia, or other psychotic disorder and are not better accounted for by another mental disorder (e.g., mood disorder, anxiety disorder, dissociative disorder, or a personality disorder).

Source. Reprinted from American Psychiatric Association: *Diagnostic and Statistical Manual of Mental Disorders,* 4th Edition. Washington, DC, American Psychiatric Association, 1994. Copyright 1994, American Psychiatric Association. Used with permission.

    2. Attention-deficit/hyperactivity disorder, predominantly inattentive type: to be used if Criterion A1 is met but Criterion A2 is not met for the past 6 months
    3. Attention-deficit/hyperactivity disorder, predominantly hyperactive-impulsive type: to be used if Criterion A2 is met but Criterion A1 is not met for the past 6 months

A word of caution is needed before I move on. Parents have access to many books on the subject of ADHD. Most are good. Some are excellent. However, popular books do not have to meet the same standards as professional books. Thus, a parent might read a book that uses the terms *attention-deficit/hyperactivity disorder* or *attention deficit disorder,* but the author might present his or her own criteria for these diagnoses. Some authors indicate at the outset that they do not follow DSM-IV guidelines;

however, some do not. Even though some of these books may do an excellent job of describing many aspects of ADHD, the criteria they use for identifying someone who has ADHD are not the same as the official guidelines. I sometimes see adults who read one of these books and concluded that they or their son or daughter has ADHD. The individual meets the characteristics described in the book but does not meet the official criteria; thus, I cannot make the diagnosis.

The Differential Diagnostic Process

The three behaviors associated with ADHD—hyperactivity, inattention, and impulsivity—were described in Chapter 5. I elaborate on some aspects of each before discussing the differential diagnostic process.

Hyperactivity

Most hyperactive children and adolescents are not running around the room or jumping on the furniture. Some might, but most do not. What we see is fidgety or squirmy behavior. Their fingers are tapping, their pencil is moving, their legs are swinging, or they are up and down from their desk or the dinner table. Something is always in motion. Parents may report that these children are equally restless at night, moving around in bed. Some individuals may show what appears to be *verbal hyperactivity*. They seem to talk constantly.

Inattention

In previous editions of DSM, this behavior was defined as *distractibility*. In DSM-IV, the term was changed to *inattention*. The difference between these two terms has not been explained clearly. Many clinicians use them interchangeably. I use the term distractibility.

Before being specific about inattention, it is important to review the broader concept of attention and attentional disorders. Researchers working on attentional disorders have clarified three tasks involved in attending:

1. The ability to seek out what needs to be attended to and focus on it
2. Once focused, the ability to maintain this attention
3. Once the activity is complete, the ability to stop attending and move on to something else

The most common cause of difficulties with the first task, seeking out and focusing, is avoidance. For example, a child or adolescent knows he or she has homework to do but keeps procrastinating or putting off the assignment. He or she might say, "I just want to watch one more TV show," or "I'll do it soon. I promise." Or, he or she might start to do the homework, then get up to get a drink, later to get a snack, later to call a friend, later to take a break. Remember what it is like when you have several tasks to do. Somehow, the one you least want to do keeps being bumped to the bottom of the list. Avoidance is best understood by looking at what is being avoided. Perhaps the student does not know how to do the homework or believes it will be too hard. Perhaps he or she has a learning disability. Avoidance is not ADHD.

Children and adolescents who are anxious, worried, or depressed might have difficulty with the second task, sustaining one's attention once the assignment is initiated. If the environment is too noisy or stimulating, for example, if a student is doing homework at the kitchen table while dinner is being prepared or is trying to work in a too-noisy classroom, he or she will have difficulty concentrating. If the work is too hard or not understood, the student's attention might wander. If the student has difficulty screening out unimportant stimuli from what is being focused on, sustaining attention will be hard. Only the last of these examples might be ADHD.

The third task, breaking away from the activity and moving one's attention to another task, might be a result of the current activity being more fun than the expected next chore. For example, a child is watching television and is told to turn off the television because it is time to go to bed. The child will not want to do so. Or, a child is playing a computer game and is told to turn off the computer and start his or her homework. These examples do not involve ADHD. Some neurological disorders result in difficulty stopping one task to start another; this difficulty is called *perseveration*. A child or adolescent with obsessive-compulsive disorder may have difficulty stopping one task to move onto another until the necessary thoughts or behaviors are completed.

ADHD is a possible cause for difficulty only with the second task, sustaining attention once a task is started. Avoiding a task or not wanting to stop doing something that is more pleasant than the required task is often misinterpreted as ADHD.

As I discussed in Chapter 5, problems with inattention or distractibility generally appear in one of two forms. Some individuals may show evidence of external distractibility and others evidence of internal distractibility.

External distractibility. Some children have difficulty screening out unimportant sounds or sights. They have auditory or visual distractibility. Individuals with auditory distractibility seem to hear everything. A student may be doing his or her homework and will hear a car going by outside, someone talking in the next room, the phone ringing, or the dog's tail wagging. In school, these children are distracted by the sound of footsteps in the hall. College students with external distractibility often say they have to study in a small room with the door shut on the top floor of the library. If they study in the main area of the library, they hear the person next to them turn the page or the sound of the pencil on the page. Adults report that they can work only when their door is shut or they wait to work until everyone else goes home. They are distracted by the sounds of co-workers talking, computers beeping, or printers printing.

Individuals with visual distractibility notice everything around them. A student who is working might start to look at the design on a rug, at a poster, or out the window. He or she might be talking to friends in the cafeteria and begin to look at what other people are wearing. A child playing soccer might start looking into the sky or at the grass. Parents might report that their child has difficulty getting dressed in the morning. The child starts to dress, and the parent leaves. Then the child sees something and starts to play with it. Then the child sees something else, and his or her attention shifts. The parent comes back in and finds the child playing and yells, "I told you to get dressed." A child or adolescent may be sent to get something by a parent or teacher but forgets what he or she is supposed to get because the child sees something on the way and gets distracted, his or her attention shifting repeatedly. Consider the following example:

A mother described to me something that happened several days before our meeting. She went into the kitchen to start dinner. As she walked in, she saw some papers on the kitchen table and decided to sit down and go over them. While working on these papers, she looked up and noticed a yellow note stuck to her telephone and remembered that she needed to make a telephone call. While she was on the phone, she noticed a magazine on the counter. When she got off the phone, she went to the counter. At this time, her children came into the kitchen and asked when dinner would be ready. But she hadn't even begun to prepare it.

Some children with both auditory and visual distractibility might experience sensory overload when in a very stimulating environment—for example, at a birthday party, a busy shopping mall, or the circus. So much stimulation is bombarding the child's brain that he or she may become overloaded. These children might be irritable, crying, covering their ears, or wanting to leave.

Parents occasionally describe their adolescent's study habits and question how he or she could have auditory distractibility. Their teen can study only with music playing in the background. So many adolescents describe why they do this in the same way that I believe their reason. If they study in total silence, they hear every little sound in the house. The music acts like white noise. They get used to it and do not pay attention to it. The music helps them not to be distracted by other sounds.

Internal distractibility. Internal distractibility is not understood fully; thus, different professionals may define it differently. It is found more commonly among adolescents and adults than among children. I see two types of internal distractibility: *drifting* and *jumping.*

Drifting means daydreaming. We all daydream at times, but for some individuals, daydreaming occurs all the time—in school, at work, with friends, or with family. Anyone could experience a given example of drifting; however, consistency over time sets some individuals apart. These individuals might start to read a page; their eyes go down the page, but their mind is somewhere else. They have no idea what they read. Or they might be in class, and the teacher is talking. Their thoughts begin to wander, and they miss what is said. Or they might be with friends, and everyone is talking. Their mind wanders, and they do not hear what is said. Parents, teachers, friends, or employers might observe a glassy or blank look in the individual's eyes. Some individuals might be called "airheads" or "space cadets." One girl joked that her friend often said, "Earth to Susan. Earth to Susan. Come in Susan." In these situations, consistency over time distinguishes drifting from normal daydreaming.

Jumping behavior is something that confuses others and frustrates the person with the problem. Our minds are always busy. Many thoughts occur at the same time. Most individuals can screen out all but the thoughts that need to be focused on. Individuals with the jumping form of internal distractibility cannot do so. They have multiple thoughts at the same time. They might make a comment from one of these multiple thoughts that has nothing to do with what is being talked about, leaving others confused about where this comment came from. They might start to do something, then their thoughts jump to another activity, and they begin to work on the other activity. If their mind jumps again, their activity may change again. These individuals have lives full of incomplete activities.

Impulsivity

Impulsive behavior is usually described as being unable to stop or having difficulty stopping to reflect before speaking or acting. Some individuals have difficulty stopping to think before speaking; others have difficulty stopping to think before acting. Most individuals have both problems.

In school, these individuals might interrupt in class, calling out before they are called on. They might blurt out an answer or interrupt a teacher while he or she is working with another student. At home, these individuals interrupt parents while they are on the phone or are talking to someone else. They may say something to a friend before thinking and hurt the friend's feelings. As soon as they say it they are sorry, but it is too late. Adolescents and adults often become aware of this problem and work at controlling it.

Young children who act before thinking might grab something, knock someone else's blocks down, push their way into line, or hit someone else. Older children might continue these behaviors. They might write down or say the first answer they think of without reflecting first. Older individuals might engage in dangerous behaviors because they do not think before they act. Adults might buy something before thinking through whether they can afford it, or they might quit a job before getting another. Adolescents and adults with ADHD might have poor driving records, having more accidents than most other drivers.

Children and adolescents who are impulsive are at risk for certain other behaviors. We do not always understand the connection, but we look for these behaviors. These individuals might still wet the bed, they might be fascinated with fire or matches, or they might steal.

Making the Diagnosis

The main difficulty in diagnosing ADHD is differentiating between the many causes of hyperactivity, distractibility, and impulsivity. The first step is data collection. The interview with parents and with the child or adolescent, the psychological test results, data from specially designed computer performance tests, and scores on rating scales will help to clarify whether an individual has one or more of these behaviors. The next step in the diagnostic process is to document that there is a chronic and pervasive history of these behaviors.

Differential Diagnosis Process

As discussed briefly in Chapter 5, there are several causes of the observed hyperactivity, inattention, and impulsivity. Let me now elaborate.

Anxiety. The most common cause of hyperactivity, distractibility, and/or impulsivity is anxiety. Anxiety can be a reflection of psychological stress or conflict or of a specific anxiety disorder. This psychological stress might be the result of an academic problem. When anxious, the child or adolescent might be physically active. As in adults, anxious feelings result in a child's need to be active, and these feelings make it difficult for the child to pay attention or maintain focus. Daydreaming or escaping into television is not uncommon. If a child or adolescent has learning disabilities, he or she might become anxious when asked to perform in an area of weakness. For example, during reading group a child might begin to fidget. When sitting at the desk doing a worksheet, this child might become frustrated and look around the room or out the window. This same child might have no problems sitting or attending when the tasks relate to strengths. For example, he or she might have excellent language skills and have no problem sitting still and attending during periods of class discussion.

Depression. Depression might reflect a psychological conflict or stress or a specific mood disorder. This psychological stress might be reflected by a poor self-image and low self-esteem resulting from learning disabilities. Depression has agitated and psychomotor retardation phases. Individuals at any age can experience depression. Sometimes it is difficult to clarify whether the individual is primarily depressed, whether the depression is a result of learning disabilities, or whether both are present, possibly along with ADHD.

Chris, a 10-year-old boy in fifth grade, was brought in for a consultation. He had been in individual and group therapy for 2 years because of his emotional problems and depression. He was unhappy in school and not doing his schoolwork in class or at home. A psychological and educational evaluation done by his school system 18 months earlier showed evidence of learning disabilities. However, the team of evaluators concluded that "his weaknesses were not great enough nor his skill levels behind enough to qualify for services."

A review of Chris's school records plus the history his parents provided revealed that Chris had been labeled as hyperactive and distractible in preschool and kindergarten. His first-grade teacher described him as overactive and unable to stay on task. His second-grade teacher made the same comments. Third grade was described as a terrible year; Chris got into fights, disrupted the classroom, and did not complete his work. Fourth grade was similar to third grade. He was falling further behind in school skills and strategies. The teachers blamed Chris's poor performance on his behavior and his "refusal" to sit still and pay attention.

The clinical history added important information to the diagnostic process. Chris was adopted by his family at age 4½ years. He had been in a foster home for 1 year before this adoption because his mother's boyfriend had sexually abused him. His mother was also neglectful, often leaving him alone. The social service agency's records indicated that Chris's mother had used alcohol and drugs when she was pregnant with him. Chris had been placed in individual and group therapy to help him cope with his past. His academic and behavior problems were seen by his therapists as secondary to his emotional problems.

During my assessment sessions with Chris, he spoke openly of his past. He knew about it and felt that he no longer worried about it. "I talked it all over in my therapy. It is behind me, and this is my family now and forever. I like them." I could find no evidence of emotional conflicts relating to his past. He did speak of his frustrations in school. He did not like school, and he knew he was not as smart as the other kids. Chris was aware that it was difficult for him to sit still in class. He also knew that he was easily distracted by any noise or activity. He blamed the fighting on the other kids teasing him.

Chris showed a chronic and pervasive history (as far as such a history could be obtained) of hyperactivity, distractibility, and impulsivity. Thus, I had to consider the diagnosis of ADHD. His mother's use of alcohol and drugs during pregnancy certainly placed him at risk for ADHD and learning disabilities. However, his history also suggested that he might still be dealing with a *posttraumatic stress disorder*. The hyperactivity, distractibility, and impulsivity might reflect anxiety or depression.

After discussing the clinical issues with Chris's therapist, I presented these diagnostic possibilities to Chris and his parents. We agreed to a trial on medication to help clarify the issues. Chris was started on methylphenidate. The dose was adjusted, and he became calmer, more on task, and less impulsive at home and in school. His teachers and his parents noticed a significant improvement. His level of work at school also improved.

After helping Chris's parents advocate for more services, school professionals agreed to identify him as having learning disabilities. He began to receive services and classroom accommodations. His grades improved. The fighting and other disruptive behaviors stopped.

In conclusion, Chris may have been struggling with anxiety and depression relating to his past life experiences, but he also had ADHD and learning disabilities.

Clinical History

The clinical history is critical to the diagnosis of ADHD. If the behaviors observed and documented started at a certain time or occur in certain situations, the clinician must consider anxiety, depression, or another neurologically based disorder. Consider the following examples:

- Billy was first described as hyperactive and impulsive in third grade. His parents had separated the previous summer.

- Allison is inattentive only in reading group or when sitting at her desk working on a report. She is very attentive during class discussions.
- Jose seems to be distracted when doing homework but at no other time while at home.

ADHD is present at birth or during the early years of life. Thus, the history of the behaviors is both chronic and pervasive. This makes sense. The child is born with the problem, and the brain is with him or her throughout life; thus, the behaviors are seen year after year. This brain is with the child or adolescent every minute of every day; thus, the behaviors occur all day.

The history is chronic.   A mother might say that her child was more active in utero or has been active all of his or her life. For example, "He started walking at 10 months, and at 10 months and 1 minute, he took off. He never stopped running." A parent might go to a school conference for his or her third-grade daughter. The teacher comments that the child does not stay in her seat or pay attention. The parent says, "You think you have problems. Her second-grade teacher complained. Her first-grade and kindergarten teachers complained. She was kicked out of nursery school because she would not sit in circle time and pay attention." Adults seeking help for these behaviors will describe their problems as being present since adolescence or childhood. With some effort, the clinician can usually find evidence to support the chronic nature of the problems.

The problems are pervasive.   The morning teachers complain about the behaviors. The lunchroom monitor complains, as do the afternoon teachers. The tutor complains. The piano teacher complains. The soccer coach complains. Sunday school teachers are not allowed to complain, but they let you know. These behaviors are not just school problems. They interfere with friendships, family life, and after-school activities.

To make the diagnosis, then, the following steps must be taken:

1. Confirm that DSM-IV criteria are satisfied to establish the presence of one or more of the three behaviors.
2. Show through the clinical history that these behaviors have been present throughout life—that is, they are chronic.

3. Show through the clinical history that these behaviors are present throughout the person's present life—that is, they are pervasive.

DSM-IV requires this chronic and pervasive history. The behaviors identified must have been present before age 7 years, and they must also interfere with functioning in two or more areas of the person's life.

Formal Instruments Used in the Diagnostic Process

Rating Scales

Rating scales are popular for assessing children's behaviors. These behavioral rating scales might be completed by parents, teachers, and/or the child or adolescent being evaluated. The results can be analyzed and compared with established norms. Important information can be obtained in an efficient way. These findings provide a baseline so that any changes can be measured.

The difficulty is in using the findings to make the diagnosis. The results will clarify whether the individual is hyperactive, inattentive, or impulsive but will not clarify the reason for these behaviors.

My bias is not to use rating scales. I have great respect for them; however, I learn more by interacting directly with the parents and child or adolescent followed by talking to the individual's teachers by telephone. This process might take more time, but it is worth it. I can learn more by talking with a teacher for 5 minutes than I can learn from any rating scale.

Rating scales are two-dimensional. The results report whether a behavior or behavioral cluster is present at a significant level. When I talk to the teacher, I can pick up more. For example, the teacher might tell me that the child is hyperactive and inattentive. The teacher would have marked the rating scale accordingly, but as we discuss the child, I would learn that these behaviors are noticed only during certain activities. Or they occurred after something happened at home or are more likely to be observed during the time the child is at one parent's home than when at the other's home. I also can pick up the teacher's affect. How upset or angry is he or she about these behaviors? "He is so disruptive that I can't teach my class!" tells me more than a check on a rating scale that indicates the child is impulsive.

However, I am in the minority. Most professionals like rating scales and use them as part of the diagnostic process. These scales operationalize the DSM criteria. The Conners series of parent and teacher rating scales are probably the most popular. Other behavioral rating scales are in use. New rating sheets are being created all the time, and some professionals have their own. Some school systems use standard rating scales that have been modified to fit the school systems' needs.

Computer-Based Tests

Several tests have been developed that use the computer to assess the child's or adolescent's ability to pay sustained attention. The results will indicate whether the individual has difficulty sustaining attention or whether he or she shows evidence of impulsivity.

Some professionals insist that they can diagnose ADHD based on the results of these studies. They cannot. The presence of difficulty maintaining attention or of impulsivity confirms only the presence of these behaviors. Unless the clinical history supports that these behaviors have been both chronic and pervasive, the diagnosis cannot be finalized. The results are to be used as part of the diagnostic process, not as the diagnostic process itself. The results might provide an excellent baseline to be used later in assessing the effect of medication on these behaviors.

The Continuous Performance Test (CPT) and the Test of Variables of Attention (TOVA) are the most frequently used computer-based tests. On each test, vigilance is assessed by having the child respond to an auditory or visual stimulus by pressing a button. The stimulus may be in the background of similar signals. For example, visual stimuli appear on a screen, and the child is asked to respond when a certain stimulus appears or when two appear in a specific sequence (e.g., when they follow each other). The task is monotonous and requires constant attention. The speed or complexity of the task can be increased. Children or adolescents with ADHD perform more poorly than do children without ADHD. They might make more errors of omission (i.e., missed signals) or more errors of commission (i.e., pressing the button in error). Errors of omission reflect inattention. Errors of commission reflect impulsivity.

Summary

All children, adolescents, and adults who are hyperactive, inattentive, and/or impulsive do not have ADHD. In reality, ADHD is probably the least most common cause of these behaviors. A clear differential diagnostic process that takes into account all possible causes for these behaviors is needed before a diagnosis can be made. A chronic and pervasive history of the hyperactivity, distractibility, and/or impulsivity must be present.

Because individuals with ADHD have a higher likelihood of having learning disabilities than do other children and adolescents, learning disabilities must also be considered in individuals given the diagnosis of ADHD. The possibility of one of the modulating disorders or a tic disorder also must be considered.

If emotional, social, or family problems are present, the clinician must help clarify whether these problems are causing the behaviors or whether these problems are secondary to the ADHD and the resulting emotional and behavior problems.

Only by understanding the total child or adolescent in his or her total world can the full clinical picture be seen. And only when the full clinical picture is known can a comprehensive treatment plan be developed.

Reference

American Psychiatric Association: Diagnostic and Statistical Manual of Mental Disorders, 4th Edition. Washington, DC, American Psychiatric Association, 1994

Part 3

Associated Disorders

Chapter 7

Specific Learning Disabilities

We all have areas in which we learn readily. Some of us even seem to excel in limited areas with very little apparent learning—thus, a few of us are natural athletes, musical geniuses, or gifted artists. We also have areas in which our abilities will never be more than average and a few areas in which we cannot seem to learn anything. Children, adolescents, and adults with learning disabilities have areas of strengths and average ability, too. These individuals, however, have larger areas, or different areas, of learning weaknesses or inabilities than most people. Each person with a learning disability displays a different pattern of strengths and weaknesses. The individual and his or her parents must understand not only the disabilities but also the abilities. What a child can do, and may indeed do well, is just as important as what he or she cannot do, because these strengths must be built on in order to compensate for the weaknesses.

Some parents report that they suspected their child had a learning disability before he or she entered school. The child may have read letters backward or confused certain letters or numbers. He or she may have misunderstood what was said or may have been slow in developing speech, language, or motor coordination. These concerns became real when the child failed to learn the basic skills taught in first or second grade. Depending on the types of learning disabilities involved, some students will begin to do poorly in first grade. Others may do well until third, sixth, or ninth grade. Only then will their disabilities interfere with academic success.

Health and mental health professionals must not respond to a parent's concerns by saying, "Your child will outgrow it," or "You are just an overworried parent. Relax," unless these professionals can validate these conclusions. Is there evidence of a developmental delay that will improve over time? Is there evidence that this parent is worried inappropriately? If no such evidence exists, these conclusions should not be made. Sometimes a child's or adolescent's school performance will finally fall apart in third, fourth, or fifth grade and the parent will say that he or she had been talking to the family doctor about these concerns since the child was age 4 years. The parent was always reassured with, "Don't worry. He will outgrow it." My advice to clinicians is to trust parents' intuition. If they are concerned, listen carefully.

To explain what is meant by learning disabilities, let me outline a simple scheme describing what the brain must do in order for learning to take place. The first step is *input*—getting information into the brain from the eyes and ears primarily but also, as I discuss later, from other senses. When this information arrives, the brain needs to make sense out of it—a process called *integration*. Next, the information is stored and later retrieved—the *memory* process. Finally, the brain reacts through talking or using muscles—the *output* process.

The brain does a great deal more than this, of course. Any learning task involves more than one of these processes. However, this simplified scheme gives you a structure for understanding learning disabilities. To summarize, the learning processes are

- Input
- Integration
- Memory
- Output

Input Disabilities

Information arrives at the brain as impulses, transmitted along neurons. This information comes primarily from our eyes and our ears. The input process takes place in the brain. It does not pertain to visual problems, such as nearsightedness or farsightedness, or to any hearing problems. This central input process of seeing, hearing, or perceiving one's environment is referred to as *perception*. Thus, individuals with perception disabilities in the area of visual input have *visual perception disabilities*, and those with disabilities in the area of auditory input have *auditory perception disabilities*. Some children have problems with one area of input, some have both kinds of perception disabilities, and some may have problems when both inputs are needed at the same time. An example would be seeing what the teacher writes on the blackboard while listening to the explanation of what is being written.

Visual Perception Disabilities

A child may have difficulty organizing the position and shape of what he or she sees. Input may be perceived with letters or numbers reversed or rotated. For example, a *u* may look like an *n;* an *E* like a *W*, a *3*, or an *M;* or a *6* like a *9*. The child may confuse similar-looking letters because of these rotations or reversals: *d, b, p,* and *q* may be confused with any one of the others. All children show this problem until about age 5½ or 6 years. This confusion with position or input becomes apparent when the child begins to copy letters, numbers, or designs or to read or write.

Another child may have what is called a *figure-ground problem*—that is, difficulty in focusing on the significant figure instead of the other visual inputs in the background. Reading requires focusing on specific letters or groups of letters, then tracking from left to right (in English), line after line. Children with this disability may have reading difficulties. They skip words or lines or read the same line twice. Many life situations require figure-ground ability. For example, a child is told to pass the saltshaker but has difficulty finding it among the many dishes and platters on the table.

Judging distance is another visual perception task that can function poorly. Some children have a *depth perception problem*. Information is received from each eye and combined to create three-dimensional vision. A child may misjudge depth, bumping into things, falling off a chair, or knocking over a drink because his or her hand got to the glass before expected. What is seen as carelessness may be this type of perception error.

Other problems are associated with visual perception disabilities. These problems occur when several areas of perception are needed at the same time. For example, while playing in an open field or gym, a child may become confused and disoriented because of trouble organizing his or her position in space. Alternatively, the child may have difficulty understanding left and right or up and down.

A common visual perception disability relates to activities, *visual-motor tasks,* in which the eyes have to tell the hands or legs what to do. When the eyes provide unreliable information, activities such as catching a ball, jumping rope, doing puzzles, or using a hammer and nail become difficult or impossible. To catch a ball, the child's eyes first must focus on the ball (i.e., visual figure-ground). The child must then keep his or her eyes on the ball so that the brain can use depth perception to perceive the correct position, speed, and path of the ball and then tell the various parts of the body exactly where to move and when to move the arms up. Children who have difficulty with figure-ground or who misperceive distance or speed may have difficulty catching, hitting, or throwing balls. Thus, they may not do well with sports that require quick eye-hand coordination (e.g., baseball or basketball). For similar reasons, these children may have difficulty playing jump rope, four-square, or hopscotch.

Auditory Perception Disabilities

A child with an auditory perception disability may have difficulty with one or several aspects of auditory perception. Some children may have difficulty distinguishing subtle differences in sound. Ours is a visual society; thus, when I mentioned subtle differences in shapes earlier, you knew I meant the 26 letters in the alphabet and the 10 shapes in our numerical system (0–9). As discussed in Chapter 2, the English language has 44 units of sound, called *phonemes.* Each letter has a sound; and vowels have two sounds, a short and a long sound. Certain combinations like *sh, th,* and *ch* have specific sounds. A child with an auditory perception disability may have difficulty distinguishing subtle differences in these phonemes. He or she may confuse words that sound alike, for example, *blue* and *blow, ball* and *bell, can* and *can't.* I may ask a child, "How are you?" and he or she may answer, "I'm nine." This child may have thought I said "old" instead of "are" or in addition to the "are."

A child may have difficulty with auditory figure-ground. For example, a child may be watching television in a room where others are playing
or talking. When a parent calls out to the child from another room, the
parent may be into his or her third sentence before the child realizes that
this voice (i.e., the auditory figure) is important to distinguish from the
other voices and sounds (i.e., the background). With this disability, the
child never seems to listen or pay attention. Intuitively, parents may have
learned early that it helped to have eye contact with the child before
speaking. They learn to go into the room, call the child's name, wait until
eye contact is made, and then speak. Consider the following example:

> I observed Mary in her fourth-grade classroom. She had been evaluated
> and found to have learning disabilities, one of which was an auditory fig-
> ure-ground problem. What I observed did not make sense to me until
> later when Mary helped me understand what happened.
>
> Mary was at her desk reading a book. Other children were talking in the
> back of the room. There was noise of movement in the hall and the usual
> noise of recess through the open window. The teacher suddenly said,
> "Children, let's do our math. Open up your book to page 38, and do prob-
> lem 5." Mary looked up to listen to her teacher as she heard "problem 5."
> She looked around and saw the other children take out their math books.
> She did the same. She then looked over the shoulder of the girl in front of
> her to see on which page she would find the problem. Mary thought she
> was being a good student. At that moment, her teacher said, "Mary, stop
> bothering Jan, and get to work." The teacher then looked at me sitting in
> the back of the room and said, "See what I mean. She never pays atten-
> tion." Mary was confused and hurt because she did not know what she
> had done wrong. (How many times has a child done something to upset
> the parents or teacher and then said in all sincerity, "I didn't do any-
> thing."?) This was the only brain she had ever had, and she did not know
> that it was different. She only knew that she was trying hard, and suddenly
> the teacher was angry with her. The teacher was frustrated with Mary be-
> cause she did not yet know of her disabilities.
>
> Later, I explained the problem to the teacher and suggested how she
> could use Mary's strength (visual figure-ground) to compensate for her
> weakness (auditory figure-ground). When the teacher wanted to give the
> class instructions, she would first say, "Class, may I have your attention."
> (She did not want to embarrass Mary by calling out only her name.) She

watched until Mary was looking at her. Then she gave the instructions. She was building on strengths to compensate for weaknesses. This approach is called *accommodation*.

Some children cannot process sound inputs as fast as other people can. Most special education professionals call this problem an *auditory lag*. Speech and language therapists may call this problem an *auditory processing disability* or a *receptive language disability*. The child has to concentrate on what he or she is hearing for a fraction of a second longer before he or she understands. Then he or she refocuses on what is being said. But by now the child has missed a word or phrase. The child soon cannot keep up and becomes lost. For example, a teacher may explain something in class. The child misses parts of what was said and is confused. He or she asks a question. The teacher becomes annoyed and says, "I just explained that. Why don't you pay attention?"

Sensory Integration Disorder

How does the brain know how to orchestrate muscle activities? For example, when a child is tying a shoe, writing on paper, or hopping, how does his or her brain know exactly which muscles or joints to use in what way in the proper sequence? We call this ability *motor planning,* as distinguished from muscle strength. Four basic sensory inputs are needed to provide the brain with the information it needs to coordinate a response. If these sensory inputs are not performing correctly or if the brain has difficulty integrating these inputs, the individual has a sensory integration disorder. These four inputs are

1. Visual perception
2. Tactile perception
3. Proprioceptive perception
4. Vestibular perception

Visual perception was discussed earlier in this chapter.

Tactile perception.   Nerve endings in our skin relay information about touch. Some of these nerve endings are near the surface and respond to light touch; others are deeper and respond to deep touch or pressure. Some children misperceive messages from these nerve endings and have a *tactile perception disability*. They are tactilely defensive. They are sensitive to touch and may perceive it as uncomfortable or even painful. From early childhood, they do not like being touched or held. The tighter a parent cuddles, the more the child cries. This is frustrating to the parent and to the child. Later, these children may complain about the tags on their clothing, they may like to wear only soft and loose clothes, or they may say their belt or the elastic in their underwear is too tight. These children may wear socks inside out, complaining that the seam bothers their feet, or they may prefer to keep their shoes off. They sit in class but are fidgety as they rearrange their clothing, move clothing tags, or take off their shoes. The scalp is rich in these nerve endings. These children may cry and be upset when parents wash, brush, comb, or cut their hair. These children seem crazy, and their behaviors are hard to understand until the reason for the behaviors is explained.

Parents learn early that they cannot grab, hold, or touch their child without warning. It is all right if the child volunteers to climb into the parent's lap. If the parent wants to touch this child, he or she has to announce the intention to do so and come toward the child's face so that the child can prepare. If a parent comes up from behind and touches, the child may jump away. Parents may have learned that the child prefers deep touch. They learn to squeeze hard and to rub deep when they hold their child.

Some children with tactile sensitivity feel defensive and try to avoid letting people getting too close. They walk around the edges of groups, they don't like to sit with the class during circle time, or they lag at the back of lines. When they walk down the school hall and another child accidentally brushes against them, they may respond as if the touch was a major blow and hit the other child.

Some children with tactile defensiveness feel deprived of touch. Thus, they may seek touch but only when they are in control. They may go around the room hugging or touching other children. Not all young children who exhibit this behavior have sensory integration disorder, but the possibility must be considered, especially when the other behaviors associated with this disorder are noted.

Proprioceptive perception. Proprioceptive nerve endings in the muscle fibers, ligaments, and joints tell the brain which muscle groups are relaxed or contracted and which parts of which joints are bent or extended. These nerve endings inform the brain of muscle tone, muscle and body movement, and body position. These inputs help individuals adapt to their environment and hold their body upright. This information also helps the brain orchestrate complex motor planning activities such as writing. Children who have difficulty with this sensory input may be confused with their body in space and may have difficulty with muscle tone and posture. These children will have difficulty changing their body position to maintain their balance. They may have difficulty with motor planning involving groups of large muscles (*gross motor activities*), for example, running, jumping, hopping, or climbing. Or they may have difficulty with motor planning involving groups of small muscles (*fine motor activities*), for example, tying shoes, using buttons or zippers, coloring, using scissors, or writing.

Some children with this disability feel deprived of proprioceptive input. They may seek such input by jumping, by stomping their feet, or by bumping into the wall.

Vestibular perception. The semicircular canals of the inner ear inform the brain of head position, which communicates the body's position in space. This information is essential to handle the effect of gravity and to maintain the correct position in space. It allows you to maintain your balance while standing on one leg or riding a two-wheel bicycle. Individuals who have a *vestibular perception disability* will have difficulty with body position in space. These problems may result in difficulty climbing on a jungle gym or riding a two-wheel bicycle. Individuals with this disability may become anxious or uncomfortable with sudden changes in body position or when their feet are not on the ground. The vestibular system helps maintain the necessary muscle tone to maintain body posture against gravity. Thus, some children with this disability have weak upper back muscles and prefer to rest their head on the desk or to lie down from time to time.

The vestibular system helps individuals navigate steps. When going upstairs, one foot at a time is brought forward and dropped. However, when going downstairs, as the foot is dropped to the next level, the head tilts forward. The vestibular system informs the brain, and the back is arched to prevent falling. Some children with this disability manage to go upstairs with little difficulty, but they continue to go downstairs one step at a time.

Some children with this problem feel deprived of vestibular stimulation. They may try to create this stimulation by spinning on their feet, by spinning in a chair, or by using a swing. Some children may sit or stand and rock their body forward and back.

The integrated system.   Sensory integration disorder refers to individuals who have combinations of the above-described problems. The gross and fine motor planning problems may be most obvious. The other problems are more difficult to observe unless the clinician knows to look for them. Occupational therapists can evaluate individuals who have these disorders, clarify their problems, and provide essential therapeutic interventions.

Other Sensory Inputs

Children and adolescents with learning disabilities may have difficulty with other sensory inputs. No research is available to validate this fact, but the clinical observations are there. If one area of the brain is functioning differently, other areas may also be involved.

Some individuals seem very sensitive to taste. Food tastes different or funny to them. They are picky eaters and complain about foods that most people like. Others may be sensitive to smell. They complain of smells most others do not detect. They avoid certain places because to them they smell funny.

Some children seem not to be as sensitive as others to temperature. They go outside without a coat in the middle of a cold winter day and seem to be fine. Some children may be less sensitive to pain. They hurt themselves and appear not to notice.

Integration Disabilities

Once information coming into the brain is registered, it has to be understood. This is a complex process. To help you understand this process, let me ask you to do something. "Print" the following three symbols in your brain:

d—o—g

Assuming you have no problem with visual perception, the symbols are printed correctly in your brain. You have to do at least three things to make sense out of, or integrate, these three symbols. First, you have to place the symbols in the right order, or sequence the inputs. Is it *d-o-g*, *g-o-d*, *o-g-d*, or what? Second, you have to infer the word's meaning from its context. For example, *the dog* and *you dog* have very different meanings. In one case, you are naming a pet, and in the other case, you are insulting someone. Thus, you have to abstract meanings from these words. Finally, now that the word is recorded properly and you know what it means, you have to take it, and all the other words that are pouring into your head, plus the many memory tracks being stimulated by these words, and pull them all together or organize them in a way that can be understood.

The process of integrating inputs or of understanding what your brain has recorded requires three steps:

1. Sequencing
2. Abstraction
3. Organization

A child may have a disability in one area or in more than one area. Because inputs are processed through both the visual and the auditory pathways, some children may have a *visual sequencing disability* or an *auditory sequencing disability*. So, too, the other integrative tasks may involve one input mode and not the other.

Sequencing Disabilities

A child with a sequencing disability may hear or read a story but in recounting it may start in the middle, go to the beginning, then shift to the end. Eventually the whole story comes out, but the sequence of events is wrong. Similarly, a child may see the arithmetic problem $16 - 3 = ?$ on the blackboard and write it on the paper as $61 - 3 = ?$ Or the child may see $2 + 3 = ?$ and write $2 + 5 = 3$. In these examples, the child knows the right answer but gets the sequence wrong. These children know their mathematics concepts but make careless errors in calculation. Similarly, children who spell words with all the right letters but in the wrong order may have this disability.

A child may memorize a sequence, for example, days of the week, months of the year, or the multiplication table, and then be unable to use the sequence. For example, he or she can recite the months of the year; however, if asked what comes after August, the child pauses before answering, "September." When asked why the pause, the child explains that he or she had to go back to January and move forward to get the answer. These children can become frustrated using the dictionary. They have to return to *a* each time to know if the next letter means going up or down the column to follow the alphabet sequence.

In other settings, a child with a sequence disability may hit a baseball, then run to third base rather than to first, or he or she may have difficulty with board games that require moving in a particular sequence. When setting the dinner table, he or she may have difficulty remembering where to place each item. The child also may have difficulty with the sequence of dressing. For example, a parent walks into the child's bedroom in the morning and does not know whether to laugh, cry, or bite his or her tongue. The child may have on his pants but is holding his underpants. Or she might have on her blouse and is holding her undershirt.

Abstraction Disabilities

After information is recorded in the brain and placed in the right sequence, an individual must be able to infer meaning. Most children who have an abstraction disability have a mild form of it. Abstraction is such a basic intellectual task that if the disability were too great, the child might be functioning below normal.

However, some children do have problems with abstraction. For example, the teacher may be doing a language-arts exercise with the class. The teacher reads a story about a police officer, then begins a discussion of police officers in general. The children are asked if they know any men or women who are police officers in their neighborhood, and if so, what do they do? A child with an abstraction disability may not be able to answer this question. He or she can talk about only the particular officer in the story and cannot generalize to all police officers. Consider the following observation I made in a regular classroom:

> The teacher was working with four children at one table. The rest of the children were at their seats doing independent work. The teacher and I were observing a child who had an abstraction disability. Two children in the back of the room began to whisper to each other. The teacher looked up and said, "Class, will you please be quiet." The child with the abstraction difficulty looked up, seemed annoyed, and complained, "I was not talking." The teacher agreed and explained that she knew he was not talking but that she was referring to the class in general. He became more upset. He had taken her statement literally. If the class was talking and he was part of the class, she meant that he was talking. But he was not talking. He continued to protest about being accused of doing something he did not do.

Older children, adolescents, or adults with abstraction problems may not understand jokes. They do not know what is so funny or when to laugh. These individual may be confused by puns or idioms. They seem to take things literally and to misunderstand what is said.

Organization Disabilities

Children or adolescents who have difficulties with organization are apparent to everyone. They are disorganized in all aspects of life. Their notebook is a mess; papers are in the wrong place, or are shoved in, or are falling out. They lose things (e.g., books, coats, or pencils), or they forget to bring things they need. They do their homework but somehow lose or forget it, so it is not turned in. Their bedroom is a disaster, no matter how many times it has been cleaned or they have been told to keep it clean. These individuals may have difficulty planning the time needed to do homework or planning ahead to be on time.

These students never seem to bring home what they need to do for homework. The teacher may give them an assignment sheet, but it does not help these students. Chaos results in the morning as they try to get everything together to take to school.

Information, once recorded, sequenced, and understood, must be integrated with a constant flow of information and must be related to previously learned information. Some students have difficulty breaking a whole concept down into its parts; others have difficulty pulling pieces of information into a whole concept. The child who has difficulty going from the whole to parts may read a book and be able to discuss the book in general, giving good information. However, this same child may have difficulty answering specific, detailed questions from the book. In contrast, the child with difficulty going from parts to the whole may read a book and provide great detail about everything that happened in the story. However, when asked about the theme of the book or about who the lead character was, this same child may not know. Students who have no difficulty going from the whole concept to parts often do well on essay examinations. Students who have difficulty taking pieces of information and recalling the whole concept may have difficulty with multiple choice examinations. For example, a student who does very well in high school, writing beautiful papers and essays, may perform poorly on the SAT examination, which is multiple choice.

Some individuals have difficulty organizing their thoughts before speaking and seem to ramble. Others have difficulty organizing their thoughts to put them on paper. They explain what they want to write in great detail, then write a confusing paper with all of the facts but in the wrong order or disconnected.

Memory Disabilities

Once information is received, recorded in the brain, and integrated, it must be stored and later retrieved. This storage and retrieval process is called *memory*. For most students with learning disabilities, two types of memory—*short-term memory* and *long-term memory*—are involved.

Short-term memory is the process by which you store and hold information by the method of concentration and repetition. The information is available while you are attending to it, but it may be lost once this attention is removed. For example, when you call the information operator for a long-distance telephone number with the area code, you get a 10-digit number. Most people can retain these numbers long enough to dial the number if they do so right away and nothing interrupts their attention. However, if someone starts to talk to you in the course of dialing, you may forget the numbers. Similarly, if you go to the store with five items in mind to buy, you may not need a list. You know you will remember. However, by the time you get to the store, so many different impressions may have intervened that you forgot some of the items. Remember in high school or college when you studied for an examination by cramming? You shoved all of the facts into your head by reviewing over and over. You studied until the minute the examination started. You probably did well. Then, weeks later, you started to study for your final. You looked at your notes and reacted as if you never saw them before. The material was in short-term memory.

Long-term memory refers to the process by which you store information that you have repeated often. You can retrieve this information quickly by thinking of it. For example, you can come up with your current home address and telephone number quite readily by thinking about it.

If your child or adolescent has a memory disability, he or she most likely has a problem with short-term memory. Like abstraction disabilities, long-term memory disabilities interfere so much with intellectual functioning that a child who has such a disability is more likely to be functioning below normal.

For example, it may take 10–15 repetitions throughout several days for a child with a short-term memory problem to retain what the average child may retain after 3–5 repetitions on one occasion. Yet this same child may have no problem with long-term memory. He or she will surprise you at times by remembering in great detail things that happened years ago that you have forgotten.

A short-term memory disability can occur with information learned through what one sees, a *visual short-term memory disability,* or with information learned through what one hears, an *auditory short-term memory disability.* Some individuals have one form of the disability; others have both.

A child may read through a spelling list one evening and really seem to know it (because he or she is concentrating on it). The next day, he or she has lost most or all of the words. Similarly, a teacher may review a mathematics concept in class until a child understands and remembers it (because he or she is concentrating on it). When the child sits down to do the homework that night, he or she has forgotten how to do the problems. If a parent does the first problem, bringing the memory back, the child can then do the rest. Likewise, a child may read a page and remember it, read the next page and remember it, and the next and the next page. Then, he or she gets to the end of the chapter and does not remember what was read.

Parents often learn the hard way that they cannot give more than one instruction at a time to a child with an auditory short-term memory disability. If they say, "Go upstairs, wash up, get into your pajamas, and then come down again for a snack," forget it. The child will not remember that many instructions at once.

Such children may make parents and teachers angry by constantly stopping in the middle of speaking and saying, "Oh, forget it" or "It's not important." If a child does this, he or she may have a short-term memory disability. The child starts to speak, knowing what he or she wants to say, but partway through, he or she forgets the flow of ideas. It is embarrassing for a child to say, "I'm sorry. What was I saying?" It is easier to say, "Oh, forget it."

| Output Disabilities

The brain communicates information with words, referred to as language output, or with muscle activity such as writing, drawing, and gesturing, referred to as motor output. An individual with a learning disability may have a *language disability* or a *motor disability*.

Language Disabilities

Spontaneous language refers to situations in which the individual initiates whatever is said. Here, the person can pick the subject and take some time to organize his or her thoughts and to find the correct words before saying anything. In a *demand language* situation, someone else asks a question or asks for a comment, to which the individual then must respond quickly. Now the individual has only a split second in which to simultaneously organize his or her thoughts, find the right words, and answer more or less appropriately.

Children with a language disability usually have no difficulty with spontaneous language; however, they often have problems with demand language. Special education professionals usually call this a *demand language disability*. Speech and language therapists call this problem an *expressive language disability*. This inconsistency in language abilities can be striking and confusing. A youngster or adult may initiate all sorts of conversations, may never keep quiet, in fact, and may sound quite normal. However, put into a situation that demands a response (e.g., "What did you do today?" or "What is the answer?"), that same individual may answer "Huh?" or "What?" or "I don't know." A child may ask you to repeat the question to gain time or may not answer at all, appearing not to be paying attention. If forced to answer, the child's response may be so confusing or circumstantial that it is difficult to follow, sounding totally unlike the person who was speaking so fluently just a minute ago. This confusion in language behavior often puzzles parents and teachers. A teacher may evaluate a child as being lazy or negative because the child speaks all the time in class, but when called on to answer a question he or she often says, "I don't know."

Motor Disabilities

The individual with a learning disability may have a *gross motor disability*, that is, difficulty coordinating groups of large muscles (e.g., arms, legs, trunk). Alternatively, he or she may have a *fine motor disability*, or difficulty coordinating groups of small muscles (e.g., those in the hands).

Gross motor disabilities may cause a child to be clumsy; to stumble, fall, or bump into things; or to have trouble with generalized physical activities such as running, climbing, jumping, or riding a bicycle.

The most common form of a fine motor disability shows up when a child begins to write. The problem lies in an inability to get the many muscles in the dominant hand to work together as a team. The child's handwriting is poor. He or she holds a pen or pencil awkwardly and writes slowly; thus, his or her hand gets tired. The child seems not to be able to get his or her hand to write as fast as the head is thinking. Watch your dominant hand as you write something. Notice the many detailed fine muscle activities involved in writing legibly. Writing requires a constant flow of such activities. Now place your pen in your nondominant hand and try to write. You suddenly have a writing disability. Going slowly is tedious, but at least your handwriting is legible. Consider how frustrating it is for your mind to be so far ahead of what you are writing. If you write at a regular pace, your hand aches and your handwriting deteriorates immediately. Shape, size, spacing, and positioning—everything about the handwriting looks awful, no matter how hard you try. A child with a fine motor disability goes through this all the time. How many times have you said to a child, "If you take your time, your handwriting will be better. When you rush, it becomes too sloppy." How did it feel for you when you slowed down to compensate?

Some children may have this fine motor problem only with writing. Usually, however, these children have a broader problem called a *written language disability*. In addition to the problems with the mechanical aspects of writing, they have difficulty getting thoughts out of their brain and onto paper. Such children may have difficulty with spelling, grammar, punctuation, or capitalization. They seem to know more than they show when they write. After they've written down the material, they can edit and correct their own errors. The difficulty is in the outflow of information. The same child who gets 100% on spelling tests may misspell the same words or simpler words when writing them in context.

A written language disability is frustrating and can be serious. Most schools do not grade students on what they know but on what they put down on a piece of paper. If a child cannot copy off of the board fast enough, take notes when the teacher is talking, or write in class, he or she has a problem. Of necessity, homework requires writing. Maybe this is why some children or adolescents resist doing homework. Think of copying off of the board. First, you have to look at the words (using visual perception). Then, you have to retain the words while you look down to write (using visual short-term memory). Finally, you have to copy the words on the paper (using fine motor skills). Children with disabilities in these areas may have to copy one word or letter at a time, never finishing the work.

Establishing the Child's Profile

The learning process is much more complex than the simple input-integration-memory-output model presented here, but this model should help clinicians understand the many different learning disabilities. The terms used here are those used in reports or at school conferences.

To advise parents on helping their child with learning disabilities, the clinician must know the child's specific profile. Each child, adolescent, or adult with a learning disability will have a different combination of disabilities and abilities. The possibilities are summarized in Table 7–1. Some reports cluster these disabilities. If they are primarily in the language areas, the individual has a *language-based learning disability*. If they are primarily in the visual input through motor output areas, the child or adolescent has a *non-language-based learning disability*.

Table 7–1. Learning disabilities

Input disabilities
   Visual perception
   Auditory perception
Integration disabilities
   Sequencing
      Auditory
      Visual
   Abstraction
      Auditory
      Visual
   Organization
      Auditory
      Visual
Memory disabilities
   Auditory short-term memory
   Visual short-term memory
Output disabilities
   Demand language
   Motor
      Gross motor
      Fine motor

In Chapter 4, I noted that for about 50% of children and adolescents with learning disabilities, such disabilities appear to have a familial pattern—that is, the problems are inherited. This means that a 50% possibility exists that one parent also will have a learning disability. As they learn about their child's disability, some parents may say, "That's me." It may be the first time they have understood why they had so many difficulties in school or in life. This new knowledge will be valuable. It may help these parents rethink the past and some of their negative experiences. This knowledge may be needed when help for the child is being discussed. As one mother once told me, "They kept telling me that I have to help my son be more organized with his work. But I have not been organized one day of my life. How can I help him when I have the same problem?"

| Another Perspective on Learning Disabilities

It is helpful for clinicians to understand the general progression of the school curriculum. This overview may explain why some students first have difficulty in the first grade, and others first have difficulty in third, sixth, or ninth grade. Although each school system establishes its own curriculum for each grade, they all follow a similar pattern.

In first grade, children are taught the basic skills. They learn *phonological awareness,* that is, the ability to attach the correct sound to each symbol and then to blend these individual sounds into a word. By the end of kindergarten, students are assumed to have learned the graphic symbols (i.e., *A* through *Z* and *0* through *9*). Children learn to print each letter of the alphabet, first in lowercase and later in uppercase. They learn the basic concepts of numbers: first, we use a base-ten system in math; second, numbers can be neither created nor made to disappear (called the *conservation of numbers*). These concepts lead to addition and subtraction.

In second grade, the skills taught in first grade are consolidated. Basically, no new skills are taught. Thus, if a student is not fully at grade level at the end of first grade, second grade may be used to improve these skills.

During third grade, a major leap is made. The first weeks are spent in review. Then, the children are assumed to know the basic skills. Thus, the focus shifts to using these skills. No longer is the question, "Can you read?" but "What have you read?" Children are expected to be able to read a book and explain what they read. Similarly, no longer is the question, "Can you write?" but "What have you written?" Students write in journals and create book reports. Spelling, grammar, punctuation, and style of writing become important topics. Children should understand the concept of conservation of numbers. Multiplication and division are introduced. Thus, if a student enters third grade without solid basic skills, he or she will start to struggle by November, following the review period. The year will become more and more difficult.

Fourth and fifth grades are spent expanding on the use of skills. Gradually, having or using the skills is not the issue. These abilities are used to study subject matter—history, science, geography, and so on. If the abilities needed in third grade are not solid, fourth and fifth grades will be difficult.

Sixth, seventh, and eighth grades—middle school—focus on subject content. Each student is expected to have both basic skills and the ability to use these skills. The student who is weak in one or more of these skills will struggle. In general, the subjects are taught in a structured way, focusing on teaching learning strategies and study skills. Because each student now has five to seven teachers and is studying that many subjects, students who have problems with organization may have difficulty managing the classes and assignments.

In high school, the focus remains on topic areas. The material is presented with the assumption that the student knows good learning strategies and study skills. Thus, students who have problems with organization or with executive functioning skills may struggle.

You can see why some students have learning disabilities that interfere with mastery of basic skills and begin to have difficulty in first and second grade. Others may have the ability to learn basic skills, but the areas of disability may interfere more with reading comprehension, written language, or higher mathematics concepts. These students will struggle in third grade. Students with learning disabilities that interfere primarily with organizational skills may not struggle until middle school. And students with difficulties in the executive functioning areas may do well until high school.

Clinical Findings Suggesting a Learning Disability

This section suggests a way for health and mental health professionals to assess a child or adolescent and to decide whether the individual has a learning disability. If such a disability is suspected, the individual could then be referred for formal testing.

This model of screening, based on the *systems review* used by physicians, is an organized approach to screen for potential areas of difficulty. If an area is identified, further questions or assessments are given. Given your knowledge of learning disabilities, the questions will appear to be logical.

Reading

- Do you like to read, or do you hate to read?
- How well do you read?
- Is it easier for you to read out loud or silently?
- Do you guess at unfamiliar words or sound them out?
- When you read, do you make mistakes like skipping lines or words or reading the same line twice? (*Yes* suggests a visual figure-ground problem.)
- Do you find that you can read the words, but you do not always understand what you have read? (*Yes* suggests a reading comprehension problem.)
- Do you find that you can read each page, but by the time you finish the chapter or book, you have forgotten what you have read? (*Yes* suggests a visual short-term memory problem.)

Writing

- How is your handwriting? Do you prefer printing or cursive? (*Printing*, after taught cursive, suggests a fine motor problem.)
- Does your hand get tired when you write? (*Yes* suggests a fine motor problem.)
- Do you find that you cannot write as fast as you are thinking? If so, do you sometimes overlap words because you are thinking of the

next word but still writing the first word? (*Yes* suggests a fine motor problem.)

- Can you copy things off of the blackboard fast enough? Can you take notes in class fast enough? (Difficulty in doing these tasks suggests fine motor difficulties.)
- How is your spelling? Grammar? Punctuation? Capitalization? (If stated to be poor, ask for a sample of writing. Individuals whose writing samples are poor may have a written language problem.)
- Do you have difficulty getting your thoughts on the page in an organized way? (*Yes* suggests a written language problem.)

Mathematics

- Do you know your multiplication tables? Can you use them? (*No* suggests a short-term memory or sequencing problem.)
- When you do math, do you make careless errors like writing *21* when you meant to write *12*, or do you mix up your columns or add when you meant to subtract? (*Yes* suggests visual perception, sequencing, or organizational problems.)
- Do you have difficulty understanding word problems? (*Yes* suggests a reading comprehension, short-term memory, or mathematics concepts problem.)

Sequencing

- When you speak or write, do you sometimes have difficulty getting everything in the right order? For example, do you start in the middle, go to the beginning, then to the end?
- Can you tell me the months of the year? (Some individuals will have difficulty doing this in order.) Fine, now what comes after August? (If there is a time lag or the answer is incorrect, ask how the answer was reached. Individuals with sequencing problems may have to go back to January and count forward.)
- When using a dictionary, do you have trouble remembering whether the next letter is before or after the letter you are on? Do you have to go back to *a* and work your way up?

Abstraction

- Do you understand jokes when your friends tell them?
- Do you sometimes get confused when people seem to say one thing but tell you they meant something else?

Organization

- What does your notebook look like? Is it a mess? Are papers in the wrong place, are they falling out, or are they shoved in?
- What about your desk? Your locker? Is your room at home always a mess?
- Do you have difficulty organizing your thoughts or the information you are learning?
- Do you have trouble taking in a lot of information and putting it together into a concept you can use?
- Do you find that you can read a chapter and understand the questions at the end of the chapter but that you are still not sure what the chapter is about?
- Do you lose things? Forget things? Do you finish your homework but somehow misplace it or forget to turn it in?
- Do you have trouble planning your time so that everything gets done on time?

Memory

- Do you find that you can learn something at night and then go to school the next day and realize that you have forgotten what you learned?
- When talking, do you sometimes know what you want to say, but halfway through you forget what you are saying? If this happens, do you have to cover up by saying something like, "Oh, forget it" or "It's not important."

Language

- When the teacher is speaking in class, do you have trouble understanding or keeping up? (*Yes* suggests a receptive language problem.)
- Do you sometimes misunderstand people and thus give the wrong answer? (*Yes* suggests a receptive language problem.)

- When people are talking, do you find that you have to concentrate so hard on what they are saying that you sometimes fall behind and have to skip quickly to what they are saying now to keep up? (*Yes* suggests a receptive language problem.)
- When the teacher speaks a lot in class, do you get lost and have trouble following along? (*Yes* suggests a receptive language problem.)
- Do you sometimes have trouble organizing your thoughts when you are speaking? (*Yes* suggests an expressive language problem.)
- Do you sometimes know what you want to say before you start to speak but find that the wrong words come out or that you can't find the words you want? (*Yes* suggests an expressive language problem.)

Motor

- Would you describe yourself as well coordinated or a little clumsy? (*Clumsy* suggests a gross motor problem.)
- Do you think you can run, jump, hop, and skip as well as your friends? (*No* suggests a gross motor problem.)
- How well do you catch, hit, or throw a ball? (*Not well* suggests a visual-motor problem.)
- Do you have difficulty tying shoes or using buttons or zippers? How about using utensils when you eat? Do you have trouble with art projects or using scissors? (*Yes* all suggest fine motor problems.)
- Are you sensitive to your clothes? Do tags on your shirt or the tightness of your underwear or your shoes feel uncomfortable? (*Yes* suggests tactile sensitivity.)

Executive Functioning

- Are you good at organizing your homework or studying for tests so that everything is done correctly without taking an excessive amount of time?
- Do you find that the way you studied for a test covered the right materials so that you were prepared?
- Do you have difficulty with reports or long-term projects?
- Do you know the best way for you to learn each subject you take?
- Can you plan your time well when studying or planning projects?

Establishing the Diagnosis

If the clinical assessment plus observations from the parents, child or adolescent, and teachers suggest a learning disability, the individual should be referred for a formal diagnostic process. These studies may be conducted by the school system or may be conducted privately.

A comprehensive study, called a *psychoeducational evaluation*, consists of psychological and educational testing administered by psychologists and educational diagnosticians. These tests usually have three parts: 1) an IQ test to assess the level of intellectual functioning and potential and to clarify the cognitive style; 2) a battery of achievement tests to clarify the level of skills in reading, writing, and mathematics; and 3) a test series that assesses each aspect of information processing: input, integration, memory, and output.

The psychological assessment may consist of a neuropsychological or a clinical psychological evaluation. IQ test results are an important aid, especially in indicating whether any discrepancies exist between the verbal and the performance IQ scores or between the individual subtest scores. Other psychological tests assess perception, cognitive, and language abilities. The educational diagnostician or the psychologists will measure the individual's current level of academic skills with standard achievement tests. If these studies suggest a discrepancy between intellectual potential and performance, further tests of processing will be given to clarify whether a learning disability is present.

If the disabilities are in the motor areas, an occupational therapist may perform further studies. If the disabilities are in the language areas, a speech and language therapist may do further assessments. Other professionals may be part of the diagnostic process if initial studies suggest other specific problem areas (e.g., audiology or neurology).

The results should establish whether a learning disability is present. If so, the data should clarify the specific areas of abilities and disabilities.

Treatment of Learning Disabilities

The treatment of choice for learning disabilities in school is special education. Professionals trained in the area work on helping the individual overcome the disabilities and compensate for those disabilities that cannot be overcome. They teach strategies for learning based on the individual's areas of strengths and weaknesses. The classroom teacher must learn to build on the individual's strengths in the classroom while helping to accommodate for the weaknesses.

The treatment of choice for learning disabilities outside of school and within the family is educating the parents and the child or adolescent. They all must learn to build on strengths while understanding and adapting to or accommodating for the weaknesses. Parents must use this knowledge to select chores, activities, and sports or camps where their child will most likely find success.

My book, *The Misunderstood Child. A Guide for Parents of Individuals With Learning Disabilities* (Times Books, 1998), expands on these concepts. It is written primarily for parents and discusses how they can build on their child's strengths rather than magnifying his or her weaknesses. It also discusses how to get the help necessary to address the learning disabilities.

| Summary

Each individual has his or her specific profile of learning disabilities and learning abilities. This chapter provides the knowledge and vocabulary needed to understand evaluation reports and comments from other professionals. Parents must fully understand their child's areas of disability and ability. It is equally important for any clinician working with such a child to fully understand these areas.

Chapter 8

Modulating Disorders and Tic Disorders

| Modulating Disorders

In Chapter 2, I introduced the concept of maintaining emotional equilibrium and the clinical problems relating to difficulties with modulation. Modulating tasks appear to be regulated within the same areas of the brain, and they appear to use the same neurotransmitter, serotonin.

Characteristics of the modulating disorders suggest they are present from birth. They are chronic, that is, they have been noticed since early infancy and childhood. They are usually pervasive, occurring in all settings. In addition, there appears to be a high frequency of a familial pattern, often up to 50%. Parents or closely related relatives are likely to have or have had the same problems.

The modulating areas of the brain modulate anxiety, anger, and mood. Thus, difficulties in modulation result in difficulties with one or more of these feelings. The individual might feel anxious, have difficulty controlling anger, or feel depressed. Obsessive-compulsive disorder appears to be a modulating disorder. The person who has this disorder has difficulty modulating or regulating specific thoughts or behaviors.

Because children and adolescents with learning disabilities or attention-deficit/hyperactivity disorder (ADHD) have a higher likelihood of having one or more of these modulating disorders than does the general population, clinicians must be aware of the possible existence of each disorder. Unless each of the possible related disorders is identified, a comprehensive treatment plan cannot be made.

Problems Modulating Anxiety

Anxiety is that emotional uneasiness associated with the anticipation of something bad happening or of danger. We distinguish it from fear, the emotional response to real danger, although the body's response to each emotion is the same. Anxiety is a common life experience. For example, you are driving down the highway and notice flashing red lights in your rearview mirror. Your first response might be to feel anxious. Your heart starts to pound, and you might begin to sweat. Then, the police car passes you and drives on, and you relax. You felt anxiety because you might have been pulled over for speeding. Anxiety is a normal feeling related to the normal stresses of life; however, anxiety also can be part of many psychiatric and other medical disorders. Each person might experience anxiety differently. These are the most common responses to anxiety:

- Related to the heart: palpitations, rapid heartbeat, increased blood pressure, flushing or pallor
- Related to breathing: feeling of shortness of breath, increased rate of breathing
- Related to the skin: blotching, rash, increase in skin temperature with sweating, funny sensations felt in the skin
- Related to the muscles: mild shaking (tremor), muscle tension, muscle cramps
- Other physical behaviors: headache, chest pain, overalertness, easy startle response, insomnia, nightmares, dizziness, fainting, urinary frequency
- Other psychological behaviors: fears; feeling scared, tense, nervous, upset, stressed, fretful, or restless; unable to think clearly
- Other social behaviors: appears clingy; needy; dependent; or shy, withdrawn, and uneasy in social situations

Children and adolescents might have a generalized feeling of anxiety. Some individuals might have excessive and unrealistic worries about competence, approval, appropriateness of past behavior, and the future. Others might show a specific feeling of anxiety. They might have a *separation anxiety*, feeling anticipatory uneasiness about separating from parents or other loved ones. Or they might develop a *phobia,* a specific fear that results in avoidance behaviors and functional and social impairment. Common phobias seen in children and adolescents include animals in general, cats, dogs, blood, fire, germs, dirt, heights, insects, small or closed spaces, snakes, spiders, strangers, and thunder. Some individuals may develop a fear of open spaces, called *agoraphobia.*

Other types of anxiety disorders may be present. Some youths develop *social phobia,* showing significant anxiety that is provoked by exposure to certain types of social or performance situations, often leading to avoidance behavior. After a traumatic experience, a child or adolescent might develop a *posttraumatic stress disorder.* These individuals are anxious and overly cautious, and they often reexperience an extremely traumatic event accompanied by symptoms of increased arousal and avoidance of stimuli associated with the trauma.

In some individuals, their anxiety level gets so high that a *fight-or-flight response,* a sympathetic nervous system discharge, is triggered. This response is seen in *panic disorders.* These individuals experience a sudden onset of intense apprehension, fearfulness, or terror, often associated with feelings of impending doom. During these attacks, the body responds with symptoms such as shortness of breath, heart palpitations, chest pain or discomfort, choking or smothering sensations, and a fear of "going crazy" or of losing control.

A summary of the DSM-IV (American Psychiatric Association 1994) classification of anxiety disorders is shown in Table 8–1.

Specific anxiety disorders are not chronic in nature and are not seen as a type of modulating disorder. If a child or adolescent develops a high level of anxiety or one of these anxiety disorders at a specific time in his or her life, the cause of the anxiety or anxiety disorder should be explored. The anxiety might be understandable. For example, many children with learning disabilities begin to show anxiety in late August as they realize school is about to start again. The anxiety might relate to family stress such as the illness or death of a close relative or tension between parents. Sometimes the cause is not readily apparent.

Chronic anxiety disorders may be manifested by anxiety or panic attacks, and the patient has a chronic history of the problem. Children with these disorders were described in early childhood as being more tense and anxious than expected. They have always been more fearful. The

---

Table 8–1.   DSM-IV anxiety disorders

Panic disorder without agoraphobia

Panic disorder with agoraphobia

Agoraphobia without history of panic disorder

Specific phobias (animal type/natural environment type/blood-injection-injury type/situational type/other type)

Social phobia

Obsessive-compulsive disorder

Posttraumatic stress disorder

Acute stress disorder

Generalized anxiety disorder

Anxiety disorder due to a general medical condition

Substance-induced anxiety disorder

Anxiety disorder not otherwise specified

---

current set of problems is only the most recent example of a long-term problem. At an earlier age, these children were afraid to be separated from their mother or afraid to go to sleep alone. Later, they might have had frequent nightmares, woken up, and needed to sleep with their parents. Now they might be afraid to be in a part of the house (e.g., on another floor) if no one else is there, or they might be afraid to play outside because there are bees. Similarly, they might be afraid to be around crowds or in noisy places, or they might be afraid to play sports.

Problems Modulating Anger

Anger, like anxiety, is a normal emotion. The important issue is how the child or adolescent handles or shows this anger. Parents usually model acceptable ways of showing anger. Thus, some youths will show anger by being negative, walking off, stomping their feet, yelling, or slamming doors. Others may throw a pillow or bang their fists. Some children and adolescents learn that it is not acceptable for them to express anger in their family. They may go to their room and beat up a pillow or a stuffed animal.

Youths with a problem modulating anger exhibit very different behavior than described above. They explode. These individuals have a chronic history of difficulty regulating anger. Parents might note that these individuals had terrible temper tantrums as an infant, violent tantrums lasting a long time as a younger child, and now have explosive behaviors.

Intermittent explosive disorder is manifested as a sudden onset of explosive behavior (see Table 8–2). The fuse or threshold point for controlling anger appears to be so short that often it may not be possible to figure out what caused the explosion. Once the child or adolescent explodes, he or she cannot be reasoned with or controlled. He or she will scream, yell, curse, throw things, hit, or break things. During an explosive episode, the individual may sound paranoid, saying things like, "Everyone hates me," or "You're trying to hurt me," or "Don't hit me." In most children and adolescents, an episode lasts anywhere from a few minutes to 15 minutes or more. Then, it stops as quickly as it started. Once an episode is over, the individual may be so tired that he or she wants to rest or sleep. There might be some show of remorse for what happened. More often, the child or adolescent does not want to talk about it. He or she just wants to watch television or engage in some other activity.

These explosive outbursts are frightening and difficult to handle or tolerate. When they occur every day or several times a day, everyone in-

---

Table 8–2. DSM-IV diagnostic criteria for intermittent explosive disorder

A. Several discrete episodes of failure to resist aggressive impulses that result in serious assaultive acts or destruction of property.

B. The degree of aggressiveness expressed during the episodes is grossly out of proportion to any precipitating psychosocial stressors.

C. The aggressive episodes are not better accounted for by another mental disorder (e.g., antisocial personality disorder, borderline personality disorder, a psychotic disorder, a manic episode, conduct disorder, or attention-deficit/hyperactivity disorder) and are not due to the direct physiological effects of a substance (e.g., a drug of abuse, a medication) or a general medical condition (e.g., head trauma, Alzheimer's disease).

Source. Reprinted from American Psychiatric Association: *Diagnostic and Statistical Manual of Mental Disorders,* 4th Edition. Washington, DC, American Psychiatric Association, 1994. Copyright 1994, American Psychiatric Association. Used with permission.

volved becomes overwhelmed and nonfunctional. Parents feel helpless. Siblings are afraid and avoid the individual. Often, children and adolescents with anger regulation problems explode only at home when parents or other significant adults are present. It is unclear whether they know they have to "hold it in" at school or at a friend's house or whether the stresses that cause the anger are associated more with family issues. Occasionally, these explosions may be seen with peers. Less often, they may be seen at school.

The treatment for intermittent explosive disorder goes beyond talking or behavior therapy. I discuss the specific treatment approaches to this disorder later in this chapter.

Problems Modulating Mood

Depression also is a normal feeling. Each major growth step experienced by a child is associated with some anxiety and depression. For example, young children learn to walk and can get around without help. There is the anxiety of moving out alone, and there is the sadness or depression of leaving behind a special kind of closeness and dependency that will no longer exist. Adolescents may be anxious about growing up and becoming an adult, and they feel the sadness or depression of giving up the special experiences and safety of childhood. A child or an adolescent who is depressed might show one or more of the following behaviors:

- Depressed or irritable mood
- Diminished interest or loss of pleasure in almost all activities
- Sleep disturbance
- Weight change or appetite disturbance
- Indecisiveness or decreased concentration
- Suicidal ideation or thoughts of death
- Agitation or slowness of thinking
- Fatigue or loss of energy
- Feelings of worthlessness or inappropriate guilt
- Irritability and increased anger (especially with children)

When a child or an adolescent shows a depressed or irritable mood that lasts a year or longer and the individual is never symptom free for more than 2 months, the disorder is called *dysthymic disorder* or *dysthymia.* Symptoms include appetite changes, sleep changes, decreased energy, low self-esteem, difficulty making decisions or concentrating, and feelings of hopelessness. If the individual shows depressed mood or the loss of interest or pleasure in activities, and evidence of changes in appetite or weight, sleep patterns, or clearness of thinking; decreased energy; feelings of worthlessness or guilt; problems with concentrating or making decisions; or recurrent thoughts of death or suicidal ideation for a period of at least 2 weeks, the disorder is called a *major depressive disorder.*

Some individuals who have a major depressive episode might also have difficulty modulating the upswing of affect. They might go into a hypomanic state manifested by an abnormal and persistently elevated, expansive, or irritable mood. They might exhibit inflated self-esteem, grandiosity, a decreased need for sleep, pressured speech, flight of ideas, distractibility, increased involvement in goal-directed activities, or psychomotor agitation. This hypomanic state might last a week or more if not treated. If a person experiences major periods of both depression and hypomania, he or she has a *bipolar disorder.* If the person experiences periods of normal feelings and depression (without mania), he or she has a *unipolar disorder.*

We do not have a complete clinical picture of these depressive disorders in young children. Often what we observe is irritability and anger. The mood swings might be from pleasant to anger rather than from normal mood to sadness. The younger the child is, the harder it is to make the diagnosis of a depressive disorder (dysthymia or major depressive episode) or a mood disorder (unipolar or bipolar).

A summary of the DSM-IV classification of mood disorders is shown in Table 8–3.

Children or adolescents can become depressed at any age. The cause of the depression might be apparent or unclear. Chronicity is a characteristic associated with modulating disorders in children or adolescents. Parents report that these individuals have always been moody, sad, or unhappy. They rarely showed happiness or enjoyment in relationships or activities. The current problem is only the most recent example of this chronic problem. I discuss treatment for these depressive disorders later in this chapter.

Table 8–3. DSM-IV mood disorders

Depressive disorders

   Major depressive disorder

   Dysthymic disorder

   Not otherwise specified

Mood disorders

   Bipolar disorders

   Due to a general medical condition

   Substance-induced mood disorder

   Not otherwise specified

Obsessive-Compulsive Disorder

Obsessions are unwanted thoughts, images, or impulses that an individual realizes are senseless or unnecessary, that intrude involuntarily into the individual's consciousness, and that cause functional impairment and distress. Despite this lack of control, the individual still recognizes that these thoughts originate in his or her own mental process. Because they arise in the mind, obsessions can take the form of any mental event—simple repetitive words, thoughts, fears, memories, or pictures.

Compulsions are actions that are responses to a perceived internal obligation to follow certain rituals or rules. They also cause functional impairment. Compulsions may be motivated directly by obsessions or efforts to ward off certain thoughts, impulses, or fears. Occasionally, children report compulsions without the perception of a mental component. Like obsessions, compulsions are often viewed as being unnecessary, excessive or senseless, and involuntary or forced. Individuals who have compulsions will often elaborate a variety of precise rules for the chronology, rate, order, duration, and number of repetitions of their acts.

A person with obsessive-compulsive disorder may have obsessions, compulsions, or both. These behaviors result in difficulty functioning. Individuals feel that they are being forced or invaded by the symptoms, and they have insight into the senselessness or excessiveness of their thoughts or acts. They might try to ignore or suppress these thoughts or actions; however, the anxiety builds and the behaviors break through.

Individuals who have obsessive-compulsive disorder exhibit the following common behaviors:

- Counting or repeating behavior: the need to touch something a certain number of times or an even or odd number of times; the need to repeat a specific behavior or pattern of behaviors; the need to count certain things until finished
- Checking or questioning behavior: the need to check and recheck something (e.g., the front door is locked, the stove is off, the car keys were brought in, or the closet light is off), the need to ask a question a specific number of times or until the individual gets the exact response he or she needs to hear
- Collecting or hoarding behavior: collecting matches, rocks, pieces of glass, or pieces of paper; hoarding newspapers or other items; becoming upset if items are thrown away
- Arranging and organizing behavior: the need to tie shoes or to dress or undress in a certain sequence or certain way; the need to organize toys, dolls, or other items in a certain way; becoming upset if anything is changed
- Cleaning and/or washing behavior: the need to lather and rinse an exact number of times while showering or to brush one's hair a certain number of times in a certain pattern; the need to wash hands repeatedly

These obsessions and compulsions may begin to appear at age 6 or 7 years. If someone has obsessive-compulsive disorder, he or she clearly reports that the behaviors were causing frustration and difficulty by early adolescence. I discuss treatment for obsessive-compulsive disorder in the next section.

Treatment of Modulating Disorders

Research in the mid- and late 1990s has begun to clarify these modulating disorders. The areas of the brain involved in these regulatory functions include the frontal cortex, the limbic system, the basal ganglia, and the reticular activating system. These areas of the brain use the same neurotransmitter, serotonin. The modulating disorders appear to be the result of a serotonin deficiency.

Awareness of this deficiency had already been observed in the depressive disorders and in obsessive-compulsive disorder. The *selective serotonin reuptake inhibitors* (SSRIs), medications that increase the level of serotonin in the modulating areas of the brain, have been established as the best treatment. These same medications have been used for children and adolescents who have a chronic pattern of anxiety or anger regulation problems. Current studies suggest strongly that they help. As the level of serotonin increases, the anxiety and angry outbursts decrease or stop. Much more research is needed in this area. For now, the clinical treatment for each of these modulating disorders is to use medications that increase the level of serotonin in these areas of the brain. Cognitive-behavioral therapy is an important intervention along with the medication. In some situations, reflective therapy or family therapy will be beneficial. At this time, four SSRIs are available:

1. Fluoxetine (Prozac)
2. Paroxetine (Paxil)
3. Sertraline (Zoloft)
4. Fluvoxamine (Luvox)

Current information on the use of SSRIs in children and adolescents does not show clear guidelines for choosing one over the other. Each clinician should follow his or her own preference regarding which medication to try first. The medication can be changed if necessary.

This book focuses on ADHD. Clinicians should understand that modulating disorders might coexist with ADHD; however, it is beyond the scope of this book to go into more detail on the treatments for the modulating disorders. The clinician should seek other references for greater detail.

| Tic Disorders

A tic disorder is not a modulating disorder; however, tic disorders are frequently found as part of the neurological continuum I discussed in Chapter 2. Most of the studies showing that tic disorders and ADHD are frequently seen together focus on one type of tic disorder, *Tourette's dis-*

order. Of all children and adolescents who have Tourette's disorder, about 50% also have ADHD. About 60% of individuals with this disorder have a learning disability, and 50% have obsessive-compulsive disorder.

A tic is a sudden, repetitive movement, gesture, or utterance that typically mimics some aspect of normal behavior. Usually of brief duration, individual tics rarely last more than a second. They tend to occur in bouts and at times have a paroxysmal character. Individual tics can occur singly or together in an orchestrated pattern. They can vary in their frequency and forcefulness. Although many tics can be suppressed temporarily, they are often experienced as being involuntary.

Muscle or motor tics vary from simple, abrupt movements, such as eye blinks, head jerks, or shoulder shrugs, to more complex, purposeful-appearing behaviors, such as facial expressions or gestures of the arms or head. In extreme cases, these movements can be obscene or self-injurious (e.g., hitting or biting). Vocal tics can range from simple throat-clearing sounds to more complex vocalizations and speech. Some vocal tics are actually motor tics. The sniffing, snorting, or grunting sounds made by tic movements of the pharyngeal muscles are an example.

If the motor or vocal tics began before age 18 and last for more than 1 month, but for less than 1 year, the disorder is called a *transient tic disorder.* This problem is not uncommon among young children. If left alone, the tics go away and never are seen again. If the motor or vocal tics began before age 18 and last for more than 1 year, the disorder is called a *chronic motor tic disorder* or *chronic vocal tic disorder.* If the person has a chronic motor tic disorder or a chronic vocal tic disorder in which the tics occur many times a day nearly every day or intermittently throughout a period of more than 1 year without a tic-free period of more than 3 consecutive months and in which the disturbance causes marked distress or significant impairment in social, occupational, or other important areas of function, the disorder is called Tourette's disorder. Individuals with Tourette's disorder frequently have a family history of this disorder.

Most individuals who have one of these tic disorders first begin to experience tics between ages 8 and 12 years. Most adults with these disorders report that their tics began during this time.

In summary, DSM-IV classifies the tic disorders as follows:

- Transient tic disorder
- Chronic motor tic disorder
- Chronic vocal tic disorder
- Tourette's disorder

Treatment of Tic Disorders

Tic disorders are not treated unless the tics create a psychological or so-cial problem for the child or adolescent or these tics are so severe as to cause muscle soreness. If the tic disorder must be treated, certain medica-tions can decrease or stop the tics. The medications most frequently used today are

- Haloperidol (Haldol)
- Pimozide (Orap)
- Clonidine (Catapres)
- Guanfacine (Tenex)

As I mentioned in my discussion of the modulating disorders, it is be-yond the scope of this book to provide detailed treatment information for the tic disorders. The clinician should seek other references.

Summary

If a child or adolescent is given a diagnosis of ADHD, it is important to evaluate for other neurologically based disorders frequently found to be comorbid with ADHD. This chapter reviews a group of modulating dis-orders and tic disorders that should be considered.

Reference

American Psychiatric Association: Diagnostic and Statistical Manual of Mental Disor-ders, 4th Edition. Washington, DC, American Psychiatric Association, 1994

Chapter 9

Secondary Psychiatric Disorders and Social Difficulties

The key to understanding the emotional and social problems of children and adolescents with attention-deficit/hyperactivity disorder (ADHD) is to see the behaviors as messages. The clinician's task is to clarify what these messages mean. If the child shows emotional problems such as sadness, anxiety, or fear, the clinician's task is to find out what these emotions mean and why they exist. If the child is aggressive with siblings and peers or gets into power struggles with and is defiant toward parents, the task is to find out what these behaviors mean and why they exist.

Being hyperactive, distractible, and/or impulsive can make a student less available for learning or for playing successfully with others. These behaviors do not automatically result in emotional or behavior problems. They are caused by the frustrations and failures these students experience. The difficulties result from the individual constantly getting feedback that he or she is unmotivated or bad, or from the individual constantly getting into trouble and not knowing what he or she did wrong. Thus, the secondary consequences of ADHD lead to the emotional and behavior problems.

All too often, the emotional and behavior problems result in the individual being referred to a mental health professional for evaluation. This professional must clarify whether the emotional or behavior problems are causing the hyperactivity, distractibility, and/or impulsivity or whether these behaviors are causing the emotional or behavior problems. Children or adolescents who are anxious or depressed can behave the same way as someone who has ADHD. Individuals who act out, getting into trouble in school, at home, and with peers may appear as if they have ADHD, and children and adolescents who have ADHD can demonstrate emotional and behavior problems.

This chapter is about these secondary emotional, behavior, and social problems. It is about difficulties that are the result of ADHD. It is not about emotional and behavior problems that might look like ADHD.

| The Secondary Psychiatric Disorders

When I prepared the first edition of this book, I used the case example of Bobby to illustrate the secondary problems associated with ADHD. Since then, I have seen far too many children like Bobby; his story remains a good example of the problems seen in ADHD.

Bobby's parents came to see me because he had just been suspended from the fourth grade because of fighting. He was 10 years old. On the phone, his mother said that Bobby had been a problem all of his life.

I met with his parents first. They reported no problems during pregnancy or delivery. Bobby's first 3 months of life were described as impossible. He had colic and slept little. He would wake up crying about every 3 hours. After several changes in formula, he improved. By about 3 months, he was eating better and crying less. Sleeping at night was still a problem, though.

Bobby's motor and speech development were normal. He began to walk at 10 months, and according to his mother, "At 10 months and 1 minute, he took off." He ran around inside the house and ran away from his parents when outside. Toilet training was started at age 2 years. He still wets the bed at night.

At age 3 years, Bobby entered a part-time nursery school. He ran around the room and refused to sit during story time or rest period. His parents were told that he was not ready for nursery school. They were not surprised, because they experienced the same behaviors at home. They described Bobby as being very active, being unable to listen to stories or entertain himself, and having a "short fuse" with his sister.

When Bobby was 4, his parents enrolled him in another nursery school. Throughout the year, his teachers complained that he would not sit still during circle time or pay attention to the group activities. Often, he would get up and wander around the room. If another child did not do what he wanted, he would hit the child.

Although kindergarten was no better, Bobby's parents felt his behavior had improved. His first-grade teacher was firm but caring and "stayed on top of him." She allowed him to walk around if he wanted.

The next year was not a good one. Bobby's second-grade teacher complained that he would not stay on task or complete his work. He got into trouble with the other children, especially during unstructured and less supervised times. His third-grade behavior was the same. He distracted the class by the noises he made or by tapping his pencil. He called out in class and forgot to raise his hand. He always seemed to be up "doing something."

Bobby started fourth grade promising his parents that he would be a good boy that year. By the end of October, his parents were called to school for a conference. Bobby's teacher told them he was moving around the room and bothering the other children. His calling out or interrupting her disrupted the other children who were trying to work. He did not complete his classwork and appeared to be daydreaming. According to his teacher, Bobby was immature and required constant attention. The other children did not like him and avoided him during lunch and recess. His parents were told to talk to Bobby about his need to "grow up" now that he was in the fourth grade. His parents knew what the teacher was describing because he was the same way at home. They had tried everything they knew, without success. They wondered what they were supposed to do.

In late December, Bobby hit a boy who was teasing him. This boy's mother called the principal to complain, and Bobby was suspended from school for 3 days. His parents were told to get him help "before he grew up to be a delinquent."

At that time, Bobby's parents came to see me. They reported that Bobby had been active and fidgety all his life. They commented that he had difficulty paying attention and staying on task. It was necessary to bring him back to task constantly when he did his homework. He always interrupted them when they were talking or on the phone. He hit his sister, grabbed toys, and screamed whenever he did not get his way.

Bobby's parents were clearly frustrated and overwhelmed with his behaviors. On specific questioning, I learned that he had tantrums when he did not get his way. Over the past year, he had begun to steal money from his parents. On a few occasions, they found him with matches, lighting paper in his room.

I met Bobby. He was a delightful, pleasant boy. During the session, he was not active. He did show a short attention span when moving from one play activity or game to another. I did not observe the Bobby described by his parents or teachers, but hyperactivity and distractibility frequently are not observed during quiet, one-to-one sessions.

Bobby clearly was not functioning in school. He had poor peer relationships, and his behavior at home resulted in constant yelling, fighting, and punishment. His teacher and his parents were overwhelmed and felt helpless.

Bobby's problems are not unique. The common theme among many children is a chronic and pervasive history of hyperactivity, distractibility, and/or impulsivity. An early history of difficulty with eating, sleeping, and irritability is common among children with ADHD. Year after year, Bobby's teachers correctly identified the behaviors, but no one recognized the probable cause. Each teacher projected his or her frustration and anger onto Bobby and his parents. By the time Bobby came to see me, emotional, social, and family problems were present; however, these problems were secondary to the unrecognized and untreated ADHD and were not the primary disorder. If individual and family psychological interventions were started, Bobby might have improved for a short period of time. However, the hyperactivity, distractibility, and impulsivity would have persisted. By treating the ADHD in addition to providing the needed individual and family help, the total clinical picture could be improved.

I evaluated an 11-year-old boy who was similar to Bobby. He experienced years of behavior problems in school and with children in his neighborhood. At home, he was negative, and every situation involved a power struggle. He had a chronic and pervasive history of hyperactivity, distractibility, and impulsivity. When I explained to his parents why I thought their son had ADHD, they expressed surprise that their pediatrician or the school professionals had not thought of this possibility. His father began to share that he thought he had the same problem. He described being a major behavior problem throughout school. He barely finished high school and did not go to college. His wife added that her husband was impulsive and explosive at home. The father asked to see me on his own.

I met with this father. He described being distractible and impulsive at work, at home with the family, and with friends. To establish whether these behaviors had been present throughout his life, I asked him to contact his mother to see if she had any memories or reports of such behavior. About 2 weeks later, he came in with every report card he had received from kindergarten through twelfth grade. The teacher comments were consistent. He was described each year as inattentive, disruptive (by calling out in class), and a troublemaker. His second-grade teacher called him immature. His third-grade teacher referred to him as "unmotivated to learn." His fifth-grade teacher described him as "a troublemaker who disrupted the class." During middle school and high school, he was constantly in trouble and frequently in detention. As he read these comments with me, he became sad. The pain of his past was still there. Finally, he added that his son would get help now. He did not want his son to have to repeat the life he had led.

Whenever I feel we are making progress in educating teachers to recognize ADHD and to recommend that students be evaluated, I meet another child like the two described above. We are making progress with some teachers, but overall, the progress is not fast enough with enough teachers.

Emotional and Behavior Problems in Children

When children experience stress, they usually react with anxiety or depression. This stress might reflect normal developmental stress. For example, when a 2-year-old child begins to master separation and moves out into "the world," the child feels anxiety about this unknown experience. The child also may feel sadness about leaving the comfort of a closer, more consistent attachment to his or her parents. So, too, with the kindergartner who starts school. The child experiences excitement and anxiety about this new adventure and sadness at not being home or in a known and comfortable preschool program.

The child who has ADHD and possibly learning disabilities may feel the stress of school and express this stress with inappropriate behaviors. This child might react with anxiety or depression. The anxiety is that he or she cannot perform as expected. The depression is the sadness of not being able to please the teacher and parents by doing what is expected.

When the stress a child experiences becomes too great, he or she must do something to cope. In general, we see children taking one of four possible approaches to coping:

1. Internalizing the stress
2. Externalizing the stress
3. Somatizing the stress
4. Using other approaches to cope with stress

Internalizing the Stress

Some children become aware of their problems and feel anxiety, depression, or both. They have these feelings at school and at home. The feelings often lift, lessen, or disappear during the summer and on school vacations.

Anxiety. Children might focus their anxiety on school, exhibiting a fear of going to school (i.e., school avoidance) or a fear of doing schoolwork. This anxiety might expand into a generalized anxiety disorder. Some children might become afraid of sleeping alone or of being in a part of the house alone. They might be afraid to ride the school bus. Some children might become so upset when faced with homework that they will not start it, or they might become upset as soon as they have any difficulty doing the work. Others might become fearful in the classroom and appear to withdraw from any potentially frustrating or uncertain situations by getting upset, resisting the work, or pulling back and becoming passive. They become unavailable for learning.

Mary, age 8, was described at home and with her friends as being a "lovely child," yet she constantly ran into difficulty at school. She called out answers without being called on first. She spoke to her friends while the teacher was talking. She often did not finish her classwork because she was "daydreaming." Everyone observed these problems, but no one tried to figure out why her behavior in and out of school was so different. She did poorly academically and was starting second grade for the second time. When I asked Mary what she did in school when the teacher became angry with her or when she did not finish her work, she replied, "I don't mean to be bad. I try to be good and to do my work." She often was afraid to go into her classroom and described being nervous all day that she might "get into trouble." She did not know why she called out or seemed not to pay attention.

Depression. Some children with ADHD do not develop the ability to cope with the pain of frustration and failure experienced at school; they experience a true sense of depression. Failures, inadequacies, and poor interactions with peers and significant adults leave these children feeling angry and devalued. Younger children, who often are unable to experience the depression internally, may express their feelings by being irritable and aggressive toward everyone. Older children may have classic symptoms of depression. They appear to be sad, they cry easily, and they may have trouble sleeping and eating. Sometimes a child turns so much anger inward that he or she becomes self-destructive, speaks of life not being worth living, or has thoughts of suicide.

Some depressed children feel so bad about themselves that they cannot accept praise. They feel they are too bad to deserve such praise. If a teacher compliments them on their work, they may feel compelled to destroy it. If a parent compliments the child, he or she might behave terribly until the parent yells or enacts a punishment.

After repeated lack of success in school, some children develop a feeling of worthlessness, resulting in a poor self-image and low self-esteem. These children see themselves as inadequate, bad, worthless people who cannot do anything right. Feedback from the outside world often encourages this self-image or, at the very least, does nothing to help correct it.

Ronnie, a markedly depressed 10-year-old boy who experienced feelings of depression, had been hyperactive since birth. Ronnie was always all over the place. His mother reported, "All he ever heard from me was 'no,' 'don't,' or 'bad boy.'" Ronnie was kicked out of nursery school for being a "monster." He grew even wilder in kindergarten and was no better in first or second grade. His ADHD undiagnosed, Ronnie repeated second grade, started third, and was then suspended from school. He had never known himself to be anything but bad, unlikable, inadequate, and stupid. He was finally found to be very bright and to have ADHD, but that did not change his self-image.

No one can talk these children out of their self-assessments because their self-image results from a collection of real experiences. They can improve, however, when they begin to see the changes that come with appropriate help and when they begin to master learning and behavioral tasks.

Depression and the resulting poor self-image or low self-esteem might be apparent in the child's comments. One hears these children say that they are bad, stupid, dumb, or "not as smart as the other kids." Class and homework challenges are met with, "I can't do that. It is too hard." There is a sense of sadness about these children. Sometimes they will say they feel sad and unhappy.

Depression might lead to regression. Some children retreat to an earlier stage of psychological or social development. Earlier behaviors or immature, infantile interactions—things you think the child has completely outgrown—recur.

The parents of 7½-year-old Debbie complained that their daughter had been happy and normal until she entered kindergarten. As her mother explained it, at this point, "she had a change of personality. She had trouble keeping up with the other children. In first grade, she just didn't learn much, so now she's repeating the grade." Her father added, "Home life is terrible. We yell at her all of the time. Since school began this year, she's gone backward, acting like a baby and talking like a baby. She's impossible. She won't listen and tunes me out. She's begun to wet her bed for the first time since she was 3. She even eats with her fingers." At a therapy session, Debbie talked about school. "I have trouble because I can't pay attention and I don't understand the work. The teacher talks, and I am listening to the kids in the next classroom. The teacher gets mad at me, and I start to hate myself."

Externalizing the Stress

Some children find the discomfort and pain of stress, with the resulting anxiety and depression, too much to cope with. Their method of coping with these feelings involves externalizing the anxiety and depression.

They project their problems onto others, accepting no responsibility for them. Suddenly, the behavioral or academic problems are because this kid did this and that kid did that. They get into three fights at school in 1 week and insist that each was the result of someone else's behavior. For example, they might say, "Billy started the fight . . . don't blame me. I didn't do it." Or "Mary made a face at me and got me mad." So, too, it becomes the teacher's fault or a parent's fault.

By projecting all the blame onto others, the child does not have to accept responsibility for his or her problems. The child may be in the principal's office because he or she got into trouble twice in the same day. The child is sitting back, not upset, saying about the first incident, "I didn't cause the problem. My teacher didn't listen to me and then got angry. It was her fault." About the other incident, the child might say, "My teacher didn't see that John kicked me under the table. I just told him to stop, and my teacher accused me of talking. John should be in here, not me."

A child who externalizes stress accepts no responsibility for his or her behavior and appears not to be anxious or depressed. Instead, the meaningful adults in the child's life—parents and teachers—feel anxious and depressed about the child. These are difficult children to help. Because they accept no responsibility for their behaviors, they do not see a need to be in therapy or they insist that there is nothing to talk about.

DSM-IV (American Psychiatric Association 1994) has two diagnostic labels for children who externalize their problems. Children who externalize primarily within the family, challenging rules, getting into difficulty, and then blaming others, are described as having an oppositional defiant disorder (see Table 9–1). Children whose behaviors expand beyond the family, leading to challenging of school and society rules, fighting, and stealing, are described as having a conduct disorder (see Table 9–2). In reality, these two diagnostic groups are only ways of describing the areas in which a child externalizes stress; neither diagnostic label explains the cause of the stress.

Sometimes, children who are described initially as anxious or depressed later are given the diagnosis of oppositional defiant disorder. Still later they may begin to exhibit the types of problems that lead to a diagnosis of conduct disorder. These diagnostic categories do not explain the cause of the behaviors, only the style the children use to cope. For these

Table 9–1. DSM-IV diagnostic criteria for oppositional defiant disorder

A. A pattern of negativistic, hostile, and defiant behavior lasting at least 6 months, during which four (or more) of the following are present:

  (1) often loses temper
  (2) often argues with adults
  (3) often actively defies or refuses to comply with adults' requests or rules
  (4) often deliberately annoys people
  (5) often blames others for his or her mistakes or misbehavior
  (6) is often touchy or easily annoyed by others
  (7) is often angry and resentful
  (8) is often spiteful or vindictive

B. The disturbance in behavior causes clinically significant impairment in social, academic, or occupational functioning.

Source. Reprinted from American Psychiatric Association: *Diagnostic and Statistical Manual of Mental Disorders,* 4th Edition. Washington, DC, American Psychiatric Association, 1994. Copyright 1994, American Psychiatric Association. Used with permission.

children, the most frequent problem is that the frustrations and failures experienced in school, with the family, and with peers lead to significant stress. This stress might be externalized as an oppositional defiant disorder or a conduct disorder. Children who have behavior and academic problems at school often develop one of these disorders. Clinicians must understand that ADHD may be the cause of these problems.

Somatizing the Stress

Some children focus their anxiety on bodily functions. A child may develop stomachaches, lower abdominal cramps, headaches, diarrhea, or increased frequency of urination or bowel movements. These complaints often occur only in the morning on a school day and rarely on weekends, holidays, or during the summer. These children have to leave class to go to the school nurse or to go home. As with any physical symptoms, the discomfort is real. The pain goes away when the child is allowed to stay home, not because he or she was faking, but because the stress of going to school was reduced.

Table 9–2. DSM-IV diagnostic criteria for conduct disorder

A. A repetitive and persistent pattern of behavior in which the basic rights of others or major age-appropriate societal norms or rules are violated, as manifested by the presence of three (or more) of the following criteria in the past 12 months, with at least one criterion present in the past 6 months:

Aggression to people and animals
 (1) often bullies, threatens, or intimidates others
 (2) often initiates physical fights
 (3) has used a weapon that can cause serious physical harm to others (e.g., a bat, brick, broken bottle, knife, gun)
 (4) has been physically cruel to people
 (5) has been physically cruel to animals
 (6) has stolen while confronting a victim (e.g., mugging, purse snatching, extortion, armed robbery)
 (7) has forced someone into sexual activity

Destruction of property
 (8) has deliberately engaged in fire setting with the intent of causing serious damage
 (9) has deliberately destroyed others' property (other than fire setting)

Deceitfulness or theft
 (10) has broken into someone else's house, building, or car
 (11) often lies to obtain goods or favors or to avoid obligations (i.e., "cons" others)
 (12) has stolen items of nontrivial value without confronting a victim (e.g., shoplifting, but without breaking and entering; forgery)

Serious violations of rules
 (13) often stays out at night despite parental prohibitions, beginning before age 13 years
 (14) has run away from home overnight at least twice while living in parental or parental surrogate home (or once without returning for a lengthy period)
 (15) often truant from school, beginning before age 13 years

B. The disturbance in behavior causes clinically significant impairment in social, academic, or occupational functioning.

Source. Reprinted from American Psychiatric Association: *Diagnostic and Statistical Manual of Mental Disorders,* 4th Edition. Washington, DC, American Psychiatric Association, 1994. Copyright 1994, American Psychiatric Association. Used with permission.

Katie, age 7, explained, "Sometimes I get into trouble because I forgot to do what the teacher said or I erase too much. . . . The teacher yells at me and I get scared. Then my stomach starts to hurt, and I have to go to the nurse."

Franklin woke up each school day with severe stomach cramps and vomiting. His mother kept him home from school, and the pains usually disappeared by noon. A complete medical examination found Franklin to be perfectly healthy. He must have guessed why he was brought to see me. His first words were, "I know my stomach trouble is because I'm afraid of school. Only it really does hurt, no kidding!"

Other children may explain their anxiety by focusing on their increasing awareness that something must be wrong with their body. They have heard parents, teachers, and doctors talking about their brain or their nervous system, and they have been through countless examinations and tests, so they express their worries by being hypochondriacal: "My back hurts," "My head aches," or "My knee feels funny" are common complaints. Sometimes this concern with the body extends to a general concern with body image or body damage. At times, these complaints become a complete rationalization for failure. For example, "I can't help it if I made a mistake. My arm hurts today."

Using Other Approaches to Cope With Stress

The class clown.   Some children cope with the stresses of school by being the class clown. Clowning can be very successful. The child learns what to do to the wrong person at the wrong time to disrupt the lesson plan or to be kicked out of class. Clowning serves several functions. It can be a way of controlling feelings of inadequacy—the child clowns around to cover up feelings of worthlessness and depression. By playing the clown or freak, the child seems to be saying, "They call me a clown, but that's only because I choose to be one. I really can turn it off if I want to, but it's too much fun this way." If the child succeeds in this behavior, he or she disrupts the lesson plan or is told to leave the group, thus avoiding the academic work, and therefore the potential failure. Clowning behavior may win a certain measure of peer acceptance. Suddenly, the child everyone teases becomes the class hero because of what he or she did. The clowning behaviors are reinforced.

In some schools, the "punishment" for being sent to the principal's office is well worth the effort—avoiding schoolwork, talking to the secretary, delivering messages, or playing with the computer.

> After 4 years of special education and psychotherapy, Jack returned to regular classes and was doing well. He saw me, and I asked him to describe what he remembered about his experiences in regular classes. "Boy, were those teachers stupid. Anytime it was my turn to read or to do anything I had trouble with, I would tease another boy or joke around. It worked great. I got sent out of the room." Then he added, "Only you got me to see that I was the stupid one. . . . You can't get help if you're not in class, and I sure didn't want to spend the rest of my life in a special class."

Handling anger.   When some children have difficulty dealing with anger, they may choose an indirect way of showing it. One such style is called *passive-aggressive.* The child's behavior is not actively aggressive in and of itself, yet the child seems to make everybody angry with him or her much of the time. While supposedly getting dressed, for instance, the child may play with his or her clothes or with toys until the parent becomes furious. The child then looks up in bewilderment and says, "Why are you so mad at me? I didn't do anything." A special education teacher once said to me of such a child, "He was so cooperative and helpful and sweet that I felt like hitting him."

Other children become *passive-dependent.* Initially, the child avoids failure and unpleasant feelings by staying out of the situations that could result in failure. But this passivity can expand into a veritable lifestyle. He or she avoids taking any initiative in anything and minimizes getting involved in everything. A truly helpless child arouses sympathy in adults. The passive-dependent child's behavior often makes people angry because the helplessness appears to be deliberate and contrived.

Occasionally, children appear to act in an *overly mature* way. Faced with feelings of being different, inadequate, and fearful that no one will like them or take care of them, these children decide to grow up quickly. They also sense that they are not making it as a child with other children and guess that it would be safer to be an adult. Often they have a compelling need to be in control and become upset if they cannot control every situation. This controlling behavior might be their way of coping with a world that they experience as out-of-control. It might be a way of becoming an adultlike person and taking control of the world. They look, act, and relate to others like serious adults. This behavior may pay off. Adults compliment them and spend more time with them. Chuck is an example of an overmature child. His parents described this 7-year-old boy as not needing anyone to take care of him.

> Chuck was totally independent; in fact, he took care of everyone else in the family and in his school class. He enjoyed most having discussions with the teacher. He had no sense of humor and was described as a "perfect little man," completely self-sufficient. In a psychiatric diagnostic session, Chuck's fantasy and play reflected great concern about dependency needs and a fear that no one would meet them. So he had to take care of himself. Chuck denied his anger and his wish to be taken care of. He used all of his emotional energies to maintain his protective facade.

Emotional and Behavior Problems in Adolescents

How well an adolescent deals with the special demands of being a teenager is based in part on how well he or she succeeded in handling the developmental stages of childhood and in part on how much the behaviors associated with ADHD interfere with the successful mastery of each phase of adolescence. Another critical factor relates to the age at which the ADHD was recognized and treated. Adolescents whose problems were not recognized until high school have a double problem—they must deal with their existing problems while trying to handle the many problems experienced in childhood before diagnosis and treatment.

Adolescence is a time when being different from peers is painful and peer acceptance is essential. Being a successful adolescent is difficult when the individual with ADHD has poor social skills, has difficulty acting like a teenager, or does not fit in. Adolescence is also the period when rebelling against authority and rules and trying to have a mind of one's own is normal. For some adolescents with ADHD, their struggles with separation and becoming independent create an even greater need to challenge authority and rules.

The first psychosocial task for adolescents is to move from being dependent to being independent. The second psychosocial task is to begin to figure out who they are, forming their own identity. The final psychosocial task is to learn to relate to adults like an adult, that is, creating intimacy. ADHD might add to the difficulty of succeeding at each of these tasks.

Independence

Becoming independent, or moving from being a child toward becoming an adult, means going out from the family and realizing successes and positive experiences on one's own. If the adolescent is insecure, has a poor self-image, and relates poorly with his or her peers, he or she will have difficulty moving away from family and being more independent. Some adolescents may cling to their dependency, turning away from outside companions, staying in the home, putting on the appearance that they would prefer to stay home and watch television. Others might find their feelings of dependency unacceptable and fight to deny them or to cover them up. Negativism; power struggles with adults; and unacceptable clothing, hairstyles, jewelry, and choice of friends are common ways of expressing one's fear of and discomfort with dependency. Parents need to be understanding and to maintain communication and availability during these periods.

Parents might be shown how to help their teenager gain confidence in the areas in which he or she feels most insecure. If relating to peers is difficult for the teenager, the parents could find an acceptable activity in which the teenager could participate in order to practice social skills. For some, a social skills group might be considered. Whether the task is using public transportation, learning to shop, handling money or a checkbook, cooking, driving a car, or interacting with friends in everyday activities, parents can work with the adolescent to develop strategies for coping and succeeding.

Identity

In a world in which value systems change, career opportunities vary, and options for the future are not always secure, establishing a positive concept of self is difficult at best. The world that today's adolescents face is different from that which their parents may have encountered. Sexual values and the importance of relationships have changed. College no longer guarantees the opportunity for social and economic advancement.

Family life has become and will continue to become more mobile. About 50% of adolescents today live in single-parent or remarriage families.

As a child moves into adolescence, he or she needs to have a positive self-image and good self-esteem. The emerging identity of the adolescent must develop from this base of feelings. We know that self-esteem in childhood is based on two major factors: success in school and peer acceptance. Many children who have ADHD, and possibly learning disabilities, have been unsuccessful in both areas. Thus, they move into adolescence with a poor self-image and a low level of self-esteem. They need to experience success if they are to rework these views of themselves and develop a positive concept of their identity.

Intimacy

The task of intimacy starts in late adolescence and continues into early adulthood. The younger adolescent dates or "hangs around with" someone who makes him or her look good. The high school senior may begin to experience "being in love" with someone who makes him or her feel good and may begin to experiment with interactions in a shared relationship.

If an adolescent has a poor self-image, low self-esteem, and a limited positive concept of his or her identity, or if he or she has poor social skills and difficulty making or keeping friendships, dating and close relationships may not be possible. The longer the limited successes or isolation exist, the greater the problems become. Even if the adolescent is able to change later, his or her reputation among peers may make it difficult to be accepted.

There are no simple answers. Psychological help is needed. Parents might seek opportunities for their teenager to have social contact in which he or she has a chance of being successful. Initially, they need to find activities that are centered around a topic or a task rather than social interactions, for example, a computer club, a nature club, a volunteer work group sponsored by a school or religious organization, or a political campaign volunteer group. The focus should be on what is learned or done rather than on talking or interacting. Ideally, this activity is adult supervised rather than peer supervised. The adolescent can begin to be part of a group activity without having to be accepted or successful with group interactions. By teaching the adult leader to be supportive and by teaching problem-solving techniques, the adolescent might begin to feel more comfortable and successful around peers. He or she is encouraged to practice relating to the others in the group. At a minimum, the adolescent will have something to do and a positive group experience. It is all the better if he or she gains some confidence and social abilities. At the best, the adolescent might start a friendship with someone who is not from the school where his or her role and reputation are known.

Specific Areas of Difficulty for Adolescents

Resistance to School and Learning

If ADHD and possible learning disabilities have gone unrecognized and untreated, or if they were addressed in grade school but not in middle or high school, the adolescent is likely to develop psychological difficulties. Some adolescents begin to resist their education and "fight" being in school or doing classwork or homework. They lie about and avoid homework. Some adolescents will try to convince parents (and themselves) that they could be successful but that they just don't care about school. You may hear from them, "School is stupid," "Who needs to learn that subject?" or "The teacher is terrible." Some students will act out in school, cutting classes or breaking school rules. Some of these young people who need special help, sadly, resist getting the help or going to a tutor or to the special education room.

Some students get the message that the school does not really want them, and they drop out. I call this *school pushout* rather than school dropout. Current statistics show that 50% of students identified by schools as having a learning disability quit high school. No statistics exist for high school students who have ADHD. I suspect the figure is at least as high. How could this happen? If a student is known to have a learning disability, how could he or she be provided such minimal services that he or she gets the message, "School is not for me."? How was the ADHD missed? Once out from under the pressures of school, these individuals may settle down, get a job, work toward a high school equivalency degree, and move on with life. For many, though, without professional help, their problems and difficulties will be carried into adulthood.

Alcohol and Drug Use

The relationship between substance use and abuse and ADHD is complex. A summary of the many studies conducted in this area suggests that if a child with ADHD is recognized early and receives all appropriate help, the likelihood of alcohol or drug problems in adolescence is no greater than would be found in the population with which he or she is growing up. However, if the ADHD is not diagnosed early or is not diagnosed at all and if minimal or no treatments were used, the likelihood of alcohol or drug problems in adolescence is greater than would be found in the population with which he or she is growing up. These findings suggest that having ADHD is not the risk factor. Having unrecognized or untreated ADHD is the risk factor.

Some reports discuss adolescents self-medicating with drugs. Adolescents with ADHD, especially those with hyperactivity and/or impulsivity, might find alcohol or marijuana relaxing and quieting. They report that they like these drugs and often do not like the other drugs that they feel make them anxious or more out of control. Some adolescents and adults with ADHD who have been alcohol or drug dependent and who are now not drinking or using drugs report that methylphenidate (Ritalin) or dextroamphetamine (Dexedrine) calms them down and helps. They report that it is easier not to return to alcohol or drugs because their need is less. The final answer on self-medication is not yet in; however, this possibility must be considered with adolescents who have ADHD.

Acting-Out Behaviors

If the adolescent is insecure and has limited academic and peer successes, he or she may have to struggle with becoming independent more than the average adolescent. As this individual struggles to resist the wish to remain safely dependent and struggles with his or her difficulties being independent, normal adolescent rebellious behaviors may worsen. More negativism and power struggles are seen in an effort to deny dependency needs. Conflicts around clothing, hairstyle, jewelry, or selected peer groups may be significant.

More extreme acting out. What happens if efforts fail to help the struggling adolescent survive and cope? Some individuals may need to move to a greater level of acting out. Their goal appears to be to numb or to deny the feelings of anxiety and depression they are struggling to avoid. These behaviors can be serious, destructive, and possibly life-threatening. Some of the more common of these extreme efforts to deny or numb the pain are

- Using, misusing, or abusing alcohol
- Using, misusing, or abusing drugs
- Running away from home
- Cutting classes or skipping school
- Engaging in delinquent behaviors
- Expressing apathy—a state of being in which the only motivation is not to feel any emotional pain for the next hour or so; the teen is self-destructive but is unable to see that what he or she is doing needs to stop
- Making suicidal gestures, attempting suicide, or committing suicide
- Engaging in increased sexual behavior—for boys, as a means of control and power; for girls, as a means of gaining attention and acceptance

Social Difficulties

Children and adolescents with ADHD often do not relate well to peers and may not be accepted by these peers. They may have problems with classmates and with neighbors. Difficulties can be found in out-of-school activities such as Boy Scouts or Girl Scouts, organized sports, and religious education. This peer rejection can be devastating and can lead to feelings of loneliness, poor self-image, and low self-esteem. Adolescents who experience these problems and feelings may have poor school performance, they may engage in juvenile delinquent behavior, and they may drop out of school. Research has shown that the longer-term outcome for children without positive peer relationships can include occupational difficulties, alcoholism, and other emotional problems.

In addition, some children and adolescents feel so out of control that they will try to dominate their environment. When among their peers, they need to control what is done and how it is done. They can be bossy and demanding. For others, their frustration may result in anger. In impulsive children, this anger can result in aggressive behaviors. Adolescents may annoy their friends with their constant activity or with their inability to pay attention.

Many adolescents with ADHD have difficulty with social skills and with reading social cues correctly. They do not recognize the tone of voice or the body language that suggests their behaviors are annoying someone. They do not understand that others perceive them as "being in their face." They may have limited age-appropriate social skills needed to interact in a positive way with peers. If they are impulsive, each of these problems is made worse. Not only do they not read the social situation well, they often act or speak before they think, resulting in behaviors that annoy or anger peers and result in peer rejection.

These problems are seen throughout the school setting—in the classroom, in the halls, and on the playground. Each of the ADHD behaviors causes difficulty. Students with ADHD can be disruptive in the classroom. They might be inattentive and require frequent comments from the teacher to return to the task at hand. They might be verbally intrusive, interrupting the teacher or other students. They might speak too loud. They might not be aware of space and get too close to others. Their increased activity level, disruptive behaviors such as calling out and making noises, increased contacts with classmates, and frequent fidgety behaviors affect everyone negatively.

Students with ADHD often have academic difficulties. Each of the behaviors associated with this disorder can interfere with a student's success in school. A student who has attentional difficulties may have a problem sustaining attention on school tasks. His or her work may be incomplete or not finished on time. A student who is impulsive may rush through work or put down his or her first thought without thinking through the answer. This lack of reflectivity may result in frequent erasures and errors, careless mistakes, and incorrect work. The overall result may be below-ability performance and possible failure. The combination of annoying behaviors in the classroom, frequent corrections by the teacher, and poor academic performance may lead other students to view these children or adolescents as dumb, thus contributing to peer rejection.

Summary

In child or adolescents with a diagnosis of ADHD, the secondary emotional and social problems must be recognized and addressed along with the ADHD. I discuss approaches to treatment in Chapters 12.

The critical question for professionals is whether these emotional and social problems are causing the hyperactivity, distractibility, and/or impulsivity or whether they are a consequence of ADHD. Each conclusion leads to a very different understanding and treatment plan.

Reference

American Psychiatric Association: Diagnostic and Statistical Manual of Mental Disorders, 4th Edition. Washington, DC, American Psychiatric Association, 1994

Part 4

Treatment

Chapter 10

Basic Treatment Concepts

The treatment of attention-deficit/hyperactivity disorder (ADHD) must involve a multimodal approach. This approach includes individual and family education, individual and family counseling, appropriate behavioral management programs, and appropriate medications. Each approach requires working closely with the family and with the school. In this chapter, I focus on an overview of the treatment for ADHD. In the following chapters, I address each part of this multimodal approach.

After ADHD has been diagnosed, the clinician must consider whether any of the related neurologically based disorders or associated emotional, social, and family problems are present. Only with a complete picture of the total individual can a comprehensive treatment plan be developed. Each of the identified problems must be addressed. Sometimes a child with ADHD will be given medication to increase his or her ability to sit and stay on task. However, the child still struggles with reading or writing. Parents and teachers believe the medication is not working, but the problem is not with the medication—the child's ADHD behaviors decreased. The problem is probably a learning disability that needs to be identified and addressed.

A team might be needed to assess all of the possibilities. For the primary care physician, the key is seeking clinical evidence suggestive of one of these problems. If a learning disability is suspected, the child or adolescent might be referred to the school's professional team or to a private practice professional. If a psychiatric disorder is suspected, a referral might be made to a child and adolescent psychiatrist or to another mental health professional. Other consultations might be considered depending on the possible clinical condition suspected.

If the professional conducting the initial evaluation is not the primary care physician, this professional needs to assess the child within his or her areas of expertise and seek consultation to assess other disorders being considered. One person on the formal or informal evaluation team must accept responsibility for integrating the findings and developing a comprehensive treatment plan. This individual needs to be sure that the parents understand the findings.

After the evaluation is complete, someone must integrate the information into a comprehensive diagnostic profile. Consider the following sample profile:

- ADHD, combined type
- Learning disabilities
- Anxiety disorder, considered secondary to the above disabilities

After a comprehensive picture of the child or adolescent is known, a treatment plan can be developed that addresses each identified problem. For example, with the above impressions, a treatment plan might read:

1. A conference with parents to review clinical impressions and proposed treatment plan. If necessary, a family session will be scheduled later.
2. A trial on methylphenidate (Ritalin), starting at 5 mg three times a day.
3. A conference with school professionals to review the child's special education needs and to develop appropriate accommodations.
4. Cognitive-behavioral therapy to address anxiety. An antianxiety medication might be used later.

Implementing the Treatment Plan

During the meeting with parents to review the evaluation findings, the professional or group of professionals should explain each diagnostic impression and how this specific conclusion was reached. The proposed treatment plan should follow from the impressions. Each treatment intervention should be explained so that parents understand what is to be done and why. If possible, the child or adolescent also needs to be informed and educated.

If the professional conducting the evaluation feels that a parent needs individual help, that both parents need parenting or marital counseling, or that the family needs counseling, the reasons should be discussed. If this professional will not conduct the interventions, he or she should make appropriate referrals.

Any medications to be used should be explained in detail. A plan should be made clear as to starting dose and follow-up monitoring. The physician should not ask parents to do what they are not capable of doing. For example, the prescribing physician should not say, "Try different doses and let me know what works best." Parents are not physicians; they need guidance at each step in the process. The clinician should arrange for a way to get feedback from the parents if side effects are noted. This interpretive meeting should not end without clear plans for each step of establishing the proper medication, dose, and timing. I discuss issues related to medication in Chapter 15.

If the school system, teachers, and school professionals play an important role, the clinician should establish a line of communication either with someone directly or through the parents. What accommodations or services are needed? If a learning disability is suspected or known, what steps are needed to finalize diagnostic studies or to implement the appropriate interventions? Who will communicate with the school system? What should the clinician ask of the school professionals? The clinician should explain to the parents what their rights are under law and how to negotiate for what is needed. I discuss these issues in Chapter 18.

If further educational efforts are needed to explain ADHD or the effect of ADHD on the child or adolescent or on his or her family, the physician should explain who will make these efforts. If the child or adolescent will need individual help, how will this help be planned and started? If a parent or both parents need help, what are the next steps? I discuss these issues in Chapter 12.

A brief evaluation resulting in the conclusion that the problem is ADHD and the subsequent writing of a prescription is not adequate. If this is the only model the family physician has the time or the expertise to follow, he or she should make appropriate referrals in order to complete the evaluation and treatment process.

Summary

A multimodal treatment plan is necessary to treat ADHD, any related neurologically based disorders, and secondary emotional, social, or family problems. Ideally, the child's or adolescent's primary care physician will coordinate the necessary assessments, integrate the multiple findings, and coordinate the treatment plan. If not, he or she should handle the medication part and refer the individual to other professionals to address the other problems.

Parents need answers to the following questions:

1. Does my son or daughter have ADHD?
2. If yes, what medication and nonmedication treatments are needed? Who will provide each treatment needed?
3. How can my family and I be helped? Who will provide what is needed?
4. What must I communicate to my school professionals? How?

Remember, the use of medication alone does not constitute treatment for ADHD. Some nonmedication interventions are needed for the child or adolescent, the parents, and the family. These interventions involve the individual, the family, and the school. The following chapters expand on each aspect of this multimodal treatment model.

Chapter 11

Educating the Individual and the Family

Before a clinician starts the educational process with parents or sees the child or adolescent, it is helpful to try to understand where they have been and where they are coming from. Before walking into the clinician's office, many parents have seen other professionals. Often, they have been told that their child's problems are because of their parenting or family. These parents may be frustrated and desperate for help. Think of their perspective.

Many of their child's behavior and school problems are confusing to them. These problems might reflect attention-deficit/hyperactivity disorder (ADHD) plus any of the associated disorders. Classroom teachers might focus on the behaviors without recognizing the underlying problems. They describe a child's inability to sit still, stay on task, or complete a task, or they describe the child's impulsive behaviors such as interrupting or fighting. The parents might have repeated the teacher's concerns to their family physician, adding their own observations and frustrations. They might have reminded this clinician that they have been expressing the same concerns for several years, only to be told that they are overworried parents or that their child will outgrow it. But the problems have persisted and possibly worsened.

Further, school professionals sometimes displace their own feelings of frustration and helplessness onto the parents. Parents rarely get a call from a teacher saying, "Your child had a great day. I want to compliment you on being such a good parent." Instead, the call is more likely to communicate that their child has been disruptive or is not paying attention or completing classwork. The nonverbal message to the parent is clear: "Do something about it . . . . Make your child behave and learn."

Children and adolescents with ADHD also will be frustrated. Their disabilities are not obvious. They have had only one brain their entire life, and they do not know that it functions differently from those of their classmates. All they know is that they want to be good, they want to be successful in school, and they try as hard as the others, yet they do not succeed and they seem to get into trouble. They are accused of being bad or lazy, of not trying, or of being a troublemaker. They do not always understand what they have done. Eventually they might begin to believe that what they are told is true. They begin to feel that they are not as bright as their classmates or that they are bad.

The critical first step in any multimodal approach to treatment must be to educate the parents and then the child or adolescent. This educational process may be needed for other significant individuals such as siblings, grandparents, and child care workers. These individuals must understand that, although invisible, these disabilities are just as debilitating as any other chronic handicapping condition. They also must understand that having these problems does not mean that the child or adolescent is bad or dumb. Finally, each must understand the treatment plan.

Over the past 30 years of working with individuals who have ADHD and often also have learning disabilities, I have followed up many of them through their childhood, adolescence, and into their young-adult life. Often, I ask them to tell me which interventions were the most helpful for them and which were least helpful. I explain that I want to learn from them so that I can better help others. The most consistent response they offer regarding the most helpful intervention is, "When you first explained who I was and what my problems were." Before this time, they saw themselves as inadequate, bad, or not smart. Afterward, they began to understand their disabilities, and with this new knowledge of themselves, they were able to rethink who they were and to begin to change their self-image.

As for any individual with a chronic problem, these children and adolescents must understand their disability and how it affects them at each stage of life. They also must understand the plans for treatment, what each intervention is to accomplish, and their critical role in what happens to them. By understanding and playing an active role in their treatment, they are more accepting of and compliant with the treatment programs. This knowledge is empowering. For the adolescent, playing an active role may be essential to minimize noncompliance.

The Educational Process

The educational process starts with the interpretive or wrap-up session when the professional or group of professionals reviews with the parents what are believed to be the problems and what is needed to address these problems. In my session, I explain each disorder or problem and my proposed treatment. A model for understanding ADHD is presented so that the parents will understand what the disability is and why specific treatments are recommended. (I review this model for understanding ADHD later in this chapter.) If the child or adolescent also has a learning disability, I explain what this disability is, using the input-integration-memory-output model I explained in Chapter 7. During this session, I try to integrate into my findings the results of all previous evaluations.

If I believe emotional, social, or family problems exist, I discuss each problem and explain whether I see these difficulties as primary and a cause of the attentional or academic difficulties or secondary and a consequence of the ADHD and possible other problems. At the end of this interpretive session, I summarize the necessary multimodal treatment plans, indicate which member of the treatment team will be responsible for each part of the plan, and clarify my role as coordinator or member of the treatment team.

My second session in the educational process is with the child or adolescent. I review the same materials I did with the parents. If I feel the parents can explain this information to the child or adolescent, I let them decide whether they will provide this education or would like me to do so. To me, the only difference between explaining ADHD to a 5-year-old, a 10-year-old, or a 15-year-old is the vocabulary and style of communicating I use. To help the child or adolescent understand, I try to use material from my diagnostic sessions. For example, "Do you remember that you told me that when you tried to do homework, it had to be quiet or you could not pay attention? Well, the problem is that it is hard for you to block out unimportant sounds. This is called auditory distractibility." I try to use similar examples to explain hyperactivity or impulsivity.

At the end of this session, I emphasize again the individual's strengths. He or she is not dumb or bad. I stress that now that we know why he or she is having difficulties in school and with family and peers, we can do many things to make his or her life better and more successful. This last theme is critical. It is not acceptable to tell someone—a child, an adolescent, or a parent—what the problems are without following up with what will be done to address these problems.

If needed or requested, my third meeting might be with the whole family. In addition to the siblings, I encourage other significant adults to attend. If a grandparent believes that nothing is wrong with his or her grandchild and that the only problem is that the parents are not strict enough, this grandparent needs to be educated. If a caregiver is part of the family, he or she might need to be educated. At this session, I again review my findings and treatment recommendations. This time, though, I try to get the child or adolescent to help me, for example, by saying, "Mary, I am not sure that I am doing a good job of explaining this problem to your brother. Can you think of an example that might help?" My intent is to educate each member of the family and to begin to change the role the child or adolescent has had in the family. He or she is not lazy, dumb, or bad. There are reasons for the child's behaviors and difficulties, and something can be done to help. It is important, also, to support parents and siblings. Some of the behaviors that they have had to put up with should not be permitted to continue. They, too, have rights in the family. During this session, it is often possible to clarify the family issues that might need to be worked on.

Some clinicians may read this section of the book and say, "Sounds great, but managed care or time restraints will not allow for three interpretive sessions." I understand these concerns. I try to find a way to follow this model, but sometimes I cannot. If I am forced to do a full evaluation in one session, I explain to the family that I can offer only a clinical impression but that I cannot do a full clinical evaluation.

This individual, parent, and family education process is critical to implementing the treatment efforts. All parties should understand what is now known and what will be done. Questions should have been answered. I believe that the knowledge base built will be valuable through-out the treatment process. Because ADHD may be a chronic disorder, this initial knowledge base can be built on over the years as new develop-mental challenges are faced.

Educating Teachers and School Professionals

The child's or adolescent's teachers must understand and accept the clin-ical findings. Classroom teachers need to understand ADHD and what accommodations might be needed. If medication is used, teachers need to know what behaviors might change and what side effects to look for. If a learning disability is suspected, the appropriate school professionals will need to conduct the necessary psychoeducational testing to clarify whether this clinical impression is correct. If it is, appropriate services and accommodations will be needed.

In Chapter 18, I provide information on education laws and parents' rights within these laws. I also review relevant civil laws and the specific procedures to use in seeking and obtaining the necessary services.

Understanding the Use of Medication

The medications I discuss in this book should not be used unless the di-agnosis is ADHD. ADHD is not a school-based disorder but a pervasive disorder that affects individuals during school time and also during fam-ily and peer interactions and during sports and other activities. Clini-cians and parents must understand this concept of helping the total child or adolescent during all of his or her life. Let me be specific:

- ADHD is not just a school disability; it is a life disability. The brain does not know the difference between 9:00 A.M. and 6:00 P.M. nor the difference between Monday and Saturday, November and August, and school days and holidays or vacations. If the clinician treats the child's ADHD only from 8:00 A.M. until 3:00 P.M. on school days, this child may do better at school; however, he or she may continue to have difficulty relating to the family, doing homework, interacting with peers, or participating in sports. The clinician must understand the need for medication during every hour of every day and must prescribe medication for each period of time when hyperactivity, distractibility, and/or impulsivity might interfere with the child's possibility of success.

- ADHD might persist beyond puberty, even into adulthood. About 50% of children with ADHD will improve by puberty; however, 50% will continue to have ADHD as adults. There is nothing magical about puberty. If the individual continues to have ADHD, he or she will continue to need treatment.

Parents must understand the neurological bases for ADHD and the need for medication. It is equally important for the child or adolescent to understand. I empathize with parents who are concerned or fearful of putting their child or adolescent on medication. Some worry that they will be drugging, sedating, or tranquilizing their child. Parents need to understand that the medications used do not drug, sedate, or tranquilize the individual. These medications correct an underlying neurochemical deficiency and allow the individual to function normally.

If parents express concerns, I listen and ask for the source of their concerns. Did they hear it on the radio or television? Did they find it on the Internet? Did they read it in a newspaper article citing someone's personal views on the subject? Or did they read it in a professional, edited, and monitored reference? I encourage educating these parents so that their misinformation does not keep their child from getting appropriate help. I might cite the study done by the American Medical Association discussed in Chapter 1.

A Model for Understanding ADHD and the Rationale for Medication

When I explain ADHD and the role of medication to parents and to their child or adolescent, I use descriptions based on research findings. I simplify some of the concepts to illustrate what can be a complex issue in a way that can be understood by nonprofessionals, but I believe I am providing the best current information on ADHD and its treatment. The model used may seem simple yet is complex, and it is an accurate reflection of what is known.

In this model, I review what research strongly supports about the understanding of ADHD. We do not yet have all the answers, but what is known provides much understanding. To help clinicians educate parents within their clinical practices, I present this model as if I were sitting in an office talking to parents about their child. I start by explaining that the child or adolescent is hyperactive, distractible, and/or impulsive (depending on the specific clinical problems present). Let me continue as if I were talking to these parents:

First, let's discuss hyperactivity. As you know, we are referring to fidgety, restless behavior. What causes this hyperactivity? An area in the brain stimulates muscle activity. This area is in the thinking part of the brain, or the cortex. I call this area the *accelerator*. Other areas in the lower parts of the brain decide how many of these messages get through to the muscles. I call these areas the *brakes*. Normally, a balance exists between the accelerator and the brakes, and the brakes appear to be the controlling factor. Children and adolescents with hyperactivity due to ADHD have brakes that are not working effectively. Thus, the accelerator is not as controlled, and the individual has an increased amount of muscle (motor) behavior. In a minute, I will come back to the brakes and why they are not working effectively.

Now let's talk about distractibility. This distractibility makes it difficult for an individual to filter out unimportant stimuli in the environment and/or to filter out his or her own thoughts so that only one thing can be focused on. The result is difficulty sustaining attention and a resulting short attention span. The brain has a series of *filter systems* that screen out unimportant stimuli or thoughts, allowing us to focus on what is important. In this way, the cortex is not cluttered with too many stimuli. In ADHD, the filter systems are not working effectively. Depending on which systems are ineffective, the individual will experience auditory distractibility, visual distractibility, and/or internal distractibility. I will explain why the filter systems are not working effectively in a moment.

Finally, let's discuss impulsivity, the inability to stop and think before talking or acting. We know less about this behavior. The brain appears to operate somewhat like a computer. Information is entered through a *keyboard*, then relayed to many areas of the brain for a rapid assessment of options. The appropriate decision is relayed through the keyboard, leading to actions. For some people, this keyboard is not working effectively. Thus, thoughts and ideas come in and decisions go back out without the brief fraction of a second of reflection needed. The result is impulsive behavior.

If I may continue to use these symbols, the brakes, the filter system, and the keyboard appear to be in similar areas of the brain. What they have in common is that each uses the same chemical to transmit messages from one nerve ending to another—the same neurotransmitter. We believe this neurotransmitter to be norepinephrine, although it might be one of its precursors, dopa or dopamine. Individuals with ADHD appear not to produce enough of this neurotransmitter in these areas of the brain. Thus, the systems that use this neurotransmitter cannot work effectively. If the brakes are not working effectively, one is hyperactive. If the filter systems are not able to screen appropriately, one is distractible. If the keyboard is not operating as it should, one is impulsive. Thus, depending on which areas of the brain are involved, the individual will be hyperactive, distractible, and/or impulsive.

What has been known for more than 60 years, certain medications can affect these areas of the brain and increase the amount of this neurotransmitter. Once the amount of neurotransmitter is raised to the normal level, the brakes begin to operate effectively, and the individual becomes less hyperactive and calmer; the filter systems begin to operate effectively, and the individual becomes less distractible and has an increased attention span; and the keyboard begins to operate effectively, and the individual becomes less impulsive and more reflective. What we understand, therefore, is that these medications do not drug, sedate, or tranquilize individuals. These medications correct an underlying neurochemical deficiency, allowing the individual to function normally. The effect is analogous to diabetes. When a diabetic is given insulin, a chemical deficiency is corrected, and he or she can function normally. This medication does not cure the diabetes. Thus, when the drug is metabolized, the person once again has difficulty regulating sugar levels. When the medications used to treat ADHD are metabolized, the person returns to being hyperactive, distractible, and/or impulsive.

To some clinicians, this method of describing the research findings that help us understand ADHD may appear to be too symbolic to be correct. I am using poetic license with anatomy and physiology. Parents usually have not gone through medical school, and these symbols and descriptions help them to understand their child. Once these terms have been introduced, they can be used during the treatment phase. For example, "He is still more fidgety than he should be. We may need more medication to get the brakes working better." This information also helps parents understand that the use of medication is not to drug their son or daughter so that others can live with him or her. The medications help their child function normally so that he or she can be successful within the family, at school, and with friends. They have no reason to feel guilty because they placed their child on medication.

Now, with this understanding that ADHD is a neurochemical disorder, it is easier to understand that the disorder exists all of the time. Therefore, to have a child or adolescent on medication only during school hours and school days makes little clinical sense. The school would be delighted with the change, but the individual, his or her parents and family, and the kids in the neighborhood would still have to live with the child's ADHD behaviors, and the child's homework still would not get done. I will stress repeatedly the need to provide medication during any hours when the ADHD behaviors prevent the individual from being successful in life. I provide specific recommendations on medication use in Chapter 15.

| Summary

Education of the child or adolescent, the parents, and the family is a critical part of addressing the treatment of ADHD. Often, this educational process is all that is needed to help the child or adolescent and his or her family move ahead with the multimodal treatment approach. Sometimes, additional efforts are needed. The individual, the parents (individually or as a couple), or the entire family may need counseling or other forms of intervention. I discuss these more intensive approaches in Chapter 12.

Chapter 12

Clinical Interventions With the Individual, Parents, or Family

The educational efforts described in Chapter 11 often result in emotional and behavioral changes in everyone and an improvement in the behavior of children and adolescents with attention-deficit/hyperactivity disorder (ADHD). Parents begin to be assertive advocates for their child, resulting in more appropriate programs within the school system. They begin to understand their child and begin to modify their parenting behaviors to better meet the needs of this family member.

If, after these efforts, the clinician decides that the parents, the child, or the entire family needs further help, specific therapeutic interventions may be necessary. Behavioral management techniques might help address specific problems. A parent or both parents might need help with their emotional difficulties or in working through their resistance or struggles with the reality of ADHD. Both parents might feel the need for help in developing more effective parenting approaches or in agreeing to a consistent behavioral management program. The child or adolescent might need help in addressing his or her emotional or behavioral difficulties or in dealing with denial or with noncompliance with the different therapeutic approaches used.

Both parents might need to enter couples therapy, the child or adolescent might need to enter a form of therapy, or the entire family might need to start in family therapy. Such decisions should be delayed until this point in the process so that the clinician can assess whether the problems have been improved or resolved through the educational process, initial counseling efforts, and the use of appropriate medications.

Whichever form of clinical intervention is started, the professional providing this help must be aware of the effect ADHD and any associated disorders might have on the child or adolescent with the disorder and on other family members. The professional also must understand how ADHD might affect the treatment process.

Helping the Child or Adolescent

ADHD often is not diagnosed until age 8 or 10 years, sometimes not until early adolescence. The years of frustration, poor school performance, negative interactions, and behavioral difficulties the individual experienced before diagnosis and treatment contribute to a poor self-image, low self-esteem, lack of peer acceptance and success, family conflicts, and possibly academic failure. Until the reason or reasons for these problems were understood, the child or adolescent might have been told that he or she was not sitting still, paying attention, or completing work or was calling out in class or disrupting the class, all because he or she wanted to be this way. All it took was a willingness to change. All was under his or her control.

Once the ADHD is diagnosed and treated, most individuals blossom. Their behavior and school performance improve, and they seem happy. For other individuals, the damage done prior to the diagnosis remains. The emotional and behavior problems described in Chapter 9 persist. Psychological help is needed to undo what has been done.

Academic Needs

If the individual has learning disabilities, these must be addressed. Progress may not be noticed until the child or adolescent benefits from remedial interventions or develops strategies to compensate for the disabilities. This takes time. Then time is needed to teach the material that was missed during the years before these disabilities were recognized. The student with ADHD might not have learning disabilities; however, he or she might not have been available for learning for years prior to the diagnosis of ADHD. This student will need special educational interventions to help fill in the gaps of knowledge not learned when it should have been learned.

The treatment approaches are similar to those used with children or adolescents who have emotional or behavior problems; however, the constant focus is on educating the children or adolescents about ADHD and the effect these behaviors have had. These individuals must develop both understanding and compensatory strategies for handling their hyperactivity, distractibility, and/or impulsivity. They must rethink their self-image and build confidence and self-esteem.

Individual Therapy

Individual psychotherapy might be helpful for the child or adolescent who is ready to understand and learn about himself or herself. For the student who externalizes the emotional stress and pain, starting work with the parents or family might be more helpful. Once the student is ready to accept ownership for his or her problems, individual efforts might be added.

Social Skills Training

If the child or adolescent with ADHD has poor social skills and limited success with peers, social skills training might be helpful. Social skills needed for social competence include physical factors (such as eye contact and posture), social responsivity (such as sharing), and interactional skills (such as initiating and maintaining conversation). In addition, as described in Chapter 9, some children and adolescents with ADHD do not appear to be able to read social cues such as facial expressions, a tone of voice, or body language. Before a child or adolescent starts in a social skills group, it is important to identify the individual's areas of social incompetence and the specific skills that appear to be missing.

The literature describes many programs for running social skills groups. In general, these programs focus on a series of steps. The first step involves helping the child or adolescent to develop a sensitivity for his or her social problems. This step is critical. Because of their impulsivity and inattention, some individuals with ADHD have only limited awareness of their socialization difficulties and may deny their problems or project the source of them onto others. Alternatively, they might not be aware that they are missing visual or auditory clues that their behaviors are bothering others. Some individuals interrupt or say the wrong things because they do not stop to think before they talk; others speak too loudly or misjudge space and get too close to another person's face. These individuals need to become aware of their behavior and how others react to it. Some group exercises focus on teaching the types of social skills most people seem to develop naturally. Through pictures or role-playing, each participant learns body language signals or voice change messages. They learn the concept of distance and personal space.

The second step involves having the child or adolescent generate alternative solutions for the identified problems. Here, the group therapist and other group members can help, asking questions such as, "How else might you handle a situation," "What else could you do," or "Have you thought about . . . ?"

The third step involves helping the child or adolescent step-by-step through the process of learning the newly identified solutions to the problems. Role-playing and practice are important ways of learning these new solutions. The individual learns and practices in the group until both awareness of the problem and the ability to try different solutions become more routine.

The final step is to help the child or adolescent link the new knowledge to past events and difficulties and to future events. He or she is encouraged to try out the new social skills and techniques in situations outside of the group and to report on the outcome. What worked? What did not work? What can be learned from what did not work? What might be tried next?

| Helping Parents

The problems of children and adolescents with ADHD go beyond hyperactivity, distractibility, and impulsivity. For many individuals, medication will minimize or control these behaviors; however, these individuals might be aggressive, oppositional, negative, or disruptive within the family. They might be anxious or depressed. They might do poorly in school, they might have no or limited peer relationships, or they might be unsuccessful in all sports efforts. It is easy to see why a parent might feel overwhelmed and helpless. It is also easy to see how such chronic stress can affect a couple's ability to agree on how to parent and how to manage these behaviors. This constant stress, year after year, also can strain or overwhelm the marital relationship.

An individual parent might need help with his or her own feelings of inadequacy and failure as a parent. He or she might be depressed or might feel so helpless that anger becomes the only response. As a couple, the two parents might feel overwhelmed as a parenting team. They might disagree on behavioral strategies, and the child or adolescent with ADHD succeeds in splitting them or causing fighting between them. One parent might want to be firm and strict, whereas the other parent wants to be understanding and permissive. One parent might relinquish his or her role by becoming passive or by minimizing time spent at home. The other parent, already overwhelmed, now has all of the parenting responsibilities. Often, the parent who elects not to parent starts to blame family problems on the way the other parent handles situations.

If stress was not already present in the marriage, it might develop. If marital stress was already present, parenting this child or adolescent might lead to a major crisis. The rate of separation and divorce is high among parents of children and adolescents with ADHD.

Add to all of this the possibility that either parent also has ADHD. His or her hyperactivity, distractibility, or impulsivity also creates stress in the family. This parent might be relieved to learn of the problem and seek help. He or she might minimize the problems and refuse help. Alternatively, the parent might get angry at the child or adolescent with ADHD because he or she does not like the same behaviors in himself or herself.

Depending on the types of difficulties found with each parent, individual therapy for one, couples therapy relating to behavioral management approaches, or couples therapy relating to marital stress might be needed. Sometimes, all of the above are necessary.

Helping the Family

When someone in the family is hurting, everyone feels the pain. Sometimes the family is under so much stress and is so dysfunctional that family therapy is needed before any educational or other therapeutic efforts can be considered. The early phases of this therapy might focus on giving control back to the parents and on helping the child or adolescent with ADHD feel safe not being in control. Specific behavioral management approaches, such as those discussed in Chapter 14, must be started. Later, when the family is functioning better, other clinical interventions can be considered as the needs are clarified.

Family therapy can help change family members' perceptions and expectations of the child or adolescent with ADHD. Sibling conflicts can be addressed. The focus is often on changing unacceptable behaviors and on strengthening the positive relationships between family members. As siblings learn to understand the disorder and as they see positive changes within the family, they can become advocates for a brother or sister who has ADHD at school, in the neighborhood, and with sports and activities. They can help with problems of peer teasing or peer rejection.

Summary

After the effect of individual and parent education and the use of appropriate medications are assessed, individual, parent, or family therapy may be necessary. Clinicians and parents must work closely with the school system at each step of the interventions.

The specific approach used will depend on the need. One professional should coordinate all efforts to be sure that each identified problem is addressed. Whatever form of individual, couples, family, or other therapy is used, the clinician must understand the effect that ADHD and any of the associated disorders might have on the problems being addressed and on the therapy model being used.

Chapter 13

Working With the School System

After the diagnosis of attention-deficit/hyperactivity disorder (ADHD) is established, the clinician and the parents need to work with the classroom teacher(s) and with the school system. The goal is to create the best classroom environment possible and to clarify the services or accommodations the student with ADHD might need. The clinician working with the student who has ADHD might be able to work directly with school personnel or might refer the family to someone else for help. In this chapter, I first review special needs relating to the classroom environment, and then I discuss broader issues relating to the school system and to school services.

The Classroom and Classroom Teacher(s)

Ideally, appropriate medication will minimize or stop the student's hyperactivity, distractibility, and/or impulsivity. If so, the classroom teacher needs to understand the medications, how they work, what side effects might occur, how to observe behaviors, and how to communicate with the clinician managing the medications. If the medication is less than successful, the classroom teacher will need to make special efforts to help the student in the classroom.

Each school system has a procedure for providing medication to students. Given the high level of awareness and concern about students taking drugs in school, children or adolescents should not be told to keep the medication with their lunch and take it quietly on their own. The price of being caught is too great. Even if the physician says it was his or her idea, the student is likely to be suspended. Follow the procedures.

Most school systems have a special form that needs to be completed by the physician and the parents. Clinicians who practice in a large region should consider keeping a supply of forms for each school system patients might be enrolled in. School personnel will need a bottle labeled specifically for the school. Thus, when writing the prescription, I ask the pharmacist to place a certain number of pills in one bottle for the school and another amount in a separate bottle for the parents. For example, if I am writing a prescription for methylphenidate (Ritalin), 5 mg three times a day, I might request a 1-month supply (i.e., 90 pills). Then I will add the instruction, "Place 20 in a bottle, label 'School Use,' give one tablet at noon. Place 70 in a bottle, label 'Home Use,' give one tablet three times a day."

The teacher and the school nurse or health technician must be sensitive to the child's or adolescent's feelings. The teacher should not call out in class, "Billy, it's time to take your pill," or, when Billy misbehaves, "Billy, did you take your pill this morning?" Even worse would be for the school nurse to use the school's intercom system to page Billy: "Will Billy please come to the health room to get his medication." These examples might sound so insensitive that no educator or nurse would do such a thing; however, I mention them because I have heard such examples many times.

General Guidelines

Establishing the best learning environment. The classroom should be modified to address the child's or adolescent's ADHD behaviors (I discuss specific approaches later in this chapter). In addition, the student should be surrounded with good role models, preferably students who will not get pulled into inappropriate behavior. The classroom should be as calm, quiet, and organized as is possible for the grade. Additional structure and supervision should be provided during out-of-classroom time, that is, in the hall, at lockers, at lunch, and on field trips. All teachers (e.g., art, music, physical education) should be informed of any special needs or understanding and how to accommodate the child in their program.

Giving instructions and assignments.   When giving instructions and assignments, the teacher should be sure to have the student's attention and should make the information clear and concise. Daily instructions and expectations should be consistent. The teacher should be sure that the student understood the directions before beginning the task. If necessary, the teacher should repeat the instructions. The student should be made to feel comfortable when seeking help. A daily assignment notebook might be helpful.

Modifying unacceptable behaviors.   Rules of the classroom should be clear and known to students. The teacher should remain calm, state the infraction of the rule, and avoid debating or arguing with the student. Having preestablished responses or consequences for inappropriate behaviors is helpful. The teacher should enforce the consequences quickly and consistently and should avoid ridiculing or criticizing the student.

Enhancing self-esteem.   Building or rebuilding self-esteem is important. The teacher should reward more than punish. Any and all good behavior and performances should be praised immediately. Ways should be found to encourage the student. If the student has difficulty, the teacher should find a way of reestablishing contact and trust so that new solutions can be found and tried.

Specific Guidelines

This section offers suggestions for handling specific behaviors. If the student remains hyperactive, distractible, and/or impulsive, each of these behaviors must be addressed. There are no general guidelines to use. The teacher should plan individually for each student and for his or her specific problem areas. The classroom teacher should try these accommodations. If these approaches do not work, it may be necessary for the school professionals to reconsider whether the student can be best handled in a regular classroom setting.

Hyperactivity. The goal is to channel excessive activity into acceptable activities. If possible, the student might be permitted to stand up or walk around the room as he or she works. More breaks might be useful. These breaks might be blended into specific tasks such as taking messages to the office, delivering something to another classroom, or getting something for the teacher. If the student sits and fidgets by tapping a pencil or his or her fingers or by playing with paper clips or other objects, the teacher might try to work out a hand signal. For example, he or she might place a hand on the student's desk to get the student's attention and then use one hand to tap the other. The student knows this signal means that he or she is fidgeting and can stop. No one else in the class needs to know of the interaction.

Inattention. Tasks might be shortened by breaking one task into smaller parts to be completed at different times. Fewer assignments might be given. Homework assignments might be shorter. Other approaches are to have the student work with other students and to try to increase the interest and novelty of the tasks.

If the student is distracted by sounds, he or she might sit in the quietest area of the classroom, away from windows, doors, or air conditioners. It might be best to have this student sit next to the teacher's desk. The teacher might work out a hand signal to point out to the student that he or she has been distracted. Perhaps the teacher could place a hand on the student's desk to get his or her attention and then touch an ear. The student knows what this means and refocuses.

If the student is distracted by visual stimuli, it would be best to decrease such stimuli. He or she might sit in the front row. (For the student who is distracted by sounds, sitting in the front row might be a problem in that most sounds are now behind him or her.) Working in a corner or with a cubicle might help. The other students would have to understand that working in a corner, facing the wall, is not for punishment. Hand signals might work. Here, the signal might be a hand on the desk and then touching an eyelid.

For the student who is distracted by his or her own thoughts, the best approach may be to have the student's desk next to the teacher's desk. The teacher might help bring the student back to task by getting his or her attention and then either whispering or using a hand signal (e.g., touching the top of the student's head) to alert the student to get back on task.

Impulsivity. Impulsivity is a difficult behavior to manage in the classroom. Efforts might be targeted at helping the student learn to wait. The child might have a piece of paper on his or her desk to write down what needs to be said or to doodle on until the teacher is free. Alternative ways of getting attention might be tried such as forming a line or handing the teacher a note. A reminder, such as a picture of a child with a finger over his or her lips on the desk, might help.

Sometimes an effort can be made after the student calls out or interrupts. If the student is receptive, a hand signal might be enough to remind the student that he or she just acted impulsively. The student might see the teacher turn toward him or her and place a finger over the lips. The student might be able to say, "I'm sorry," and wait.

Overview. Ideally, the student should be taking the appropriate medication at the right dose so that he or she is not hyperactive, distractible, or impulsive. If this approach is not possible, the classroom adaptations discussed here often will help. If, even with these efforts, the student is unavailable for learning or is disruptive in the classroom, the classroom teacher and the parents should request a meeting with the other school professionals either to rethink the classroom placement or to consider what additional services might be provided to the classroom teacher to help. Examples of such services would be a psychologist who could work out a behavioral management program or a counselor who might try group therapy.

The School System

Ideally, the child or adolescent is taking medication, and the medication is working well. If the medication is not helping, alternative medications

151

should be considered (see Chapter 15). If parents refuse to have their child on medication, the school must design a program to handle the student's hyperactivity, distractibility, and/or impulsivity. The school system must address the following four concerns:

1. If the student is taking medication, the classroom teacher will need to understand the medication, its effects, its side effects, and what observations need to be communicated to the parents and to the physician.
2. If the student is not taking medication or the medication is not effective in reducing the behaviors, the classroom teacher and other professionals will need to develop strategies for handling these behaviors.
3. If the student also has learning disabilities, school professionals will need to provide appropriate special education services and accommodations.
4. If the student does not have learning disabilities but has gaps in specific skill or knowledge areas because he or she was less available for learning before diagnosis and treatment, remedial interventions might be needed to fill the gaps.

School Guidelines and Procedures

The federal guidelines issued by the U.S. Department of Education for school systems to use when working with students who have ADHD reflect the concerns listed in the previous section. These guidelines state that two primary *decision factors* should be used in planning the school program:

1. Is the child or adolescent successfully using medication?
2. Does the child or adolescent also have a learning disability?

Schools use two different sets of legal guidelines when addressing these federal guidelines: education law and civil law. The education law is the Individuals With Disabilities Education Act (IDEA). The civil law refers to the Rehabilitation Act of 1973, especially to Section 504 of this act and to the more current Americans With Disabilities Act. I discuss these important pieces of legislation in detail in Chapter 18.

The regulations for IDEA clarify the criteria to be used to classify (or code) a student as having a disability. If a student is coded, appropriate services and accommodations must be provided in the least restrictive environment possible. The so-called Section 504 guidelines also clarify what criteria are used to identify an individual as having a disability; however, if so identified, only accommodations are necessary. If a student is coded under IDEA, he or she will get special education services and accommodations. If he or she is identified under Section 504 guidelines, only accommodations are provided. Thus, whenever possible, parents should use the education law and have their child identified under IDEA rather than Section 504. Let me elaborate.

The IDEA guidelines have no category for ADHD. The federal regulations have three options under IDEA for students who have ADHD:

1. If the student also has a learning disability, he or she can be coded as having a *learning disability* (and thus be eligible for both services and accommodations).
2. If the student has significant emotional problems that make him or her unavailable for learning or that so disrupt the classroom that others cannot learn, he or she can be coded as being *seriously emotionally disturbed* (and thus be eligible for both services and accommodations.)
3. If the student does not qualify as having a learning disability or is not seriously emotionally disturbed, he or she may be coded as *other health impaired* (and thus be eligible for both services and accommodations.)

If the school professionals do not feel that the student with ADHD meets one of the these categories under IDEA, they can use Section 504 guidelines; however, under these guidelines the student will receive only accommodations. The student might receive more time to take tests or other helpful adaptations, but no specific interventions will be made. The difficulty is often with the student who has ADHD and learning disabilities but where the degree of discrepancy between ability and educational performance is not great enough to code the student as having a learning disability. He or she still needs services but will not get them under Section 504.

Summary

The clinician and the parents should work closely with the classroom teacher and with the school professionals who must develop the most appropriate school environment and program for the student with ADHD. To be informed and assertive advocates, parents should understand both the needs of their child and their right to specific services or accommodations. The clinician may have to educate them.

If parents are not successful with their child's teacher or with the school system, they might seek help from a parent advocate or from a parent support group. Information on support groups is listed in the Appendix.

Chapter 14

Behavioral Management

No specific behavioral approaches work best with individuals who have attention-deficit/hyperactivity disorder (ADHD). With any approach, the clinician needs to be aware of the effect the ADHD behaviors have on the plan to be implemented. This concept is especially important during the times when the child or adolescent is not taking medication. For example, if the child takes methylphenidate (Ritalin) at 8:00 A.M. and noon, he or she is off medication from 4:00 P.M. on. Similarly, if the child takes Ritalin at 8:00 A.M., noon, and 4:00 P.M., he or she is off medication from the time he or she wakes up until about 8:45 A.M. and from 8:00 P.M. until bedtime.

A child's noncompliance with getting dressed in the morning might reflect distractibility that results before the medication starts to work. Noncompliance with evening routines might reflect the time after the third dose has worn off. Most, if not all, behavioral programs are unsuccessful if the child is impulsive. The whole concept behind controlling impulsivity is to think before one acts. If you do a certain behavior, a consequence results. When a child or adolescent is impulsive, he or she acts and then thinks. Only after acting will this person remember the consequence.

If you have a behavioral management model that you are competent with, use it. For clinicians who do not have such a model, I present one in this chapter. The model is not unique, nor did I create it. It is a blend of several models that I find helpful when working with families who have a child or adolescent with ADHD.

| A Model for Changing Unacceptable Behaviors

The first step is assessing the behaviors and collecting data. The second step is developing and implementing a plan. I always assume that a child or adolescent will find "loopholes" in any plan; thus, adjustments will be needed.

These approaches must be applied actively. If the approach does not work, the strategy must be rethought and tried again. This approach will work with most children and adolescents, but it takes time, effort, and commitment. Further, this commitment must come from both parents.

Sometimes a parent calls me and describes his or her child to me. The child sounds like a tyrant who must have his or her way or all hell breaks loose. The child screams, throws things, hits his or her siblings, or messes up his or her room. Later, I meet this "tyrant,"—a 4-foot, 70-pound little kid with a sweet smile who could be picked up and carried under one arm. Where is the monster?

After I begin to work with the family, I soon find out. This child's behavior dominates the family. The parents avoid too many confrontations because they do not want to face the consequences. They "look the other way" until pushed so far that they have to react. By that time, feeling helpless, the only possible reaction often is anger. They yell, hit, or give out a punishment, for example, prohibiting the child from watching television for 1 week, but then they have to back down because they have no way to enforce the punishment or because enforcing it leads to more confrontations and fights.

As my evaluation progresses, I gain clues about the dynamics within the child or within the family that explain the behaviors. More often, I cannot clarify the underlying issues but can see that something has to be done and quickly. The clinician needs to "put out the fire" before an in-depth assessment can be considered. What is clear is that the child is in control, and the parents are not in control or are equally out of control. What may also be clear is that the parents disagree, and rather than supporting one another, they are split and fight with each other. This family situation is anxiety producing for the child and is not compatible with healthy psychosocial development. This situation is dysfunctional for the parents and for the other family members.

Perhaps I will find patterns. For example, without meaning to do so, the parents reinforce the very behaviors they do not want. The child acts badly and gets a lot of attention—negative attention. The parents get upset, and this proves to the child that he or she can control one part of the world—the family. This, along with getting what the child wants, is the reward for bad behavior. The other children see the parents forced to give in. They become angry. Soon, they may learn that the only way to get attention or to get what they want in this family is to be bad.

Whatever the dynamics or the initial cause, the family dysfunction must be addressed first. Parents must regain control. The child or adolescent must feel that he or she can be controlled. These changes are essential for the parents, for the child, and for the family. Such negative control of parents is unhealthy and unproductive for the child. He or she must learn different behavioral patterns before they spread to the school, to peers, or to the community.

After the behaviors are under better control, the child or adolescent can begin to learn new and better techniques to function within the family and to cope with stress. Parents and children can rework styles of interacting and roles within the family. First come the behavioral changes, then come awareness and insight.

Related to this goal is an important concern when the child or adolescent also has ADHD and is impulsive. As noted earlier, behavioral programs do not work well with impulsive individuals. The goal of the program is to help these individuals think before they act. For example, "If you do this behavior, you will have to spend time in your room." If an individual is impulsive, he or she acts and then thinks. The consequences are remembered after the act. Thus, the awareness of a consequence is not present to help the individual think twice before acting. Children and adolescents with ADHD who are impulsive must take medication properly before a behavioral program will be successful.

Often, the same child or adolescent who is out of control at home is functioning well in school, at friends' houses, or at play with friends away from the house. Sunday school teachers, activity leaders, sports coaches, and other parents might think the child is great and a perfect lady or gentleman when around them. In this case, one might assume that the behavioral difficulties are not neurologically driven or they would occur in every setting. If the behaviors are expressed only at home, they may reflect family dynamics or conflict. Alternatively, the child or adolescent might hold in his or her frustration and anger all day so as not to get into trouble. He or she comes home where it is safe to let out these feelings, and any little frustration leads to an explosion. As one child told me, "I can't act this way at school. The principal will suspend me. But my parents love me and will never get rid of me. So I can get away with acting this way at home." Another possibility is that the child has ADHD and is taking the appropriate medication and dosage when he or she is out of the house; thus, no behavior problems occur at those times. If the medication covers only school hours, however, the child is off medication when at home, and the hyperactivity, distractibility, and/or impulsivity cause behavioral difficulties at those times. Giving the child medication in the evenings and on weekends might lead to a significant improvement in home behaviors.

If the unacceptable behaviors are found only at home, a behavioral management program will be needed for the home and the family. If these behaviors expand into the school, a similar program might be needed at school. If these behaviors also expand into after-school activities or settings, a behavioral management program might be needed throughout each day.

Basic Concepts of Behavioral Management

 Any behavioral plan, to be successful, must be based on two basic behavioral concepts:

1. One is more likely to succeed in changing behavior by rewarding what is seen as desired behavior than by punishing what is seen as undesirable behavior.
2. For a plan to work, the responses to acceptable and to unacceptable behaviors must be consistent and must occur each time. Inconsistent response patterns may reinforce the negative behaviors.

Parents must understand that there is no right or wrong way to raise children. They must collaborate with the clinician in developing a plan with which each parent can be comfortable and can agree. Then they must follow the plan in a consistent and persistent way. No more splitting. No more parents disagreeing in front of the family about how best to handle behaviors. The child experiences the same responses from both parents. When the child shares two households, as in divorced families, this approach is harder to follow, but it must be the goal.

Initially, parents should be taught to be omnipotent. No more reasoning, bargaining, bribing, threatening, or trying to provoke guilt or shame. Parents make the rules; parents enforce the rules; parents' decisions are final. Life may not seem to be fair to the child or adolescent, but this is what is expected. Parents must learn that if they "step into the arena" and agree to debate or argue with the child, they will lose. If a parent says it is time to go to sleep and the child says, "I want to stay up 15 minutes more," the answer must be, "I did not ask you what time you wanted to go to sleep. I said it is bedtime." Argue about the 15 minutes and it will become 20 minutes, and then 30 minutes. Soon, the parent's frustration and anger will result in fighting. Later in the plan there can be flexibility but not initially.

Developing the Initial Intervention Strategy

Initially, parents are usually overwhelmed. They have exhausted their choices of actions, and none has worked. They may feel helpless or feel they are failures as parents. If there are two parents in the family, stress may exist between the two; for example, they may disagree on how to handle the behaviors or they may blame each other for the problems. One, often the father, may feel so frustrated and unsuccessful that he finds ways to work later and later, coming home after the kids are in bed.

The first step is to teach the parents how to collect data on their observations of the behaviors. Each parent should collect data separately. The differences between the parents' observations will be useful. Ask them not to be embarrassed by what they do. Record what really happens without worrying what someone will think. We already know that things are not working well. They should record what they live with so that changes can begin.

A structure will be needed to collect these data. The easiest model to use is called an *ABC chart*. This type of chart records three things: the antecedent to the behavior (A), the behavior observed (B), and the consequences of the behavior (C). A typical entry might look like the example in Table 14–1.

Each parent will see and record different things. In part, this reflects when each parent is home and with the child or adolescent. One parent may be the firm disciplinarian and the other the easygoing, "give them another chance" type. Each parent has different experiences and expectations. The father may come home at 6:30 P.M. looking forward to being with the children and playing with them. Frustrated and short of temper, the mother may have had it by then and wants the kids to be quiet and to get their homework and other chores done so that they can go to bed.

Neither parent is right or wrong. The important goal is for both parents to agree on their expectations and to be consistent in asking that these expectations be met. Consistency is the key. Inconsistency reinforces the behavior; consistency lessens or stops the behavior.

Certain patterns should become clear for each column in the chart and for overall behaviors. Certain antecedents lead to certain behaviors. The consequences that follow the same behaviors are inconsistent. One parent might become mad and yell at everything, or other family members might be punished as much as the child who caused the problems. A common theme may be that when a child or adolescent does not get what he or she wants or is asked to do something he or she does not want to do, this child or adolescent misbehaves.

After the data are collected, they are analyzed. Patterns are looked for. The first task is to define clearly the unacceptable behaviors that need to be changed. Parents often start with a long list of behaviors to change. Once the data are studied, the unacceptable behaviors might be clustered into two or three major areas. By doing this, the parents will not be as overwhelmed. They are not dealing with an impossible list of problems but can focus on a few major areas.

Frequently, the unacceptable behaviors fall into one of three basic groups. Parents should try to divide their lists into these groups.

Table 14–1. Typical entry for an ABC chart

Date/Time	Antecedent	Behavior	Consequence
Monday			
4:30 P.M.	Don't know; not there	He hit sister; she hit him back	Told both to go to room
6:00 P.M.	Talking to sister	He teased her; she cried	Yelled at Billy
9:00 P.M.	Told Billy to get ready for bed	Refused to take bath, get in PJs; yelled at me when told	Took 30 minutes of reminding; finally hit him and he went to take his bath

Physical abuse. Physical abuse includes hitting, threatening to hit, breaking something, or threatening to break something. Thus, hurting a pet or damaging property would be included.

Verbal abuse. Verbal abuse includes any words, tone of voice, or sounds the parents wish to identify as verbal abuse. Yelling, cursing, teasing, or taunting could be included. Parents could identify something as verbal abuse at any time by saying, "The next time you do that behavior, I will call it verbal abuse."

Noncompliance. Noncompliance includes not completing a required or requested chore, not listening to what is said, or refusing to do what a parent asks. Often, three warnings are given. Following the third warning, action is taken. For example, "If I have to ask you to hang up your coat again, it will be for the third time, and the consequence for noncompliance will be given."

Once the behaviors are identified, it is useful for the clinician to study the relationship between the antecedents and the behaviors. Look for themes. Consider the following examples. The behaviors are more likely to occur

- When the child is tired, hungry, or about to be sick
- During the first hour after coming home from school
- During times of transition, whether leaving or returning to the house
- When routines are disrupted or planned activities have to be changed
- When the child is off medication or the medication is wearing off
- When the child does not get what he or she wants or is asked to do something he or she does not want to do

The behaviors might relate to the child's learning disabilities or sensory integration disorder. Maybe the child was given too many instructions at once. Maybe the assigned chore was too difficult. Maybe the child is frustrated with homework or wants to avoid doing it because he or she does not understand it or thinks it is too hard.

These themes might lead to possible interventions, and they will also make parents more sensitive to the times or situations when problems are most likely to occur. Try to identify these themes and think of how this information can help parents to understand and address the problem behaviors.

Finally, study the pattern of consequences. Are they consistent? Do the parents use consequences and later give in and not carry them out? Do they use consequences that cannot be enforced and, thus, have to back down?

Setting Up the Initial Program

Once the clinician identifies the behaviors that need to be changed, a plan can be developed. Working with the parents, the clinician defines the behaviors as clearly as possible and works out a consequence that can be imposed consistently and that is compatible with the family's philosophy and values. Work out the plan in great detail, and then have the parents introduce it to the family. The plan should be for all siblings. Even if the other children or adolescents do not cause problems, it will not affect them negatively to be part of the program. They might benefit by being rewarded for their good behavior. The "bad" child may have required so much attention that the "good" child was ignored or not thanked for being good. This plan will help parents remember to reward their children for being good. If a sibling is provoking or encouraging the negative behavior, it will become clear if he or she also is on the plan.

Several basic principles must be applied in order to reverse the pattern of punishing bad behavior and usually ignoring or inconsistently rewarding good or positive behavior. This plan will reward positive behaviors and withhold rewards for negative behaviors. Furthermore, each parent will have planned responses that can be used every time. The child or adolescent cannot catch a parent off guard, making him or her feel helpless and therefore angry. Each time a behavior occurs, either parent will have the same response.

Let me illustrate the point about consistency. Suppose a boy hits his sister five times in 1 week. On one occasion, his mother was in such a rush that she yelled at him, but there was no consequence for hitting. On another occasion, she was tired and did not want to deal with him, so she pretended that she did not see what happened. On the other three occasions, she did punish him by making him go to his room. If this child gives up hitting his sister because his mother tells him to do so, he has to give up hitting her 100% of the time. If he continues to hit her, he has a 40% chance of getting away with it. He is punished only three out of five times. He would be a fool to give up the behavior. If a parent is consistent, the behaviors will decrease and then stop. If the parent is anything less than consistent, the behavior might persist or get worse.

Step One

The day should be divided into parts. For example, a typical school day has three parts: 1) from the time the child or adolescent gets up until he or she leaves for school, 2) from the time he or she returns from school until the end of the evening meal, and 3) from the end of this meal until bedtime. Weekend, holiday, or summer days can be divided into four parts by using meals as the dividers: 1) from the time the child or adolescent wakes up until the end of breakfast, 2) from the end of breakfast to the end of lunch, 3) from the end of lunch to the end of dinner, and 4) from the end of dinner until bedtime.

Step Two

The clinician and parents should make a list of the child's or adolescent's unacceptable behaviors. This list should be brief and limited to the major problems. If the three basic unacceptable behaviors noted earlier are used, a list might read as follows:

1. No physical abuse (define in detail for the child; e.g., hitting brother, pulling cat's tail, kicking mother, or breaking toys).
2. No verbal abuse (define in detail for the child; e.g., cursing, calling someone stupid, or teasing).
3. No noncompliance (define in detail for the child; e.g., refusing to do what you are told to do). For younger children, the term *not listening* might be used. Make it clear that you will make a request several times. Then you will say, "If I have to ask you again, I will call it non-

compliance." Any behavior that continues after this warning is considered to be noncompliance. In this way, the child or adolescent can never say, "But, you never told me I had to do this."

Step Three

The plan's purpose is to reward positive behaviors. Negative behaviors are not mentioned as such. The child or adolescent can earn 1 point for each behavior he or she does not do during a unit of time. I discuss *time-out* in the next section. With time-out, too, the focus is on the positive and not the negative. The wording is important. The parent says, "What you did is so unacceptable in this family that you must go to your room and think about the need to change what you do." The parent does not say, "Go to your room!" with the connotation that doing so is punishment.

The child can earn points by not doing the unacceptable behaviors. He or she can earn 1 point for each negative behavior not done during a unit of time. For example, suppose a boy gets up in the morning, does all of his chores, and gets to breakfast on time. He does not hit anyone, but he does call his sister "stupid." As he leaves for school, the parent would say, "I am pleased that you earned 2 points this morning. You followed all the rules, and you did not hit anyone. I wish I could have given you the third point, but you did call your sister a name, and that is verbal abuse." This parent might say to the sister, "I am happy that you earned all 3 of your points. Thank you for not calling your brother a name when he called you one." Remember, behavior is changed by rewarding what you want and not by punishing what you do not want.

The points should be recorded in a book or chart. If the child is too young to understand points, stars can be pasted onto a calendar or chart. For some children, a more concrete approach would be to fill a jar with marbles to represent each point earned.

Each part of the day is handled in the same way. In the model designed above (i.e., with three units of time on school days and four units of time on other days), the maximum number of points that can be earned on a school day is 9, and the maximum on other days is 12. The total for a week will be 69 points. These points can be used in three ways: for a daily reward, a weekly reward, or a special reward.

The points are counted daily and then continue to be counted weekly or cumulatively. The child or adolescent should participate in developing the rewards. Parents make the final decisions, but suggestions are welcome. If the child or adolescent says, "This is stupid. I won't participate," the parent replies, "The plan starts tomorrow. Either you suggest what you might like to work toward, or I will make the decisions for you."

Each reward must be individualized for each family member and must be compatible with the family's style of child rearing and family philosophy. Rewards that involve interpersonal experiences are preferred to material rewards. Examples of daily rewards include an additional 30 minutes of television time that is watched with a parent; being able to stay up 30 minutes later, reading a book or playing a game with a parent; or 30 minutes of special time with one parent. For example, let's say that a child is expected to be in his or her room by 8:30 P.M. with lights out by 9:00 P.M. Usually the half-hour in the room is spent in quiet activities such as talking or reading together. If this child earns the daily reward, he or she could stay up until 9:30 P.M. and have an extra half-hour of time with a parent. However, if he or she did not earn the daily reward, this child must be in the room by 8:00 P.M. with the lights out by 8:30 P.M. He or she loses a half-hour of time with the family.

Again, we are trying to reverse the pattern of rewarding unacceptable behavior by spending time with the child or adolescent when such behavior occurs, at the expense of other family members. Often less time or no time is spent with the child when his or her behavior is appropriate. Now, if the child behaves appropriately, he or she has special time together with the family; if the child behaves inappropriately, he or she gets less time with the family.

The weekly reward might be going to a movie, going out to eat with the family, having a friend sleep over, or any other special activity. If possible, the activity is decided on earlier in the week. For example, "On Sunday, the family is going to the park to play and then have a picnic." Points are counted from Saturday morning to Friday night; thus, parents know if the child or adolescent has enough points before the weekend starts. In this way, a sitter can be lined up or other arrangements can be made before any family activity begins. In the past, this child might have been impossible all week, yet he or she would go out with the family on the weekend. His or her behavior might spoil the fun of this weekend activity. Now, this child or adolescent stays home and misses time with the family, while those members of the family who earned their points get to spend positive time with the family.

A special reward might be something important that must be worked toward. A new bicycle, a special toy, or a special trip might be selected. This reward should be planned so that the child will need at least 1 month to accumulate enough points.

For the daily and weekly rewards, set a goal initially of earning 80% of the maximum number of points possible. After several months of success, this goal might be increased to 90%. It is best not to set the goal at 100%. No one can be perfect all the time. Any negative behavior early in the day or week could destroy all hope of a reward, and the child or adolescent might give up.

For the plan described here, the child or adolescent would need 7 points each weekday evening to get the reward (i.e., 80% of 9 points). He or she would need 55 points by Friday night for the weekend reward (i.e., 80% of 69 points).

Time-Out

Before starting the plan, the parents should define which behaviors will be considered so unacceptable to the family that they will result in the child not only not earning a point but also being removed from the family for a period of time so that he or she can think about the need to change this behavior. I always include physical abuse as "so unacceptable that you must spend time in your room thinking about the need to change." Parents could consider using time-out only for these behaviors.

Parents might start by saying that this time can be spent in a different part of the house than the rest of the family is in, as long as the child or adolescent is quiet and stays isolated. If he or she cannot handle this location, the child or adolescent might have to be in his or her bedroom. If he or she cannot stay in the bedroom with the door open, the door will be shut. Parents might be concerned that their child's bedroom is full of fun distractions and that the child or adolescent will not sit quietly and think. That is okay. The main idea is that the child loses time with the family.

While the child is in his or her room, the rest of the family is interacting. If parents feel a need to do so, they can pick a guest room or the laundry room.

Time-out is to be spent quietly, thinking about what happened and why the child needs to change behavior patterns. Quiet time means quiet time. If the child calls out or yells, the timer is reset. If the child comes out, he or she is sent back and the timer is reset. (Later in this section, I discuss what to do if a parent cannot get a child or adolescent into the time-out room or if the child will not stay in the room.)

This time to think should not be too short. Except for young children, a few minutes have little meaning. For children older than 8 years, I often suggest 30 minutes. For adolescents, I suggest 1 hour. If the child will not be quiet or stay in the time-out room, the initial 30 minutes might turn into hours.

Time-out also can be used out of the home. The parents should try to plan ahead. For example, the parents might say, "We are going to Aunt Sara's house. I spoke to her, and she told me that if you need a time-out room to think about your behavior while we are at her house, you can use the guest room." If at a restaurant and it is safe, parents can take the child or adolescent to the car or ask that he or she sit in the waiting area at the front of the restaurant. If in a shopping mall and it is considered safe, parents can place the child on a bench and say that they will return at a certain time. If parents feel more secure watching the child, they can move to another area of the mall but stay within eyesight. There will be times when parents cannot use time-out immediately, for example, in the car. As soon as the family returns home, the child or adolescent is expected to go to the time-out room for the assigned time.

For the plan to work, it must be exact as to expectations, behaviors that are rewarded, and consequences. Once initiated, I can promise that any child will find loopholes in the plan. That's okay. If the clinician and parents put their heads together, they will find a way to close the loopholes. The parents are in control, not the child.

Issues that could prevent this plan from being implemented should be resolved before starting it. The most common problem involves children who will not go to their room for time-out or who will not stay in their room. Parents should not have to chase their child around the house. They should not have to drag their child to the room, fighting all of the way. It should not be necessary to hold the door shut as the child bangs on the door and tries to open it. A solution to these problems must be created and implemented. If parents find that they really cannot control their child, more intensive professional help will be needed.

I usually recommend a plan for the child who will not go to the time-out room that requires the cooperation of only one person, the parent. I assume that the child cannot be forced to go to the time-out room. I assume that the father or mother has control only over himself or herself. This plan has two parts to it. Parents should discuss the plan before the full program is implemented, and it should be used whenever the child refuses to go to the time-out room or stay there.

First, the parent announces how much time is acceptable for the child or adolescent to take to get to the room. For example, "I will give you 3 minutes to get to your room so that you can begin to think about the need to change." The child is informed that every minute it takes him or her to get to the room after the time limit has elapsed will be doubled and added to the original time. For example, if the original time is 30 minutes and it takes the child 30 minutes to give in and go to the room, he or she now must spend 90 minutes in the room.

The second part of the plan may sound difficult, but it is not. The parent announces that he or she will always love this child. Love is unconditional. However, during the time that this child chooses to abuse the parent by not listening to him or her, the parent chooses not to parent the child. The parent does not take away love but takes away being a parent. The message is clear: if you abuse me as a parent, I do not choose to parent you. What does this mean? The parent does not talk to this child or interact in any way. When mealtime comes, a place is set for everyone in the family but this child. If he or she wants to eat, he or she can make his or her own meal and sit somewhere else. If the parent was to drive the child to a meeting, to sports practice, or to a game, the parent will not do so. The child or adolescent will have to face the consequences of not attending the event. The parent will not write an excuse. If the behavior persists until bedtime, the parent will not respond to the child or adolescent nor put him or her to bed. When it is time for the parent to go to sleep, he or she will turn out the lights and go to bed. The child or adolescent will be left in the dark and alone. Once this individual goes to his or her room to spend the quiet time, parenting starts again.

Suppose this child or adolescent runs outside if told to go to his or her room. The plan must include informing this child or adolescent that if he or she runs outside, the parent will not chase. The time it takes the child to come in and go to his or her room will be counted, doubled, and added to the original amount. If it gets dark, the parent will call the police and report a missing child. It is no fun hiding behind a bush as it gets dark and cold if no one is going to chase you.

Some parents find the "I love you, but if you abuse me as a parent, I do not choose to parent you" approach too painful to consider. I remind these parents that allowing the unacceptable behaviors and teaching their child or adolescent that he or she can be in control is more painful and potentially more harmful to the child than is the suggested model.

If the child or adolescent will not stay in the time-out room, there is a problem. It may be possible to put a lock on the door. For example, the parents can buy a bathroom door set and install it in reverse so that the lock is outside. Should it be necessary to lock the door, a parent must remain in the hall to listen in case it becomes necessary to enter the child's room. The child may put up a real battle not to let the parent win. If locked in, he or she might trash the room. If this happens, the next day, while the child is in school, parents are to put everything from the child's room into another room and leave nothing but the mattress on the floor. The child can earn back the furniture one piece at a time.

I have been teaching this model in various forms for 30 years, so I know that other loopholes exist. If the child or adolescent commits an act of physical abuse, he or she does not earn a point and must go to his or her room for a given unit of time. For any further such behaviors during the same time unit, he or she will have to return to the room. But, what about verbal abuse? For the first event, he or she will not earn a point. What does the parent do for the remainder of the time in this period if the child or adolescent is verbally abusive again? I suggest that for the second occurrence and for every other occurrence during the period, the child or adolescent must have a time-out. I usually use half of the time assigned for physical abuse. If the child is verbally abusive all the way to the room, by the time he or she reaches the room, the time to be spent might be four or five times more than when the first event started.

What about noncompliance, for example, when a parent asks the child to do a chore and he or she refuses? The child does not earn the point for that period. What then? He or she already did not get the reward, so why listen? Does the parent now have to do the chore? Later in this chapter, I suggest strategies to use for noncompliance.

This reward-point system along with the time-out plan will work. The key is consistency. Parents must develop a plan that is feasible and then implement the plan. The child or adolescent will test and test, but parents must stick to the plan. No child or adolescent wants to give up being the boss of the family. It will take time, but the plan will work. Once the external controls work and this child begins to have internal controls, everyone will be happier and less frustrated. Once this improvement is noticed, the plan must be continued. If stopped too soon, the behaviors will return.

Setting Up the Second Phase of the Plan

The goal of the second phase of intervention is to help the child or adolescent internalize the controls. The first phase provided external controls. Now, the effort shifts to helping build these controls into the child's or adolescent's behavior patterns. The first phase continues; however, the parents now use a more interactive rather than omnipotent approach. As with the first part of this plan, parents need to learn how to interact in a different way, bringing in examples and role-playing how to respond.

Once the unacceptable behaviors are under better control, *reflective talking* can be introduced. Initially, these discussions are held after the fact. The best time might be at night while sitting on the child's bed. For example, a child may have been in a fight or a yelling match. He has spent time in his room. Later in the evening, a parent sits with this child in private and discusses what happened. The parent might say, "You know, all day long at work I just could not wait to come home so that I could spend time with you. I feel so disappointed that your behavior resulted in you being in your room so that I could not spend that time with you. What else could you have done?" Another approach is to say, "I am sorry you had so much trouble this afternoon. I love you, and I do not like being angry with your behavior or having to ask you to remove yourself from the family. What do you think we can do to stop such things from happening?"

Let this child talk. At first he may only make angry accusations of unfairness or of others causing the trouble and getting away with it. The parent might respond, "I don't know if your brother was teasing you before you hit him or not. I was not there. But let's suppose that he did. What else could you have done? By hitting him you got into trouble and he did not. There must be a better way. Maybe you could have told me what you thought he was doing." Such conversations may have to occur many times as the parents try to get their child to accept responsibility for his or her behaviors and to think about the need to change. Parents should not only point out the behavior but also offer alternative solutions.

Gradually, it will be possible to point out themes and then make suggestions. For example, "You know, Mary, I notice that you are most likely to get into difficulty right after you come home from school. Do you suppose that you hold in all of your problems with the schoolwork or the kids until you get home so that you will not get into trouble at school? Then, you let it out the first time you are upset at home. If so, maybe you and I can do something to help. Maybe, as soon as you come in the house we can sit in the kitchen and have a snack. We can talk about your day, and you can tell me about the problems you have had. You may feel better and then will not have to let your unhappy feelings out at the family."

Soon, it will be possible to do the reflective thinking before the fact. For example, "John, you and I have learned that if you keep playing with your brother after the teasing starts, there will be a fight. Do you remember what we talked about? What else could you do? Isn't this a good time to try out that new idea?" Here's another example: "Juanita, you are forcing me to be the police and to yell at you or punish you. I do not like doing that. I'd rather enjoy being with you than yelling at you or punishing you. Why do you think you force me to be the police? Remember what we talked about the other night? Do you want to try some of the ideas we talked about? Why don't we both take a 5-minute break to calm down and then try to talk about the problem." Gradually, the child or adolescent will begin to try the new behaviors.

The child can learn from hearing his or her parents discuss their feelings and thoughts openly. The parents should let the child understand their feelings of anger, sadness, fear, or worry. Parents can model how to handle these feelings. For example, a parent might say, "I am so angry with what you did that I cannot talk to you now. I am going into the other room to calm down. Later, we can talk." Not only will this parent feel more in control later, but he or she will have demonstrated a way to handle angry feelings.

Parents should begin to explain or to model acceptable ways for their child to handle feelings. Many families are quick to tell their children that they may not show anger, sadness, or disappointment, but they do not teach them acceptable ways of handling these feelings. Anger is a normal feeling, and children and adolescents must learn how to handle this feeling in an acceptable way in the family. Can they yell as long as they do not curse? Can they stamp their feet or slam the door shut as long as they do not break anything? Parents need to watch out for confusing messages. For example, one parent in a family yells or throws things when angry; the other parent pouts or goes to a room alone when angry. When the child gets angry and starts to yell, he or she is told, "You may not yell at me." If he or she walks off pouting, the parent says, "You come back here. I am talking to you." It is acceptable for families to have different rules for adults and for children; however, parents must then teach their children acceptable ways to express feelings within the family.

Handling Noncompliance

The reward system described earlier in this chapter may not work if the child or adolescent has caught on that once the point is not earned, there is no reason to comply. For example, a child may think, "You put away my toys. I lost my point, so why should I do it now?" Parents need a strategy to handle these situations. The basic concepts described earlier in this chapter should be used. The parents are in control, and the rules and consequences are consistent and persistent. Let me suggest a few strategies to try. The clinician and the parents might come up with other approaches.

Handling Chores

To avoid any confusion about chores or other duties expected by the family, parents must make a detailed list of expectations. For example, individual chores might include putting dirty clothes in the hamper, making one's bed, and picking things up off the floor. Family chores might include setting the table, loading or emptying the dishwasher, or vacuuming. Keep the list in an obvious place. Clarify whether completion of these chores is to be rewarded by money or whether it is expected as part of family responsibility. If family chores are to be shared on different days, make a list that clarifies what each child is to do each day. For example, "Francine clears the table on even-numbered days, and Charlie clears the table on odd-numbered days."

If the expected chores are not done, what will be the consistent consequence? What can parents do if the child forgets or does not do an expected chore? Should they continue to nag and then shout? The next sections suggest several models. Each suggestion gives the parents the control. If a task is not done, a clear consequence results. The choice is the child's or adolescent's. If the child does the chore, he or she receives the expected reward. If the child does not do the chore, he or she experiences the expected consequence.

"Maid service." Parents should establish that all "parent services" are not supplied free of charge. If chores are not done by a preset time, a parent will do the chores but not for free. The parents should make a list of the required chores and the exact time by which they should be finished. For example, "Bed must be made before leaving for school," "Dinner table must be set by 6:00 P.M.," or "Bike must be in garage by the time it gets dark." Write down a reasonable fee next to each chore if a parent must do it. Parents should be realistic about the age and financial resources of the child or adolescent. For example, reasonable fees might be 50 cents to make the bed, 25 cents to pick up things from the floor of the child's room, 50 cents to put a bike in the garage. Then, the parents should stop arguing, reminding, or nagging this child. If the chore is done by the preset time, fine. He or she earns a point and a thank-you. If it is not done, a parent does the chore without comment. At the end of each day or week, the parents submit a bill for their services. If the child gets an allowance, the parents might present a bill like this:

Allowance:	$5.00
Maid service:	$3.75
Balance due:	$1.25

The child might get upset and ask how lunch, snacks, or drinks are to be bought. The parent would reply calmly, "Think about that next week when you decide not to do a chore." If the child does not get an allowance, parents might be able to use birthday or savings money. If there is no such money or if the child owes much more than the allowance, he or she should be given specific work details to earn the money owed. For example, "I will pay you $3.00 an hour to clean the garage. You owe me $3.00, so I expect you to work 1 hour this weekend."

If money cannot be used, parents should explore ways of using the equivalent as barter. Television time or time playing computer games could be used. First, the parents set a starting value. For example, "You are entitled to play 5 hours of computer games each week." Then, the list of chores would include the equivalent units of time that each chore will cost if a parent must complete it. At the end of the week, the bill for maid service might read:

Computer time allowed:	5 hours
Maid service:	3 hours, 15 minutes
Time remaining to use:	1 hour, 45 minutes

The child will get upset, but the computer game is locked up and is given out for only the amount of time earned that week. For the parents, there will be no more getting angry, no more reminding, and no more fights. The child has two choices: do the chores and get the rewards, or don't do the chores and pay someone (i.e., a parent) to do them.

"The Sunday box." Parents can set up a "box" in a secure place, for example, a closet or room that can be locked or the trunk of a car. They should make it clear to the child that any items (e.g., toys, bikes, books, coats, or shoes) left where they should not be after a predetermined time of the day will be placed in this box. (For bikes, put the front wheel in the box.) The box is emptied every Sunday morning. This means that if a favorite game, a bike, or a piece of sports equipment is left out or not put away on time, it is lost until Sunday. If the objects are clothes or shoes and the child cannot do without them, the child must pay in money or loss of time with the computer or television to retrieve them early.

This plan has worked so well in some families that one parent placed the other parent on the plan. For example, if the father's clothes, work papers, and other objects had been left lying around, they disappeared into the Sunday box.

Handling Property Damage

When a child damages property during an outburst, the initial response from parents will be based on the plan in place. If this behavior is called physical abuse, the child will not earn a point and must spend time in a quiet room thinking about the behavior and the need to change. A more severe consequence might be needed. The child or adolescent could be made to pay to repair or replace the item. The money could come out of an allowance. If the cost is high, the money might come out in installments until the item is paid for. If this model for payment is not possible because the child or adolescent does not have an allowance or birthday money, he or she could be given a way to earn the money. For example, parents can pay by the hour for other-than-expected tasks such as cutting the grass, washing clothes, washing the kitchen floor, cleaning the garage, helping a neighbor, or doing community service. The first time a child or adolescent gets angry and kicks over a lamp, breaking it, and then learns that it will cost $50 to replace the lamp and that he or she will have to work for 20 hours to pay for the damage, may be the first time that he or she starts to think before acting. This is the goal, getting the child or adolescent to stop before acting and to think about the consequences of his or her behavior.

Handling Dawdling

Many parents reinforce dawdling by reminding, nagging, yelling, screaming, and then, in anger, doing the task with or for the child. This behavior teaches the child that he or she can get away with this behavior, force a parent to help, or succeed in getting a parent upset. Instead, parents should define the limits for a behavior and then establish clear consequences.

For example, a child might not get dressed on time. She is not openly oppositional but is so busy playing or looking out the window that tasks just never get done. As the time for the school bus gets closer, she has not yet dressed or eaten because she is dawdling and playing. Then, the parent probably goes into the bedroom, yells at the child, and quickly dresses her so that she will have time to eat and then catch the bus. This child has succeeded in getting the parent upset and angry and in getting the parent to help. In this situation, the parent needs to think through whether the child's difficulty getting dressed might relate to a learning disability (e.g., sequencing, organization, or fine motor problems) or to ADHD behaviors present because the child has not taken medication before leaving for school.

For this type of behavior, parents might first establish the rules. For example, the kitchen is open until 7:30 A.M. You must be dressed to enter. If you come in before 7:15 A.M., you may have a hot breakfast. If you come in after 7:15 A.M., there is only time for cold cereal. No food is served after 7:30 A.M. You will have to go to school hungry and wait for lunch. You are expected to be ready to leave for the bus by 7:40 A.M.

What do parents do if it is 7:40 A.M., and the child still is not dressed? An older child or adolescent should be told that if he or she misses the bus or car pool, the parent will not be able to take the child to school or can take him or her but not until later when the parent was planning to go out. The child could use public transportation, if available. Further, the parent will not write a note if the child is late or absent; thus, the child might receive detention at school. Finally, the parent could comment, "The problem is yours, not mine. Maybe tomorrow you will get dressed on time." Another plan to consider, if family location and circumstances allow, involves using a taxi. If parents must also leave early, they could arrange for a contract with a reliable taxi service. This means that the child could call a cab when ready to go to school and only has to sign a voucher to pay the driver. This child is then expected to pay back or work off the cost of the cab. Again, the parents will not write an excuse explaining the child's lateness. He or she will have to accept the consequences.

If the child decides to stay home, he or she must stay in his or her bedroom without watching television or interacting with the parents during school hours. The parents will not write an excuse explaining the child's absence.

If the child is young, and the school personnel are willing to cooperate, another plan can be developed with the help of the bus driver, the classroom teacher, and the principal. The child is told the plan in advance. When it is time to leave for the bus, the parent quietly takes all of the clothes that have not yet been put on and places them in a bag. The child is wrapped in a robe or coat and walked to the bus, pajamas and all. The bus driver, having been briefed, smiles and says hello. The child gets on the bus with the bag of clothes. The parent then calls to alert the principal. If the child finishes dressing on the bus, fine. If he or she arrives at school in pajamas, the teacher quietly asks, "Would you like to go to the bathroom and get dressed?" The child will not starve without breakfast on this day. He or she will not have succeeded in defeating the parent. This child will learn that dawdling no longer works. Only he or she is affected by the behavior.

This approach might work in other situations. At bedtime, whether the child is in pajamas or still in street clothes, the parents should put him or her in bed and turn out the lights. Similarly, when the family is ready to leave for a movie, a visit, or a shopping trip, and the child is not ready by the requested time, parents should leave with the rest of the family. If the child cannot be left alone, the parents should have a sitter on call for the early phase of this approach so that they can follow through with the plan. Once the sitter is called, it is too late to change plans. Even if the child dresses quickly, he or she stays home. After one or two times, when the child or adolescent loses rather than the parents or the rest of the family, this individual will get the message: "Finish your tasks on time or accept the consequences. You lose, not the rest of us."

| Summary

When a consistent behavioral plan is used in a family, unacceptable behaviors begin to change to more acceptable behaviors. Both parents regain control and confidence in their ability to parent. Children and adolescents learn that they can be controlled and that they will not be overwhelmed by not being in control. They are usually happier. Now, all of the positive experiences within the family reinforce the behaviors.

If this plan does not work or does not work as well as desired because the ADHD or learning disabilities are not managed fully, these issues must be addressed. If the plan does not work because both parents do not follow the plan or defeat the plan or because the child or adolescent has such serious emotional problems that he or she cannot give up the need to be in control or to be bad or be punished, more intensive help will be needed.

The child or adolescent with ADHD often develops secondary emotional, social, and family problems. Sometimes a parent or both parents will become as stressed or dysfunctional as the child or adolescent.

With the help of the clinician, the plan described here for addressing unacceptable behaviors can be implemented. If the child or adolescent can change and parents can feel more competent, this might be enough. If not, more or different help may be needed.

Chapter 15

Psychopharmacology

The material I cover in this chapter is not meant to substitute for the fuller literature provided by pharmaceutical companies as published in the *Physicians' Desk Reference*. This information is intended as a general review of medications used to treat attention-deficit/hyperactivity disorder (ADHD). The information provided is based on clinical research and professional guidelines. It is presented in a practical way as a clinical guide. For physicians, the material will focus on the practical day-to-day decisions that must be made. For other professionals reading this book, the material will provide the information needed to understand the medications that the individuals with whom you work might be taking.

The necessary differential diagnostic process must be considered before establishing the diagnosis of ADHD. If the clinician establishes this diagnosis, the behaviors are presumed not to be the result of anxiety or depression but are neurologically based; therefore, ADHD is both chronic and pervasive. As I discussed in Chapter 6, the behaviors are present all of the time, every day, not just during school hours. Some physicians insist that children and adolescents take medication only during school hours. These individuals are off medication during evenings, weekends, holidays, and summers. They often have behavior, social, and family problems during these times and have difficulty doing homework. During the summer, they might do poorly at camp or in other activities. The issue of when to use medication can be used to illustrate the difficulty clinicians have with keeping current on clinical research.

A study conducted in the 1970s on a small number of children suggested that methylphenidate (Ritalin) might inhibit the production of growth hormone and, thus, stunt a child's growth. "Vacations" from Ritalin were suggested so that the body could catch up with this deficiency. Many physicians heard of this concern and began to insist that their patients take a break from the medication. Since this initial study was conducted, several major studies have shown that Ritalin does not decrease the production of growth hormone. Any decrease in height is considered negligible (less than 1 inch), and even this finding is questioned. The general understanding is that Ritalin does not affect a child's growth and that the medication can be used whenever it is needed. However, not all physicians are aware of these more recent studies or of the current understanding.

Another example of information not getting out to every practitioner relates to the use of medication following puberty. We used to teach that by puberty everyone "outgrew" what is now called ADHD. Thus, medications were no longer needed. It became clear in the 1980s that about 50% of children continued to have ADHD into adulthood. This is why a parent so often reports that he or she, too, has ADHD. The disorder does not always go away. Some practitioners, not knowing this, take all children off of medication when they reach puberty. It is not too surprising that about 50% of these children begin to do poorly. Adults respond to the medications for ADHD in the same way as do children. My discussion of the treatment for ADHD in children and adolescents applies equally to adults.

Another problem occurs from time to time in the professional literature. A specific finding is observed and reported, and until this problem is understood, cautious guidelines are appropriately suggested. Gradually, the initial findings are better understood, and these guidelines are softened or dropped. Later in this chapter, several examples will be given where an initial alarm was followed over time with a decrease in concern. It can be difficult for clinicians to keep up with these changes.

The use of medication to treat what is now called ADHD was first described in 1937 when an epidemic of viral encephalitis occurred. Some of the children, as they recovered from this disease, were observed to be hyperactive and distractible. A pediatrician, Dr. Charles Bradley, gave the children amphetamine sulfate (Benzadrine), a stimulant medication, and the children became less active and distractible. The stimulant medications have been used to treat these behaviors for more than 60 years. ADHD may be a more popular diagnosis and the public may know more about it in the 1990s, but it is not a new disorder.

About 80% of children and adolescents with ADHD show improvement while taking the appropriate medication in the proper way. These medications decrease or stop the hyperactivity, distractibility, and/or impulsivity. They do not treat learning disabilities if they also are present. For some individuals with ADHD, medication may result in improved motor control and possibly in improved handwriting. Although the effect is not understood, some children and adolescents with a language disability show improved speech and language when taking stimulant medications; however, the underlying processing problems seen with learning disabilities do not improve.

Some of the material I present here might contradict the views or practices of other physicians. Nevertheless, I believe that I am presenting the most current information.

How is it that some physicians are not current on the use of medications to treat ADHD? Physicians work very hard to keep up with their field. They read their journals and newsletters, discuss new medications with pharmaceutical representatives, and attend conferences. They know of the newest concepts and treatments for infectious diseases, metabolic diseases, and other commonly seen problems. However, most of the research and clinical literature on ADHD appears in the child and adolescent psychiatry and general psychiatry literature and in some of the psychology journals. Most family practitioners and pediatricians do not receive these publications; thus, they find it difficult to keep up with the ever-expanding literature on ADHD.

There is no established protocol for treating ADHD with medication. In the following section, I present an approach I find helpful. The protocol I discuss should be seen as one possible model for thinking through each step of the clinical treatment process. Each clinician might use a variation of this model.

Clinical Protocol

In treating ADHD, I first try the stimulant medications, which I call the Group One medications. If these medications do not help or if the side effects create problems that cannot be resolved clinically, I try a second group of medications, mostly *tricyclic antidepressants* (TCAs). I call these the Group Two medications. If these medications do not help or they help to control only some of the behaviors, I might prescribe a combination of Group One and Group Two medications. Usually, up to 85% of correctly diagnosed ADHD in children, adolescents, and adults will respond to one or the other group or to a combination of the groups. I discuss so-called *nonresponders* later in this section.

Recall that ADHD is caused by a deficiency of a specific neurotransmitter, norepinephrine. The goal of medication is to increase the level of this neurotransmitter at the nerve interfaces in the areas of the brain involved. Currently two different mechanisms accomplish this increase. I like to use the analogy of a lake without enough water in it. One could increase the level of water in the lake in one of two ways. First, one could pour more water into the lake. Alternatively, one could build a dam. No more water is flowing into the lake than before, but the water flows out more slowly; thus, the water level goes up.

One mechanism for increasing the level of norepinephrine produces more of it. The stimulants (Group One medications) appear to work by stimulating the nerve endings to produce more norepinephrine. The other mechanism, like a dam, decreases the breakdown or metabolism of the neurotransmitter, causing the norepinephrine that is produced to stay around longer. The relative amount of norepinephrine then goes up. The TCAs and other Group Two medications appear to inhibit the uptake of norepinephrine, resulting in an increase in the amount at the nerve interface.

Each medication has a generic or chemical name and a trade name. Table 15–1 lists the medications used to treat ADHD. The generic name is listed first, and the trade name is given in parentheses.

In this chapter, I discuss in detail each of the medications in these two groups. But first let me discuss the nonresponder group. The most frequent reason that a child or adolescent does not respond to one of these medications is that the medication is not being used correctly. Either the

Table 15–1.   Medications used to treat ADHD

Group One medications

Methylphenidate (Ritalin)

Dextroamphetamine (Dexedrine, Dextro-Stat)

Pemoline (Cylert)

Dextroamphetamine and levoamphetamine mixture (Adderall)

Group Two medications

Imipramine (Tofranil)

Desipramine (Norpramin)

Nortriptyline (Pamelor)

Bupropion (Wellbutrin)

Clonidine (Catapres)

Guanfacine (Tenex)

---

dosage or the coverage is not correct. The second most frequent reason is that the parents' understanding of the role the medication plays is misunderstood. A parent might call me and say his or her child has taken every medication and has not improved. When I ask for more information, I learn that the child is calmer and more focused but still cannot read well or spell. I need to explain that these medications treat ADHD but not learning disabilities. A parent might say that the child is better focused but is still oppositional and defiant. I need to explain that these medications treat ADHD but not oppositional defiant disorder. A different clinical intervention is needed for this disorder. The third reason is that the diagnosis is not correct. The hyperactivity, distractibility, and/or impulsivity may be a reflection of anxiety, depression, learning disabilities, or another psychiatric disorder but not of ADHD.

There is a small group of true nonresponders. These children and adolescents often have several or all of the neurological disorders I discussed in Chapter 2. They might have ADHD, but they also have a learning, language, or motor disability; one or more of the modulating disorders; and/or a tic disorder. The medications might help the ADHD, but other medications are needed to address the other disorders.

In this chapter, I discuss treatment with the Group One and Group Two medications and also discuss indications for combining medications from each group. Later I discuss the medication treatment for the child or adolescent who has ADHD and other related disorders. Because clinicians and parents are more likely to be familiar with the trade names, I use those names in my discussion. Refer to Table 15–1 for the generic names.

I firmly believe that parents must know as much as the physicians do about the medications their children are taking. Thus, the physician should discuss with the parents each medication in detail, including how the dosage is selected and adjusted, what the side effects might be, and how to address these side effects.

Group One Medications: Stimulants

It is difficult to predict whether a child or adolescent with ADHD will respond better to one stimulant medication than another. Some children will respond poorly to one and have a positive response to another. Some will have side effects with one and not with another. Clinicians must use their own judgment as to which one to try first.

Each of these medications has shared characteristics, effects, and side effects. Ritalin and Dexedrine come in short-acting and long-acting forms. Cylert comes in only a long-acting form. Adderall lasts for 5–6 hours.

Caffeine is sometimes considered among the stimulants. It has not proven to be a useful medication for treating ADHD.

Before starting a patient on one of the stimulant medications, the physician should give the patient a general medical examination, including measurements of height, weight, pulse rate, and blood pressure. A personal or family history of a tic disorder should be noted. Follow-up examinations should include observations for tics and involuntary movements and recordings of height, weight, pulse rate, and blood pressure. If Cylert is used, blood studies of liver function should be conducted every 6 months (see later in this chapter).

Stimulant medications may aggravate symptoms of anxiety, tension, and agitation; thus, they should be used with caution when these symptoms are present. These medications might also exacerbate a tic disorder, and this possibility must be considered. Cylert should not be taken by individuals with known impairment of liver function.

Dosage and Use

Ritalin is available in 5-, 10-, and 20-mg tablets and in a long-acting Ritalin-SR 20-mg tablet. Ritalin-SR is designed to release 10 mg initially and 10 mg 4 hours later (for a total of 20 mg). The short-acting Ritalin tablet lasts an average of 4 hours; however, in some individuals, it may last more or less time. Although some references indicate the amount of Ritalin needed based on body weight, the amount needed by each individual does not seem to relate to body weight. I elaborate on this concept later in this chapter. The recommended upper limit for Ritalin is 20 mg four times a day.

Dexedrine is available in 5-mg tablets and in long-acting Spansule capsules of 5-, 10-, and 15-mg strength. Each tablet lasts an average of 4 hours. The Spansule capsules last 8 hours. Dexedrine is approved for use starting at age 3 years. The upper dosage limit is the same as with Ritalin, 20 mg four times a day. Dextroamphetamine is also available as Dextro-Stat, which comes in 5- and 10-mg tablets, each lasting an average of 4 hours. A new medication in this same group is Adderall. This medication is a mixture of several different salts of amphetamine. It is unknown whether this mixture of amphetamine salts offers benefits over the single-salt dextroamphetamine. Adderall comes in 5-, 10-, and 20-mg tablets and is designed to last 5–6 hours.

Cylert is available in 18.75-, 37.5-, and 75-mg tablets and in a 37.5-mg chewable tablet. It is administered as a single oral dose each morning and lasts for 24 hours. The recommended starting dosage is 37.5 mg/day. The dosage is increased gradually by 18.75 mg each week; the maximum recommended daily dosage is 112.5 mg. Cylert is approved for use starting at age 6 years. During early 1997, several cases were reported of children on Cylert developing acute liver function problems. The drug's manufacturer issued an alert. For this reason, many professionals are hesitant to use Cylert at this time. It may be that like other sudden alerts, the problem will be of less concern over time.

Because Ritalin is the most frequently used of the Group One medications, I use it as a prototype for this group of medications. I discuss in detail its use and management. Unless I note an exception, you can assume that the material I present applies to all Group One medications.

The short-acting Ritalin tablet begins to work in 30–45 minutes and lasts about 4 hours. It does not accumulate; thus, at the end of 4 hours, it is no longer found in the blood. If a child takes 10 mg three times a day, one does not say that he or she is taking 30 mg a day. One says that at any moment during the day he or she has 10 mg in the blood. Studies show that there is little difference between taking Ritalin on an empty versus a full stomach. Food does not impair absorption; thus, the drug can be given before, with, or after a meal. As noted earlier, the dosage is based not on body weight but on how rapidly the individual metabolizes the medication. Once the therapeutic benefits are noted, the blood level appears to be the same for the individual who needs 5, 10, 15, or 20 mg/dose.

When Ritalin is used, three clinical questions must be addressed. These same questions are relevant for the other stimulants:

1. How much medication is needed per dose?
2. At what time interval is the medication taken?
3. During which time periods should the medication be taken?

How much medication is needed per dose? The dosage needed to reach clinical benefit appears not to be related to body weight but to how rapidly each individual metabolizes the medication. I have 200-pound adults taking 5 mg and 30-pound children taking 20 mg. Each person seems to need a specific amount to reach benefit. No readily available tests measure the blood level of Ritalin; thus, clinical observations are used to establish the dosage. I start the individual on 5 mg/dose. With very young children, I might start at 2.5 mg/dose. At 5-day intervals, I get feedback from parents and teachers. If no benefits are noted, I increase the dosage by 5 mg on each of 5 days until a decrease in hyperactivity, distractibility, and/or impulsivity is reported.

Two side effects—emotional lability and hyperfocused or "spacey" behavior—would suggest that the dosage of Ritalin or any of the other stimulants is too high for that individual. I discuss these side effects in more detail later in this chapter. Unless one of these side effects is noted,

I raise the dosage every 5 days. If I reach 20 mg/dose with no noted benefits, I rethink the diagnosis or the use of the medication. Often, I increase each dose separately. For example, I might want to assess the effect of an increase in dosage. Thus, I might increase the morning dose but leave the noon and afternoon doses the same. Then, I will ask parents and teachers if they notice a difference between the morning and afternoon parts of the school day. If I find that the child or adolescent is doing much better in the morning than in the afternoon, I increase the noon and afternoon doses.

Feedback from parents and teachers is critical in adjusting the dosage. One efficient way for the physician to gather this feedback is to ask a parent to discuss the child's or adolescent's improvement with the teacher at the end of the school day and then to call the physician. In this way, feedback from school and home can be obtained with one telephone call. Rating scales can be used if a more formal feedback model is desired.

I find it best to start with a short-acting form of Ritalin until the appropriate dosage and time of dosing is established. Then, if needed, a longer-acting form might be considered. With Ritalin, the long-acting Ritalin-SR can be used only if two consecutive doses are 10 mg, or 20 mg total. For other dosages, Dexedrine Spansule capsules or Adderall might be needed.

At what time interval is the medication taken? The average length of action for a short-acting tablet is 4 hours; however, for some individuals the medication may last 2 or 3 hours, and for others it might last up to 5 hours. Thus, the dose interval must be established for each individual. There is nothing absolute about taking Ritalin every 4 hours.

The dose interval is determined clinically, using feedback from parents, the individual, and teachers. As an example, a child is administered Ritalin, 5 mg at 8:00 A.M., noon, and 4:00 P.M. daily. If the feedback throughout the day is good, the dose interval in place may be best. The teacher says, "You know, John is great in the morning, but at about 11:00 A.M. or 11:30 A.M. he begins to wiggle in his seat and cannot stay on task. He is much better after the noon medication is given." Perhaps the dose interval for John is 3 hours. He may need his medication at 8:00 A.M., 11:00 A.M., and 2:00 P.M., with a 5:00 P.M. dose added, if needed.

Similarly, suppose the teacher reports, "Alicia is great in the morning, but between 12:30 P.M. and 1:00 P.M. she gets so upset. If I look at her the wrong way, she cries," or "Between 12:30 P.M. and 1:00 P.M. she appears so spacey that she seems out of it. By 1:00 P.M. or 1:30 P.M. she is fine again." How do we explain this? Two behaviors suggest that the medication dosage is too high for this child. One is that she is emotionally fragile; that is, she is more irritable and tearful than usual. The other is that she becomes so overfocused that she appears to be spacey. It is possible that for Alicia, each dose lasts 5 hours. She gets the next dose in 4 hours and for about 1 hour she is on the remains of the first dose plus the second dose. For her, the combined dose is too high; thus, the side effects occur. For Alicia, each dose should be 5 hours apart.

During which time periods should the medication be taken?   ADHD is a neurologically based disorder having to do with how the brain functions. Thus, the hyperactivity, distractibility, and/or impulsivity will be present throughout the day, every day. Medication should be used whenever these behaviors interfere with the individual's success in life.

Medication is not used to make parents or teachers happy. Medication is used to help the child or adolescent be successful in the family, in school, with friends, in activities, and in sports—that is, everywhere. For some individuals, medication will be needed only during school and homework hours. For most, however, medication will be needed all day, every day.

As I noted earlier, the misinformation that Ritalin inhibited growth hormone, and thus stunted growth, led to the concept of vacations from the medication during evenings, weekends, holidays, and summers. Too many family physicians do not know that concern about growth is no longer an issue, so medication often is used only at 8:00 A.M. and noon, Monday through Friday, September through June. The individual struggles with homework and has difficulty getting along at home, with friends, and everywhere he or she goes.

My preference is to give the child or adolescent medication all day, every day, and ask parents to observe. If they find that the medication is helpful only related to school, I will set up a plan to cover school and homework time only. Parents are taught how to use a single dose for special occasions like going on a long car ride. More frequently, parents report that the medication helps their child function better at home and with all out-of-home activities. Some parents note, "He actually sat through a whole meal and talked with us," "She can now entertain herself," "He plays better with his friends," or "I asked her to do something, and she actually did it." Unless parents can observe their child or adolescent in all situations, it is difficult to assess when medication is needed.

The key is to think of the behaviors—hyperactivity, distractibility, and/or impulsivity. When do these behaviors interfere with the individual's success in life? Let me give a few examples. A parent reports that the medication works well. His son gets his doses at 8:00 A.M. as he leaves for school, at noon, and at 4:00 P.M., but between the time he gets up and the time he leaves for school, he is impossible. He plays with his toys rather than getting dressed, he runs around the house, he jumps on his sister's bed, he talks loudly, and he gets everyone angry with him. Finally, at 8:00 A.M. his father gives him his medication, hands him a piece of bread and butter, and shoves him out the door. This situation is not good for the parent, the sibling, or the child with ADHD. The problem is clear. The first dose is given at 8:00 A.M. From the time the child gets up until about 8:45 A.M. his ADHD is uncontrolled. The solution is also clear. I asked the father what time his son gets up on school mornings. He said, "7:00 A.M." I asked him to wake up his son at 6:15 A.M., give him his medication, and let him go back to sleep. The child then wakes up at 7:00 A.M., pleasant and cooperative. He gets dressed, comes to the kitchen, has a good breakfast, and leaves for school with hugs and kisses. He gets his other doses at 10:45 A.M., 2:45 P.M., and if necessary at 6:45 P.M.

Suppose a child gets her medication at 8:00 A.M. as she leaves for school and the second dose at noon. She is about to be suspended from the school bus because on the morning trip she runs up and down the aisles and won't stay in her seat. The problem is that the medication does not start to work until she is already in school. The noon dose lasts till 4:00 P.M. and covers the trip home. She needs the first dose at 7:15 A.M. so that it is working before she gets on the bus.

For some children and adolescents who take their medication at 8:00 A.M., noon, and 4:00 P.M., the difficult time is from 8:00 P.M. until bedtime. An additional dose at 8:00 P.M. may be needed. With each of the examples given here, the key is that medication is used whenever it is needed to help the individual be successful in life.

The need for medication might vary depending on the child's age and grade in school, the school's academic demands, and the family's style. For example, a first or second grader might have little or no homework. If he or she is primarily distractible, medication will be needed during school hours but not for after-school hours. However, this same child, when older and in a higher grade, might have homework and need medication during after-school hours. Similarly, a hyperactive child might need medication during school hours; however, if he or she is young and spends most of the after-school hours playing outside and if the family does not mind the fidgetiness, medication might not be needed at home. This same child might need medication for these hours when he or she is older and homework or family demands increase.

Each situation should be thought through based on the guidelines noted in this chapter. Suppose a family plans to drive to the grandparents' house, a 4-hour car trip. Once there, the child will run around and play with cousins all weekend. Then there is the 4-hour ride home. This child might need medication for the car ride there and back. While there, he or she might not need medication or might need it only for the quieter family dinner times.

Side Effects and Their Management

In this section, I use Ritalin again to demonstrate the Group One stimulant medications. I review the drug's possible side effects and how these side effects are managed. As necessary, I note any unique side effects found with the other medications in this group.

The two side effects found most frequently with Ritalin are loss of appetite and difficulty falling asleep at night. Less frequently, some individuals complain of a stomachache or headache after most doses. Even less frequently, some individuals develop tics or other less common side effects. As discussed earlier, two side effects suggest that the dosage of the medication is too high: emotional lability and a hyperfocused or spacey state.

Loss of appetite.   Ritalin might decrease an individual's appetite. This side effect may lessen over the first several weeks and cease to be a problem. If it persists, something should be done. The first effort is to observe the child's eating patterns. The medication may take the edge off of the appetite; thus, the child or adolescent might not finish his or her meals but may eat candy, cake, or other sweets. If this behavior is observed, parents need to limit sweets until after the meal is eaten. Some children taking three doses a day will eat breakfast (because the first dose has not started to work), show no appetite for lunch or dinner, and then come into the kitchen at 8:00 P.M. starving and eat everything they can find.

Parents can try to overcome this problem by creating "windows of opportunity." They should try to get their child to eat a good breakfast before the first dose starts to work and then accept that lunch will be a lost cause. Maybe the child will eat part of a jelly sandwich, but often he or she will eat nothing. Parents should then try to delay the 4:00 P.M. dose until 5:30 P.M. or 6:00 P.M. During this time, the parents may need to provide more structure and supervision and not expect the child to do his or her homework. It is hoped that the child's appetite will return in time for dinner. Then the third dose is given.

If this approach does not work and the child is losing weight or not gaining weight, Ritalin will have to be stopped and another medication tried. For reasons we do not understand, some children will experience less appetite suppression with one of the stimulant medications than the others. Thus, the physician might try one of these other medications. If the problem continues, the physician should discontinue the stimulant medications and try a Group Two medication.

Sleep difficulties. Some children and adolescents taking Ritalin have difficulty going to sleep at night. They can stay up for hours before finally falling asleep. This problem often lessens or goes away over several weeks. If it does not, intervention is needed. For some children, the medication keeps them awake; for others, the lack of medication keeps them awake. Each possibility must be explored, as each leads to a different management approach.

The clinician cannot predict which of these situations is the reason for an individual's sleep problem. Trial and error is the only way to determine the cause of the sleep problem. For example, I pick an evening when a sleep problem might not be a disaster because the child can sleep later the next day, maybe a Friday or Saturday night. I ask the parents to give their child another dose at 8:00 P.M. If the child goes right to sleep, I know that a lack of medication caused the difficulty. If he or she is even more wired and unable to sleep, I know that the medication is causing the difficulty. On such a night, I do not want the child to be up all night. Thus, I will have the parents give the child Benadryl so that he or she can sleep through the night.

If the medication results in difficulty falling asleep at night, and the problem occurs only occasionally, Benadryl might help the child get to sleep. A dose of 25–50 mg, depending on the child's weight, might help him or her to fall asleep. If Benadryl is used, the child should know that Benadryl is not a sedative. The child cannot read or play until he or she gets sleepy. If the child waits about 45 minutes until the medication is absorbed and working, then lies quietly in the dark and tries to sleep, the medication may help him or her to fall asleep. This medication may be used on occasion; if it is used every night, the effect might be lost.

If the sleep problem persists, the 4:00 P.M. dose might be decreased or stopped. If this change creates behavior problems in the afternoon and evening or makes it difficult for the child to do his or her homework, a change to a Group Two medication might be needed.

If a lack of medication causes the sleep problem, another approach is needed. If the child or adolescent takes three doses a day, he or she is functioning normally from about 8:00 A.M. until about 8:00 P.M. Then, the medication wears off and he or she is not used to being hyperactive, distractible, and/or impulsive. In bed, this individual cannot lie still. He or she hears every sound in the house and cannot turn off his or her mind. For this individual, a fourth dose at 8:00 P.M. may make it easier to go to sleep.

If every medication in Group One and Group Two has been tried and the physician has concluded that Ritalin or one of the other stimulant medications works the best but that this medication causes significant sleep problems, another approach may be used. Catapres, a Group Two medication, can be added 1 hour before bedtime. (Catapres is described in more detail later in this chapter.)

Stomachache. The reason for the side effect of a stomachache is not understood. No one has suggested a solution that seems to work. If a dose is taken on an empty stomach, trying to eat something first might help. If the stomachaches persist, it is usually necessary to change to a Group Two medication.

Headache. The reason for the side effect of headaches is not known. If headaches persist, a Group Two medication must be tried.

Tics. I described tics and tic disorders in Chapter 8. Motor tics are sudden, involuntary movements of specific muscle groups. The tics seen most frequently involve blinking or moving of the eyes or twitching of the face, mouth, neck, or shoulder muscles. If the pharyngeal muscles are involved, the individual might make sniffing, snorting, or coughing sounds. Sometimes the tics begin immediately or soon after the medication is started. Occasionally they start later. At times the tics are noted only after the dosage has been increased.

If tics occur, it is best to stop the medication and try one of the Group Two medications. For most individuals, the tics will stop immediately. For others, the tics might be a problem for several months before going away.

If a family history of a tic disorder is present, the child or adolescent may be genetically loaded to develop a tic disorder. In this case, the medication might trigger this disorder earlier than it might have otherwise started. Stopping the medication will not stop the tics. Here, the medication did not cause the tics, but the medication caused a disorder that would have started later to start earlier. For most individuals who are going to develop a tic disorder, the tics start between ages 8 and 12 years. The closer the child is to adolescence without evidence of tics, the less likely that Ritalin or one of the other stimulants will set off a tic disorder that was probably genetically determined. If a child has a family history of a tic disorder, the physician might start with one of the Group Two medications as a precaution. When a child is adopted and no family history is available, the possibility of tics should be discussed with the parents, who, with the physician, will decide whether to use a Group One medication.

If all of the possible medications have been tried, and only one of the stimulant medications works, but it causes tics, the parents must make a decision with the help of the physician. Should the stimulant be used and another medication be added to treat the tic disorder? In some cases, the result of not treating the ADHD is so harmful to the child or adolescent that the decision to continue the medication and to treat the tic disorder is necessary.

Emotional lability or spacey behavior. Emotional lability and spacey behavior suggest that the dosage is too high and should be reduced. Being emotionally labile means that, based on that individual's normal behavior, he or she is more tearful or irritable. Spacey behavior means that the child or adolescent is so overfocused that he or she seems to be in a cloud or seems "zombielike." Sometimes this problem is noted as a *blunting* of the individual's personality. A parent may note that the spark is missing from the child's personality or that the child's personality may seem flat.

Neither of these behaviors should be accepted. The medication dosage needs to be lowered. If lowering the dosage results in a loss of effectiveness, another medication should be tried. As with the other side effects, one of the other stimulant medications might not cause the same side effects and should be tried. Usually, however, if one medication causes side effects, the others also will.

Other side effects. Some children and adolescents show a rebound effect about 20–30 minutes after the last dose wears off. For those individuals taking three doses a day, this effect occurs at about 8:30 P.M. to 9:00 P.M. For 30 minutes or more, the child may become very hyperactive and talk constantly or may be excitable or impulsive. If this side effect becomes a concern, the last dose may be reduced to see if it makes a difference. Another approach, if the medication does not cause sleep problems, is to give a fourth dose at 8:00 P.M. so that the medication does not wear off until the child is asleep.

Other uncommon side effects may be present. Some children might become explosive with limited ability to control their anger. Some might become depressed or very anxious. Others might become obsessive (having intrusive thoughts) or compulsive (needing to do certain behaviors or patterns of behavior). With each of these side effects, if the medication is stopped the behaviors return to normal either immediately or within a few days.

Long-Acting Stimulants

Ritalin comes in a long-acting form, called Ritalin-SR, meaning Ritalin, sustained release, for a total of 20 mg. This form releases 10 mg immediately and 10 mg in 4 hours. (Many parents believe that the SR form releases 20 mg each time; they need to understand that the 20 mg refers to the total amount released.) Experience shows that this form does not always work as it should. For some individuals, the total effect is only about 5 hours. For others, each release lasts 3 hours. Thus, these individuals do well from, say, 8:00 A.M. to 11:00 A.M., then they have difficulty until about 12:30 P.M. or 1:00 P.M. They then do well for about 3 hours. We now understand that if the surface of the Ritalin-SR tablet is broken (e.g., if the tablet is chewed or cut in half), the whole dose is released at once. The child or adolescent gets the full dose immediately and nothing 4 hours later. For some children, the effect involves emotional lability or spacey behavior during the first 4 hours and hyperactivity, distractibility, and/or impulsivity during the second 4 hours.

Dexedrine comes in a capsule form, called a Spansule. Three dosages are available: 5 mg, 10 mg, and 15 mg. Each dose lasts 8 hours and releases the medication reasonably evenly. The capsule can be opened and sprinkled over food if necessary without affecting the medication's absorption pattern and length of action.

Special Issues

At what age can a child be started on the Group One medications? Dexedrine is approved at age 3 years. The other stimulants are approved at age 6 years. However, it is not unusual for all of the stimulant medications except Cylert to be used starting at age 3 years.

Clinical observations to date do not show that children and adolescents taking one of the stimulant medications develop tolerance, requiring a gradual increase in dosage. Many individuals need the same dosage for years. Because the amount needed is not based on body weight, it is not necessary to raise the dosage with growth. For some individuals, however, the dosage may have to be increased slightly over time.

Cylert is long-acting; thus, it is always in the bloodstream. For this reason, liver function must be monitored in patients taking this drug. A blood test is usually given about every 6 months. I provide more information on the need to monitor liver function with long-acting medications later in this chapter.

Earlier literature raised the question of what is called *state-dependent* learning. That is, if a child learns something while taking a medication, will he or she retain this information when not taking the medication? All studies show no such problems with any of the Group One medications.

The question of addiction is noted in the pharmaceutical literature. Reference is made to the possibility of abuse. At the dosages used to treat ADHD, however, addiction has not been reported to be an issue. Newspaper articles have mentioned the increased use of Ritalin by students to get a "high." Most reports noted that the students ground up the Ritalin and sniffed it; thus, the entire dose was absorbed into the bloodstream at once rather than being absorbed slowly over time, as when taken properly. These students reported feeling high and stimulated. Such feelings are not reported if the medication is taken properly by mouth.

My understanding of the literature relating to the stimulants and addiction is that if the individual has ADHD that is properly managed by medication and he or she also has appropriate nonmedication help, the likelihood of substance abuse is no greater than expected for that individual's peer group. If the individual with ADHD is not taking medication or the ADHD is not managed properly by medication, or if the necessary nonmedication interventions are not in place, the likelihood of substance abuse may be higher than would be expected for that individual's peer group. The conclusion I reach is that using medication to treat ADHD does not increase the possibility of substance abuse. The lack of recognition of the disorder, the absence of treatment, or incomplete treatment—with the resulting frustrations and failures—might result in an increase in substance abuse. The disorder or the medication is not the issue.

Earlier literature also noted concern with the use of a stimulant medication if the individual had a seizure disorder. The current guidelines suggest that this issue need not be a concern. The physician should decide on an individual basis whether to prescribe a stimulant medication for a child or adolescent who has ADHD and a seizure disorder.

Parents might be concerned about the long-term use of Ritalin or the other stimulants. How safe are they? No side effects were noted in long-term follow-up studies of children who took Ritalin in the 1960s but stopped by adolescence. However, at present, an individual might start taking a stimulant medication as a child and use it into adulthood.

We do not yet have follow-up reports on this type of long-term use. The best evidence to date suggests that there will be no long-term side effects. Parents must understand that hard data are not in at this time on the effects of using these medications continuously over many years.

| Group Two Medications

The Group Two medications are used if the Group One medications do not work or if the Group One medications produce side effects that cannot be managed clinically. Alternatively, the Group Two medications might be used in an attempt to obtain a smoother, more even effect from the medication. If the Group One medication lasts only 2–3 hours, a long-acting Group Two medication might be added to get more even coverage by filling in the gaps when the stimulant is not working.

Most of the Group Two medications are in the TCA family of medications; thus, most clinicians refer to the whole group as TCAs. However, several medications in this group are not TCAs. The common characteristic of this group is that the mechanism of action results in a decrease in the breakdown or absorption of norepinephrine at the nerve ending, resulting in an increase in norepinephrine.

There are several reasons that the medications in this group are our second choice when treating ADHD. First, they do not always address each of the three behaviors seen with ADHD. The Group One medications produce a decrease in hyperactivity, distractibility, and/or impulsivity. For reasons we do not yet understand, the Group Two medications do not cover all of these behaviors. The TCAs (i.e., Tofranil, Norpramin, and Pamelor) and Wellbutrin seem to help with the hyperactivity and distractibility; however, often they do not address the impulsivity. Thus, a second medication might need to be added to address the impulsivity. Catapres and Tenex seem to help with impulsivity but often will not address the hyperactivity or distractibility. Again, a second medication might have to be added.

Second, these long-acting medications must be managed differently than short-acting medications. When a medication is in the bloodstream all the time (even if Ritalin is used three times a day, it is out of the bloodstream half of each day), the patient's liver function must be monitored about every 6 months. Although the possibility of the drug affecting liver function negatively is negligible, the 6-month time interval is thought to allow for early enough recognition of such a problem that the medication can be stopped before damage occurs. This step is a precaution because the liver metabolizes most medications. This precaution is not unique to these medications. The same need would exist if the child or adolescent were taking medications for asthma, arthritis, or other medical disorders. Similarly, on rare occasions, the TCAs might result in a decrease in a particular type of white blood cell (neutrophils); thus, a complete blood count also is taken every 6 months.

Tofranil is the most frequently used Group Two medication. Thus, I use it as the prototype for this group. Later, I discuss the unique features of other medications in this group.

Dosage and Use

Tofranil is available in 10-, 25-, and 50-mg tablets. Because it is long-acting, the medication often is taken in the morning and in the evening, so that the child need not take medication at school. The suggested guideline is that it be used in individuals age 6 years and older. As with the stimulant medications, there appears to be no relation between the dosage needed to treat ADHD and body weight. The dosage should be determined by clinical observation. In children, 10–20 mg twice a day often is enough. Sometimes the dosage may go up to 100–150 mg, given in divided doses.

Tofranil and the other TCAs also are used to treat depression in adolescents and adults. The dosage needed for depression is often 200–300 mg/day. Thus, one cannot use the blood level of Tofranil to determine the dosage needed. The range used by laboratories to define "therapeutic range" is based on these higher dosages to treat adult depression. Also, the side effects noted in the material provided by the pharmacist are not accurate for the ADHD population. These side effects are seen at the higher dosages used to treat depression and not at the lower dosages used to treat ADHD.

Tofranil may take 1–2 weeks to begin to work or for the effects of a dosage increase to be observable. Thus, the dosage is usually increased every 1–2 weeks until the desired effects are noted. If two doses a day cause fatigue or the child seems to do less well in the late afternoon, the total dosage could be divided into three doses a day. For convenience, these doses can be given in the morning, afternoon, and evening.

Side Effects and Their Management

The most frequent side effect of Tofranil is tiredness or sleepiness. This side effect often decreases over time as the individual gets used to the medication. If this does not happen, the dosage can be decreased or divided into three smaller doses each day. If these shifts do not help, it may be that Tofranil cannot be used. As with the stimulant medications, sometimes a different TCA might work without this side effect and should be considered.

Less common side effects are constipation, dry mouth, or blurred vision. If these side effects occur, another medication should be considered. A very uncommon side effect is morning insomnia. The child may wake up at 4:00 A.M. and want to play. This problem often can be minimized by giving the child more of the Tofranil in the morning. If not, a different medication may be needed.

Tofranil and the other TCAs might affect brain wave activity. Thus, if the child or adolescent has a seizure disorder, the medication might cause a seizure. Each child or adolescent must be considered individually.

If a TCA is stopped, it must be tapered off slowly. If the medication is stopped abruptly, the child or adolescent might develop flulike symptoms.

Tricyclic Antidepressants and Heart Function

TCAs can cause a slight shift in the electrical conduction pattern of the heart. Most studies show that this shift is minimal and does not cause symptoms. A very small percentage of children and adolescents have what is called a subclinically abnormal electrical conduction pattern of the heart. That is, there are no clinical symptoms of the abnormal pattern. If a TCA is given to these children, the effect of the medication added to the underlying shift might combine to cause a rapid heartbeat (tachycardia). These individuals will complain of their heart pounding or racing in their chest and of their neck feeling full. This side effect is uncommon. Some of the literature on the TCAs recommends that an electrocardiogram (ECG) be done prior to starting the medication and again after the dosage is stabilized. Other reports suggest that the possibility of tachycardia is minimal and the effect is not life-threatening; thus, getting an ECG is not considered essential. Clearly, if a child or adolescent has a known history of a conduction problem, these medications should not be used. Physicians will have to decide on a case-by-case basis whether a child should have an ECG prior to starting this medication.

Other Group Two Medications

Wellbutrin is not a TCA, but it is similar in structure. It works in a similar way to Tofranil and the other TCAs. Wellbutrin is recommended only after age 18 years. The side effects are the same as for other Group Two medications. It comes in 75-mg and 100-mg tablets.

Catapres and Tenex, two medications used to decrease high blood pressure in adults, can at lower dosages increase the amount of norepinephrine at the nerve endings. The exact mechanism by which this occurs is different from that in the other Group Two medications, but the result is the same.

Whereas the other Group Two medications decrease hyperactivity and distractibility but not impulsivity, Catapres and Tenex seem to have minimal benefit with hyperactivity and distractibility, but they decrease impulsivity. Thus, they are used along with the other Group Two medications when impulsivity is an issue. Catapres comes in 0.1-, 0.2-, and 0.3-mg tablets. Tenex comes in 1.0- and 2.0-mg tablets.

The main side effect of these drugs is sedation. Tofranil will make the child tired in class. Catapres or Tenex might make him or her fall asleep. Thus, minimal dosages are given. With Catapres, each dose will last about 6 hours. Often, a 0.1-mg tablet will be used, and one-half or one-fourth of a tablet will be given to the child in the morning and a similar amount at about 3:00 P.M. Even this low dosage can sedate some children, in which case even lower dosages should be tried. With Tenex, often one-half of a 1.0-mg tablet will be used in the morning and in the afternoon.

If either Catapres or Tenex is stopped, it should be tapered off slowly. If the medication is stopped abruptly, some children or adolescents complain of headaches or dizziness.

As mentioned earlier, if a child or adolescent has been tried on many medications and one of the short-acting stimulants seems to be the only one that helps and this medication makes it difficult for the individual to go to sleep, Catapres can be used at bedtime. Catapres also may help with impulsivity. We take advantage of the sedating effect and use a slightly higher dose than would be used during the day. This dose is given 1 hour before planned bedtime and frequently helps the child or adolescent go to sleep. There was a brief concern about using Ritalin and Catapres in this way because of one reported death. A more detailed study of this case and of the use of these medications resulted in a report that this mixture is safe.

Catapres also comes in a slow-absorption transdermal patch. The medication is in a small gauze pad. A waterproof cover can also be used. Each patch releases the medication slowly over 7 days. These patches come in various dosages and can be selected to provide steady coverage over 1 week with a decreased likelihood of sedation. If Catapres is helpful but sedation is a problem, the slow release provided by the patch over an extended period might minimize the sedation and should be considered. The patch has two problems. First, some children do not like the patches and pull them off. Second, the patches can cause a skin rash that itches.

Other Medications for ADHD

Only the medications discussed in this chapter have been found to be effective in the treatment of ADHD. If a child or adolescent has other problems in addition to the ADHD, other medications might be tried. In Chapter 2, I reviewed other neurologically based disorders that might be comorbid with ADHD. These include disorders reflecting problems with modulation of anxiety, anger, or mood; obsessive-compulsive disorder; and tic disorders. Each of these problems may need to be treated (see Chapter 8).

Summary

Medication to treat ADHD must be seen as part of a multimodal approach that includes education, counseling, behavioral management, and family work. If any of the associated disorders are present, they must also be addressed.

The information provided in this chapter is meant to be a clinical guide and not a substitute for the fuller literature provided by the pharmaceutical companies and the U.S. Food and Drug Administration.

Chapter 16

Controversial Therapies

O ur knowledge of learning disabilities and attention-deficit/hyperactivity disorder (ADHD) is incomplete. We have treatment approaches that are based on research and are considered to be accepted practices. I have already discussed these interventions. I now discuss the less acceptable or more controversial treatment approaches. The controversy might be based on the theory behind the treatment, on the way the treatment is carried out, or on the lack of research data to support findings reported by individuals using the treatment approach.

Controversial therapies have been with us throughout history. (Remember when ground-up apricot pits were said to cure cancer?) Professionals who study controversial therapies comment on four specific characteristics of most of these therapies, whether for cancer or for learning disabilities:

1. The individual who publicizes and pushes for the treatment claims to have research to prove what is being stated, but no research is provided from respected journals.
2. The individual stresses that practitioners of "traditional medicine" are too conservative and refuse to accept what does not fit what they already know.
3. The individual provides literature said to prove claims for cure or improvement. One is left to wonder why, if the claim is accurate, the treatment is not used by most professionals in the field.

4. The individual seems to be saying, "I'm a genius," or "I'm a quack," and it is up to the public and the establishment to prove which is true.

Parents often turn to their family physician for guidance, only to learn that he or she does not know any more than they do. The difficulty is that many professionals and nonprofessionals propose treatment approaches. If research has been conducted to support a particular approach, it will be published in professional journals that are reviewed carefully to ensure that the results reported are accurate. Usually, others try to replicate the findings found by the first researcher. If others support the treatment findings, the approach is accepted by the professional groups. It is difficult to evaluate claims communicated through self-published books, popular books and magazines, newspapers, and television shows. Thus, professionals know only what they have read or heard through these sources or from parents who have told them about a particular treatment approach.

In this chapter, I discuss controversial treatment approaches that have been proposed and are still being used. I do not review controversial research that focuses on cause but has not resulted in proposed treatment approaches. When research shows that the proposed treatment does not work, I review this research. When all of the facts are not yet in or agreed on, I review the information known from both perspectives and let you decide for yourself.

Learning disabilities are lifetime disabilities. The approaches we now use take time and money and must be used over years. The treatment for ADHD works only during the hours the child or adolescent is taking medication. If the medication wears off, the individual's ADHD is again apparent. Thus, I can understand why parents would want to try almost any approach that might work better and faster for their child. I can especially understand a parent wanting a cure rather than an intervention. Parents must be informed so that they can be intelligent consumers. The following rule of thumb is helpful: if the treatment approach being proposed is so successful, why doesn't everyone in the country use it? No professional, regardless of discipline, would avoid using a treatment that has been shown to work.

I find it helpful to categorize these controversial therapies according to the disorder they treat: learning disabilities or ADHD. Table 16–1 lists

---

Table 16–1. Controversial therapies

Learning disabilities
  Physiological
    Patterning
    Optometric visual training
    Vestibular dysfunction
    Applied kinesiology
    Auditory processing training
  Chemical
    Megavitamins
    Trace elements
  Other approaches
    Allergies
    Tinted lenses
Attention-deficit/hyperactivity disorder
  Physiological
    Biofeedback
  Chemical
    Megavitamins
    Trace elements
    Food additives
    Refined sugars
    Herbs
  Other approaches
    Allergies

---

these therapies in this manner. Within each category, I group the therapies by the proposed mechanism of action: physiological changes or
chemical changes. A few proposed treatments do not fit this model and
are listed separately. *Physiological changes* refers to the concept that by
stimulating specific sensory inputs or exercising specific motor patterns,
one can retrain, recircuit, or in some way improve the functioning of a
part of the nervous system. *Chemical changes* refers to the concept of

207

orthomolecular medicine, a term introduced by Dr. Linus Pauling, referring to the treatment of mental and other disorders by the provision of the optimum concentrations of substances normally present in the human body.

Patterning

The theory and technique of patterning was developed by Dr. Glenn Doman and Dr. Carl Delacato. The underlying concept follows the principle that failures to pass properly through a certain sequence of developmental stages in mobility, language, and competence in the manual, visual, auditory, and tactile areas reflect poor neurological organization and may indicate brain damage. The proposed treatments involve repetitive activities using specific muscle patterns in the order the child should have learned them if development had been normal; for example, rolling over, then crawling, then standing, then walking, and so forth. The method is described in the developers' literature as reaching, " . . . all of the stimuli normally provided by this environment but with such intensity and frequency as to draw, ultimately, a response from the corresponding motor systems."

Reports from the American Academy of Pediatrics and other professional organizations based on a review of the research literature deny any evidence of this approach's success. The report from the American Academy of Pediatrics concluded "that the patterning treatment offers no special merit, that the claims of its advocates are unproven, and that the demands on families are so great that in some cases there may be harm in its use."

This approach remains popular in the United States and around the world. Parents must know that patterning will not improve their child's learning disabilities or ADHD.

Optometric Visual Training

Although this treatment approach for learning disabilities is popular, some professionals believe that it is controversial and does not work. Parents often are caught in the middle. Ophthalmologists believe that this treatment approach does not improve reading and should not be used. Many optometrists believe that it is effective and should be used.

Both professional groups believe that if a child has a learning disability, it is important to rule out or treat any refractory problems (e.g., nearsightedness, farsightedness, or astigmatism); any imbalance in the use of the eye muscles that might interfere with vision, pursuit of visual stimuli, or convergence; or any other medical problems. After this process, ophthalmologists believe that the treatment of choice for learning disabilities is special education and that the child should be referred for this help. Many optometrists believe that visual training will be of help in treating learning disabilities.

Optometric visual training focuses on visual perception and on the ability of eye muscles to pursue visual stimuli and to converge. Other educational and sensory-motor training techniques might also be used.

The ophthalmological literature questions the benefits of visual training, stressing that reading is a central brain process and not an eye process. The newer research on reading that shows that reading is an auditory process requiring phonological awareness and not a visual processing task is noted in support of this view. Some reports show that optometric visual training does not work. The optometric literature presents research to support the theory and therapy. Research also is presented to show the benefits of this therapy.

Parents will turn to their health or mental health professional for advice, but in the end, they will have to make their own decision.

Vestibular Dysfunction

Several investigators have suggested that the vestibular system is important in learning. The vestibular system consists of a sensory organ in each inner ear that monitors head position and the effect of gravity and relays this information to the brain, primarily to the cerebellum. Investigators claim that a clear relationship exists between vestibular disorders and poor academic performance in children with learning disabilities.

Dr. A. Jean Ayres was the first investigator to stress this view. She proposed a theory in which sensory integration is needed for the development of higher learning and intellectual functioning. Her theory proposes the interrelationship among the visual, vestibular, tactile, and proprioceptive senses. Much of her research and that of others explores these interrelationships. Controversy exists about aspects of her theory of sensory integration. The treatment model that evolved from her theory is called *sensory integration therapy*. Some individuals question the usefulness of this approach for children and adults who have learning disabilities with visual perception, motor planning, vestibular, and tactile difficulties. The majority view of the field is positive about sensory integration therapy.

Dr. Harold Levinson has written several books describing his views on the causative role of the vestibular system and the vestibular-cerebellar systems in dyslexia. He proposes the treatment of dyslexia with anti-motion-sickness medication to correct the vestibular dysfunction. His books do not present research published in scientific journals. Most of the research noted in his books is his own. Little evidence supports his theory or the effectiveness of his treatment. In one of his recent books, he proposes multiple other interventions along with the anti-motion-sickness medication, including many other medications and special education.

Much research has been done on the vestibular system. The consistent finding is that no significant differences exist between children who are normal learners and those with learning disabilities either in the intensity of vestibular responsivity or in the prevalence of vestibular dysfunction. Furthermore, these researchers point out that the technique used by Dr. Levinson to diagnose vestibular dysfunction (i.e., the child reporting when a picture on a rotating cylinder is no longer clear) is a measure of *blurring speed* and, thus, a measure of visual stimulation, not of vestibular stimulation.

Dr. Levinson continues to write and publish his books. Much of the publicity for his approach is through these books and appearances on television talk shows. Other professionals have not started to practice what he proposes. Yet, he remains popular and busy.

Applied Kinesiology

Several years ago, chiropractors and chiropractic clinics in the United States actively advertised and sent out flyers claiming that they could cure dyslexia and learning disabilities. The literature referred to the use of *applied kinesiology* and to the work of Dr. Carl A. Ferreri. The claim was that this treatment could result in an astounding reversal of all dyslexic and learning disability conditions. This literature often stated that "this technique produces measurable results immediately, that is, after just one treatment."

The basis for the theory and treatment was published in *Breakthrough for Dyslexia and Learning Disabilities*, a book written by Dr. Ferreri and Dr. Richard Wainwright. This book was published by a small publisher and distributed by Dr. Ferreri in his own practice. No research was conducted on the theory or the treatment. One reference, a paper written by Dr. Ferreri, was cited over and over as proof. I tracked down this article. It was in a free, unedited publication distributed to chiropractors. The paper was 1-page long and simply described Dr. Ferreri's theory.

In Dr. Ferreri and Dr. Wainwright's book, the authors theorize that learning disabilities are caused by two specific bones of the skull shifting out of position and applying pressure on the brain. They also discuss an imbalance within the "reflex centers" of the pelvis, inner ear, head, and neck. The treatment consists of manipulating the bones of the skull, especially those around the eyes, and other bones and muscles of the body. I saw videotapes of Dr. Ferreri administering this treatment. It appeared to be painful to the child.

The proponents of this approach report that after specific bones of the skull are back in place, the learning disabilities are no longer present. They report that special education tutoring will be needed to correct the problems that existed before the cure and that the bones might slip out of place again, requiring further treatment.

Parents began to have their children treated. The Board of Education of one city in California ruled that all special education students in their system would receive this treatment. Chiropractic clinics began to advertise actively.

This proposed treatment is not based on any known research. Some of it is based on anatomical concepts that are not considered valid by the majority of anatomists. No research supports the proposed cures. No follow-up studies document the claimed results. Since the professional organization of chiropractors has become critical of Dr. Ferreri and his proposed treatment, less has been heard of this treatment.

Auditory Processing Training

Several treatment approaches for improving auditory processing have become available in the United States. Organizations offering auditory processing training have advertised this method as a treatment for learning disabilities and ADHD. These advertisements mention no supporting research, and none is known to have been published. As with other promised treatments, many parents read the advertisements and started their children in this expensive treatment.

One treatment is called *Auditory Integration Training*, based on the theory of Guy Bernard, a physician in France. Another treatment is called the *Listening Training Program*, based on the theory of Alfred A. Tomatis, also a physician in France. The first method uses amplified sound; the second method focuses on purported overly sensitive hearing.

The only literature available for study were the advertising flyers and instruction booklets supplied by the providers of the service. Two reviews of these approaches were published by the Edmonton (Canada) Public School System and the Manitoba (Canada) Speech and Hearing Association. Each of these reviews expressed caution about the treatment approaches and concern about the lack of research data. I describe here the methods and the concern with the lack of research.

Bernard's method is based on the theory that some individuals have auditory perception defects such that they hear distortions of sound, have unusually sensitive hearing, or have uneven patterns of auditory sensitivity that are within the range of normal hearing yet are uncomfortable. Auditory testing is conducted using a device called an Audiokinetron to determine the frequencies at which a person has hyperacute or hypoacute hearing. Based on the resulting *audiogram*, various compact discs are selected containing music determined to be the best for the person receiving the training. This music is played through the Audiokinetron, which has been set based on the individual's audiogram to amplify some frequencies and to filter out other frequencies of the sound spectrum. During 20 half-hour sessions (two per day), the frequencies that are hyperacute and painful are filtered out. This approach is described as similar to immobilizing painful joints or muscles until they heal. According to the program developer, after the treatment, the audiometric curve tends to flatten, and hearing is normalized. This treatment then allows the auditory cortex to reorganize. In addition, the exercise is said to strengthen the muscles that control the three bones of the middle ear, preventing sensory overload.

Tomatis's method is based on the theory that some children lose or turn off their ability to listen to certain parts of the normal sound spectrum. They do not effectively absorb, comprehend, and interpret what they hear. These children's normal language development and their relationship to the world beyond themselves can be affected. The intervention is done through a controlled process of auditory stimulation using sophisticated electronic equipment and special control interviews with the child and the parents. Treatment typically involves a 3-week treatment session followed by a 6-week rest period and then another 3-week session. During the sessions, the child listens to filtered music and other sounds to "help the ear focus on the sounds he hears." In the later phases of treatment, the child is to repeat what is heard through earphones in order "to strengthen the now sensitized ear."

The ads and flyers are full of claims of success. Parents are almost made to feel guilty if they do not avail their child of this treatment. No research supports the theory or claims. It may be too early to report whether these approaches help students with learning disabilities. These treatments are controversial because they are being used before any research has shown validity for the theory or any benefit from the treatment.

Newer approaches exist for improving phonological awareness and thus reading skills. These approaches are based on solid research and apply the findings of this research. They should not be confused with the two auditory processing approaches described in this section.

Megavitamins

Using massive doses of vitamins to treat emotional or cognitive disorders was first proposed in the 1940s for the treatment of schizophrenia. It was argued that this disorder was the result of a biochemical problem and that this problem could be avoided by the use of massive amounts of vitamins, especially the B vitamins. No research supported the theory or the treatment, and few professionals consider this approach today.

In the early 1970s, Dr. Allen Cott proposed that learning disabilities could be treated successfully with megavitamins. As with other professionals mentioned in this chapter, he presented his concepts in his own book, citing no research to support his concepts. The American Academy of Pediatrics issued a report specifically focusing on megavitamin therapy to treat learning disabilities. The conclusion: "There is no validity to the concept or treatment."

Within the past several years, the concept of megavitamins to treat learning disabilities (and ADHD) has resurfaced. I discuss these approaches in the section on herbs.

Trace Elements

Trace elements are chemicals found in minute amounts in the body that are essential to normal functioning. They include copper, zinc, magnesium, manganese, and chromium along with the more common chemicals calcium, sodium, and iron. In recent years, iodine, aluminum, and cadmium have been discussed in relation to learning disabilities and ADHD.

Individuals are evaluated for the level of these trace elements in their body. Hair or nail clippings are used for this analysis. If deficiencies are found, replacement therapy is given. No data have been published to support the theory that deficiencies in one or more of these elements cause learning disabilities. No formal studies by professionals, other than those offering the diagnosis and treatment, have validated the proposed successes; however, this concept remains popular in this country. Centers are available to diagnose deficiencies and to treat learning disabilities with trace elements.

Allergies

Professionals who work with children have reported for many years that they see a higher percentage of children and adolescents in their practice with allergies who also have learning disabilities and/or ADHD than would be expected in the normal population. Many studies have examined the possible relationships between allergies and learning disabilities. I discuss Dr. Feingold, a pediatric allergist who focused on ADHD, later in this chapter.

A relationship appears to exist between allergies and brain functioning; however, no clear cause and effect have been found. Two clinicians have written about specific issues relating allergies to learning disabilities and ADHD. Each has proposed a treatment plan. As with other approaches, the theory and treatment concepts are presented in books written by the clinicians themselves, sometimes self-published. Little, if any, research is presented. Pediatric allergists do not accept these treatments.

Dr. Doris Rapp believes that a relationship exists between food or other sensitivities and learning or hyperactivity. She proposes as a treatment a diet that eliminates the identified foods or the avoidance of other suspected allergens. She believes that the traditional allergy skin testing does not always detect the foods that cause problems. Her critics say that her challenge test, which involves placing a solution under the tongue, is not a valid measure of allergies.

Dr. Rapp identifies certain foods or food groups to which children might be allergic: milk, chocolate, eggs, wheat, corn, peanuts, pork, and sugar. She suggests that parents try a specific elimination diet described in her books. This diet consists of eliminating all the possible allergy-producing foods, and then adding one back each week to see if a change in behaviors occurs.

Dr. Rapp tests other possible allergens by using a food extract solution placed under the tongue. If the child is sensitive to certain foods or chemicals in the environment (e.g., paste, glue, paint, mold, or chemicals found in new carpets), these items are eliminated or avoided. She reports an improvement in the behaviors of the child. Most specifically, she reports less aggressive or oppositional behavior and less hyperactivity. Other professionals have not been able to duplicate her findings.

Dr. William Crook has written extensively on the relationship between allergies and general health, learning disabilities, and ADHD. He writes of the *allergic-tension-fatigue syndrome*. He also reports that specific allergies can result in hyperactivity and distractibility.

Many of his more recent publications and presentations focus on a possible allergic reaction to specific yeast and the development of specific behaviors following a yeast infection. He reports that treatment of the yeast infection improves or corrects the problem. No clinical or research studies have confirmed his theories or proposed treatment program.

Tinted Lenses

Helen Irlen proposes the treatment of certain types of dyslexia with colored or tinted lenses or templates. She specifically focuses on a group of problems she refers to as *scotopic sensitivity syndrome*. Individuals with this syndrome show difficulty in six areas: 1) *photophobia*, or sensitivity to light; 2) eye strain; 3) poor visual resolution; 4) reduced span of focus; 5) impaired depth perception; and 6) poor sustained focus. She points out that her proposed treatment is not a substitute for corrective refractive lenses.

Ms. Irlen's papers and other publications cite her research, but this research was presented at a national meeting (American Psychological Association, August 1993), not in a professional journal. In this presentation, she proposed that a small percentage of individuals with dyslexia have scotopic sensitivity syndrome. For this group, the use of tinted lenses will improve the dyslexia. Her treatment with tinted lenses was demonstrated on the television show "60 Minutes," showing a child who could not read and who then used the proper tinted lenses and began to read. Ms. Irlen became very popular.

Since Ms. Irlen's presentation at a national meeting, studies have tested her treatment approach. Some published papers support her concept and some do not. The final facts are not in on the concept or the treatment.

The controversy is that before the facts are in and the effectiveness of this treatment has been studied, Irlen Centers opened around the country. At these centers, a screening test for scotopic sensitivity syndrome is given, and tinted lenses are sold. Of further concern is that Ms. Irlen reported initially that a small percentage of individuals with dyslexia, those with scotopic sensitivity syndrome, would benefit from tinted lenses. How objectively is dyslexia being diagnosed and this syndrome identified before lenses are sold? Should any treatment be advertised and sold before the facts are in?

Biofeedback

A professional in California proposed that ADHD is a result of an altered pattern of brain waves and that this pattern can be identified on an electroencephalogram (EEG). Thus, the EEG could be used as a diagnostic tool. This approach is controversial.

Further, by using a biofeedback technique, clinicians are supposed to be able to teach individuals to change their brain wave pattern. Once the pattern is corrected, the ADHD is improved or treated. Greater controversy relates to this use of EEG biofeedback as a treatment for ADHD, yet the equipment is sold and many professionals throughout the United States use this form of treatment.

The Professional Advisory Board of the organization Children and Adults With Attention Deficit Disorder (CHADD) published a position statement after these professionals reviewed all of the literature on these concepts. In their statement, they challenged the use of EEG biofeedback for ADHD, and parents were advised not to use this treatment approach.

Food Additives

In 1975, Dr. Benjamin Feingold published the book *Why Your Child Is Hyperactive*. He proposed that synthetic flavors and colors in the diet were related to hyperactivity. He reported that the elimination of all foods containing artificial colors, artificial flavors, salicylates, and certain other additives stopped the hyperactivity. In none of Dr. Feingold's publications, including his book, did he present research data to support this theory. All findings in the book were based on his clinical experience. He and his book received wide publicity. Parent groups advocating for the Feingold diet formed all over the country. It was left to others to document whether he was correct.

Because of a hope that he might be correct and because of a need to either counter his claims or prove he was correct, the federal government sponsored several major research projects to study this theory and the treatment. In 1982, the National Institutes of Health held what is called a consensus conference on this issue. A panel of experts were brought together. They reviewed the results of these research studies, read all available literature, held hearings to allow anyone who wished to present evidence to do so, and questioned experts. The panel members then spent time synthesizing what was known and finally wrote a consensus on the topic.

They concluded that there appears to be a subset of children with behavioral disturbances who respond to some aspects of Feingold's diet. However, this group is very small, possibly 1% of the children studied. They also commented that with notable exceptions, the specific elimination of synthetic food colors from the diet does not appear to be a major factor in the reported responses of most of these children. They concluded that the defined diets should not be used universally in the treatment of childhood hyperactivity.

Two studies reached the same conclusions after this consensus conference. The Feingold diet is not effective in treating hyperactivity in children. For reasons that are not clear, a small group, perhaps 1%, appears to respond positively to the diet.

There is no way for physicians to identify in advance which patients might be part of this 1% group. Sometimes a parent will report that if his or her child eats foods (e.g., Kool-Aid, Hawaiian Punch, or certain cereals) that have specific food colors or takes a medication with specific food colors (e.g., penicillin with red or yellow food dye), he or she will become more hyperactive. Perhaps this is a child with ADHD who might respond to a diet that eliminates a specific food color; however, the basic ADHD would still be present and need treatment.

| Refined Sugars

Clinical observations and parent reports suggest that refined sugar promotes adverse behavioral reactions in children. Hyperactive behavior is most commonly reported.

Several formal studies have been conducted to clarify and/or verify these parent claims. Each study used what is called a *challenge study*. Children who were reported by parents to become more hyperactive when they ate refined sugar were challenged with refined sugar (glucose), natural sugar (fructose), or a placebo. The results failed to support the parent observations.

Another study explored whether the reported increase in activity level among children who ate a high-sugar snack or meal might be related to the amount of refined sugar eaten and not to the exposure to the sugar. In this study, each child was given a breakfast. This breakfast was high in fat, carbohydrates, or protein. The children were then given the challenge test with refined sugar, natural sugar, or a placebo. The researchers found that some children appeared to be more active after a high carbohydrate breakfast and exposure to refined sugars. Possibly, then, some children with ADHD will become more hyperactive if they eat high levels of refined sugar in foods and snacks throughout a period of time (e.g., sugared cereal for breakfast, cookies at snack-time, a jelly sandwich and candy for lunch, and cake for an after-school snack).

Herbs

The use of alternative medicines is popular around the world. Herbs, spices, and other ingredients have been known to be therapeutic in certain situations. The extension of these concepts to the treatment of ADHD and possibly to the treatment of learning disabilities has become widespread within the past several years. As with most of the controversial treatments discussed in this chapter, most of what is known is found in flyers and advertisements distributed by the individuals selling the products. No research is presented, but claims are made about the effectiveness of the treatment.

In preparation for the update of this book, I sent a written request for more information on several products I saw advertised or found exhibited at a meeting or for which I had received advertisements in the mail. I was struck by the absence of anything more than advertisements. Furthermore, for three of the products for which I requested more information, the information I received included an offer for me to be the exclusive salesperson for the product in my area. I was told how much good I would do for children by making them aware of this treatment.

The uniform theme among these products is that no research is provided to defend the claims they make. The information I received often contained testimonials and large technical words. The material seemed to imply that if I did not use the product, I was preventing my child from making progress. I list these products below so that physicians can inform parents of the most common products available at the time this book was finalized. It is not a complete list. Certainly other products are out there. The product descriptions come from the literature provided with the product or from the product labels.

- God's Recipe: a mixture of colloidal minerals, antioxidants with Ginkgo Biloba, and multienzymes
- Pedi-Active ADD: phosphatidy/serine, stated to be the "most advanced neuronutrients available"; includes a diversified combination of other ingredients
- Kids Plex Jr: contains multivitamins, amino acids, and a mixture of "ergogens and Krebs cycle intermediates and lipotropics"
- Calms Kids: a mixture of vitamins, minerals, and amino acids
- Pycnogenol: a "water processed extract from the bark of the French Maritine Pine Tree . . . (the most) potent nutritional antioxidant discovered by science"
- New Vision: a mixture of 16 juices and 18 fruit blends made into a capsule
- Super Blue Green Algae: comes in many forms; benefits are stated to result because algae is the "very basis of the entire food chain—it is largely responsible for creating and renewing all life on earth"

No other details were available for these products. For example, which vitamins or amino acids or are included? Many of the descriptive terms used were not defined and made little sense. No evidence was given to support the claims. I encourage parents to think carefully before buying these products.

| Summary

When a parent learns of a new treatment for ADHD, he or she has good reason for showing interest. We all want a better and faster way to help children and adolescents with ADHD. Parents need to become as informed as possible. They should be taught to ask why a new treatment is not used by everyone. If the person proposing the treatment tells the parents that "Most professionals are biased and do not believe these findings because they are different from the usual treatments," parents should ask to see the data supporting the concept and treatment. They should not accept popular books published as validated facts by the person proposing the theory or treatment. Parents should discuss new approaches with their family physician, other professionals, and other parents.

The information in this chapter should help clinicians be better informed when parents request guidance. The known information can be provided to counter the information parents might have.

Part 5

Special Topics

Chapter 17

Attention-Deficit/ Hyperactivity Disorder in Adults

The exact percentage of children and adolescents who continue to have attention-deficit/hyperactivity disorder (ADHD) as adults is not known. It is estimated that about 50% of adolescents with ADHD will continue to have this disability as adults. If the current estimate that 3%–6% of youths have ADHD is correct, we might expect 1.5%–3% of adults to have ADHD.

The awareness that adults might have ADHD is relatively recent; thus, many physicians who treat adults are not familiar with this possibility. Mental health professionals who work only with adults also might not know to consider this possibility. With the increase in books and other literature on adult ADHD and the frequent coverage of this topic in the media, more adults are asking whether they might have this disorder. Unfortunately, they might have difficulty finding a professional to evaluate them.

The process for establishing the diagnosis of ADHD in an adult is the same as in children and adolescents—the presence of a chronic and pervasive history of hyperactivity, inattention/distractibility, and/or impulsivity. The medications used for treating the disorder in children and adolescents work the same way in adults. The effect of ADHD on the adult might be the same as it was for the individual as a child or adolescent but will be reflected in different settings, for example, in postsecondary school, on the job, and interactions with adult friends and the adult's family.

This book is primarily about ADHD in children and adolescents. This chapter focuses on many issues relating to adults but may not cover these issues in as much depth as a clinician working with adults might want. Many excellent books are available on adult ADHD. They can be found in most bookstores, or a list can be obtained from Children and Adults With Attention Deficit Disorder (CHADD), the national organization for individuals with ADHD. (See Appendix for information on CHADD.)

ADHD Behaviors in Adults

Hyperactivity

Adults with ADHD often find careers and lifestyles that are compatible with being more active. They might seek jobs that require or permit moving about rather than sitting at a desk. They seem to find other adults who accept their activity level. The behavior is there, however. They might sit, but their knees are moving up and down, their leg is swinging, or their fingers are tapping. They have a difficult time sitting through long meals or a movie.

I have met many adults who find that the only way they can relax is to exercise to the point of exhaustion. If they go to the gym and work out or if they jog long distances, they can relax more during the hours after this activity. Others make sure that their work demands allow them to keep an active pace all day.

For some adults, the hyperactivity does not become an issue until they become so successful on the job that they get promoted to middle management. Now they have to sit at a desk and organize the work of others, and they cannot. For others, the stress begins when marriage and children create the need to be more calm, to sit for longer periods of time, that is, to be still.

Inattention

As discussed earlier in this book, adults might have the same problem with external distractibility as children. They might show greater problems with internal distractibility. Their mind jumps from thought to thought, or they find themselves trying to pay attention but drifting off. As with hyperactivity, these problems escalate with career success and promotion to more demanding levels of performance. Marriage and the demands of children add to these difficulties.

Impulsivity

Adults, like children or adolescents, might speak or act before they think. Many adults become aware of this problem and concentrate on controlling themselves. As they go into a meeting, they might say to themselves, "Keep your mouth shut." However, they still interrupt people or say things before thinking, hurting the feelings of others or sounding foolish. Others act impulsively. They might buy things before they think about whether they have the money, or they might start to do something without thinking about whether they have enough time to complete the activity.

Some adults steal, gamble, lie, or have other impulse-control problems. Some drive poorly. They speed, take risks, and change lanes without looking and thinking. They tend to have more traffic accidents and get more tickets than nonimpulsive persons.

| Organizational Problems

Every article or book on ADHD discusses organizational problems and the problems of the "organizationally impaired." Adults with ADHD, like children and adolescents with ADHD, can have major organizational problems.

Adults have problems organizing materials at work or home, and they have difficulty organizing schedules and time. Their whole life can seem to be one big disorganized problem—at their job, on their personal time, and with their family. Is organization one of the characteristic problems of ADHD? We do not yet know, but I would like to offer my views on this issue.

I believe that organization is a significant problem for many children, adolescents, and adults with ADHD. I also believe that disorganization has several possible causes. For some, it is a result of inattention and distractibility; thus, it is seen in individuals who have ADHD. For some, it is a result of a learning disability or an executive function problem; thus, disorganization is seen in adults who have these problems. Because a high percentage of individuals with organizational problems also have ADHD, this behavior might be seen in adults who have ADHD.

Organizational problems secondary to distractibility. The adult gets up to do something. On the way, something visually distracts the individual and his or her attention shifts. Recall the woman described in Chapter 6 who went into the kitchen to start dinner. She walked into the kitchen, and her attention shifted immediately to some papers she saw on the kitchen table, then to a note she saw on the telephone (prompting her to make a telephone call), and finally to a magazine she saw on the counter. Twenty minutes after she entered the kitchen, her children came in asking about dinner. Suddenly, she remembered why she came into the kitchen. Her life was full of similar examples of visual distractibility, resulting in a life of disorganization. The disorganization was a consequence of her ADHD.

Other adults might describe starting to do a task at home (e.g., laundry, housecleaning, or bill paying). Suddenly, their mind jumps to something else and they start to do this other activity. Then, their mind jumps again and off they go. Their day is full of incomplete tasks, and their life is disorganized. Here, the internal distractibility associated with ADHD results in the disorganization.

I believe that many adults who have problems with organization and completing tasks have this disorganization as a secondary consequence of their external or internal distractibility. Thus, I can see why many books on adults with ADHD focus on problems with organization.

Organizational problems secondary to learning disabilities. Recall that one of the processing tasks of integration is organization. With the processing model, organization means the ability to organize pieces of information together into a concept or the ability to break a concept into its parts. Organization also refers to the ability to organize one's thoughts, materials, and time. A characteristic of children and adolescents who have an organizational disability as part of their pattern of learning disabilities is that their notebooks, papers, and materials are a mess. These individuals lose and forget things. They complete work and misplace it before they can turn it in. They can't organize their desk or room, and they get overwhelmed when their environment is disorganized. They have difficulty organizing time. Clearly, we see adults who have the same problems in college, on the job, and within the family. Sorting, folding, and distributing laundry can be as overwhelming a task to an adult as organizing notebooks and homework is to a child.

Adults with an organizational disability as part of their learning disabilities might have difficulty deciding how to subdivide or put together materials. Their office or home may be cluttered with piles of papers or other materials. Their desk is cluttered. They "sort of know" which pile to look through to get what they want, but others think they are disorganized and messy. Partners do not like living with such clutter. These adults will tell you that they do not know how to subdivide material into categories so that they can file the material. If they file it, they would never know where to look to find it again; thus, it is better to put everything in visible piles—at least they know what pile to look for.

Adults with organizational problems secondary to learning disabilities might have major difficulty with time planning. They just can't get themselves organized or plan their day to get everything done. They make schedules but somehow can't follow them. They misjudge how long a task or errand will take and seem to be late constantly.

Another example of learning disabilities leading to disorganization is seen in adults who have short-term memory problems. They never remember what they were supposed to do or where they were supposed to be. They make lists to help them but lose the lists or forget to look at them. Their lives are disorganized.

Organizational problems secondary to executive function disorder. Recall that *executive functions* refers to the ability to define and assess a task, plan a strategy for carrying it out, begin this process, make any adjustments needed along the way, and complete the task. Some adults with

ADHD describe an inability to take on tasks. They have difficulty deciding how to solve the problem, or they start but get lost or stuck. Again, their lives are disorganized. Here, though, psychoeducational testing might clarify that this problem is not the result of ADHD but rather the processing problem we call executive function disorder.

Recognition and Diagnosis

Few physicians and mental health professionals who see adults are familiar with ADHD; thus, this diagnosis often is missed. Individuals seeking help sometimes know more about this disability than do the professionals they see.

For some individuals, the diagnosis becomes apparent when their child receives a diagnosis of ADHD. "That's me," they might say. "I have had the same problems all of my life." One parent might point to the other and say, "He is just like our child." For others, a newspaper or magazine article, a book, or a television special might make them aware that there might be a reason for the problems they have had most of their life. Consider the following case examples:

Fran was diagnosed as having learning disabilities when she was in third grade. Although she attended special classes all through high school, she had increasing difficulty doing her schoolwork. Fran's teachers and her parents complained that she would not stay on task or make an effort to complete her work. During her senior year of high school, she began psychotherapy for her "lack of seriousness about school." Her psychiatrist thought she was depressed and prescribed an antidepressant medication for her, but it had no effect.

She went to a college that offered resource help and accommodations for her learning disabilities, but she found the work difficult. She couldn't concentrate when she studied in the dormitory and began to worry that she might not succeed. On the advice of her former psychotherapist, she went to the college mental health service. The psychologist who saw her asked if she might have ADHD and referred her to me.

Fran had a classic history of hyperactivity, distractibility, and impulsivity throughout her life. She was fidgety and had been so "forever." Her friends, even the new ones in college, teased her about her constant need to

move some part of her body. Any sound would distract her. She could recall examples from elementary school when she would listen to what was
going on in the hall rather than in class. Fran cried as she described her
impulsivity. She constantly hurt her friends' feelings by saying things before thinking, and her teachers often yelled at her for answering out of
turn.

With Fran's permission, I invited her mother to a session. We asked
her to bring all of Fran's old report cards and the psychoeducational evaluation reports from the past. The hyperactivity, distractibility, and
impulsivity were described year after year, starting in kindergarten. Her
teachers and parents assumed these problems were part of her learning
disabilities.

I started Fran on methylphenidate (Ritalin). She showed significant
improvement at a dose of 10 mg three times a day: "It's a miracle. I feel so
relaxed. I can concentrate so much better, even in the dorm. I am getting
my work done so much quicker and better. My friends have commented
that I seem so different. I pay attention when they are talking to me, and
I don't interrupt them when they are talking . . . "

Fran then added, "Why was I not given this medication when I was a
child?" This last question opened up her feelings of anger and sadness
with which she had had to struggle for so long. She also felt the pain of
years of being told it was all her fault and that she could do better if she
tried. We continued to work together to help her with these concerns and
feelings.

During my interpretive session with Howard's parents, I explained why
I felt he had ADHD and how I wanted to approach helping him. Both parents agreed with the diagnosis, the need for medication, and the need for
further educational efforts. The next day, his mother called me. She mentioned that she was never comfortable talking about her husband during
our meetings, but she was worried about him.

Her husband was described as explosive at home. He would yell, throw
things, and "explode." On several occasions, he punched holes in the wall
with his fists. She also commented that he dropped out of college and that
he had difficulty keeping jobs because of complaints about his not getting
his work done. She thought he had ADHD. We agreed that I would try to
explore this theme during our follow-up meeting.

When I met with Howard's parents to discuss behavioral management
issues within the family, I mentioned that in about 50% of children with
ADHD, one of the parents had the same problems. I then reviewed how

these problems might appear in an adult. I asked each parent if any of what I was describing sounded familiar. After a brief silence, Howard's father commented that he had been thinking about himself since our last meeting. The more he opened up and described himself as a child, adolescent, college student, and adult, the more he showed evidence of hyperactivity, distractibility, and impulsivity. He agreed to see me on his own.

The history I obtained confirmed the diagnosis. He agreed to start medication and showed significant improvement in all areas. He felt that his work performance improved. His wife reported that he was so much more relaxed and into being part of the family. He was not losing his temper.

I arranged for Howard's father to work with someone who helped him focus on his work-related difficulties. He also decided to disclose his problem to his supervisor at work. We had to think this approach through to clarify what he wanted to say and what he wanted to have as accommodations on the job.

As the preceding case examples show, the diagnosis of ADHD in adults starts with establishing clinical evidence of one or more of the three behaviors. Then the presence of these behaviors must be shown to be pervasive—to affect two or more areas of the adult's life. Finally, these behaviors must be documented to have existed since at least age 7 years. Often, this chronic theme is based only on the adult's memory. Sometimes the adult will remember that he or she used to take medication in grade school so that he or she could sit still or pay attention. Preferably, previous records or information from parents or siblings can be obtained to validate this history.

Treatment With Medication

The use of appropriate medications is just as essential in adults as it is in children. Because the dosage of these medications is not based on body weight, the amount used might be the same in an adult as in a child. The correct dosage must be determined based on an evaluation of the individual.

Mr. A, a 30 year-old attorney, came to see me after reading an article in the newspaper. He told me that from age 9 to 16 he had taken medication because of overactivity and trouble concentrating. He remembered that two of his sisters took the same medication. At my request, he contacted his mother, who contacted the family doctor. We learned that he had been taking dextroamphetamine (Dexedrine).

During college and law school, Mr. A. occasionally was able to get Dexedrine from his friends. When he took it, he studied better and more efficiently. Now he was working for a law firm and having great difficulty staying on task and getting his work done. He said he was frustrated with his performance. He knew he could do the work, but he had great difficulty staying organized and keeping track of his billable hours. He also found that it was difficult to get any work done during the day because of the talking and noise in the office. He worked best late at night or when he took his work home.

I prescribed Dexedrine for Mr. A. At a dose of 5 mg every 4 hours, he reported a dramatic improvement. He was able to concentrate and stay on task. He was able to work despite the activity around him. His thoughts were more organized, and he became effective and efficient at work. Even his direct supervisor noted the changes.

If an adult responds to medication, the concept of using medication whenever it is needed is just as important as it is in children and adolescents. Adults might need coverage during evenings and weekends in order to function better within their family.

Some adults have agreed that the medication helped them be more calm and less impulsive, yet they liked the way they were before they started taking it. They were used to their level of activity and liked the level of excitement they experienced. Knowing how the medication worked, they elected not to take it. I supported their decision.

Nonmedication Treatments

As with children, ADHD interferes with all aspects of an adult's life, including success in postsecondary education, on-the-job relationships and performance abilities, interactions with friends and more casual relationships, ability to participate in recreational activities, and success with more intimate relationships with a significant other. For many adults, the major area of difficulty is work. For others, the major area of difficulty is the family.

For some adults, the emotional consequences of ADHD throughout life might result in problems that need to be addressed. The resulting anxiety or depression or the difficulty with anger control or with relationships is as important to treat as the basic ADHD. For others, it is clear that they have ADHD plus one or more of the related disorders discussed earlier in this book. These problems also must be identified and addressed.

ADHD might have significantly affected the individual's academic success in high school and in postsecondary programs. Once ADHD is diagnosed, the individual might need to be assessed for educational, vocational, or career needs. This need is especially great for the adult who has had limited success in the world of work or who did not complete an education he or she really wanted.

After the diagnosis is made, several questions should be considered. First, does the individual need help with any secondary emotional, social, or family problems? Second, are any of the related disorders present? The disorder found most frequently is a learning disability. If so, each disorder must be addressed. Third, what job- or career-related difficulties exist and how might they be approached? I find that the selection of a medication and the adjustment of the dosage and timing is often the easiest part of the treatment program. Addressing these other areas requires time, networking, and effort.

Some adults find that once their ADHD behaviors are under better control and their learning disabilities, if present, are understood, they can rethink many aspects of their life and move forward. Others might need vocational testing, vocational guidance, or accommodations in their current job. Some might want to return to college, and appropriate accommodations will be needed. In Chapter 18, I review the legal issues of importance when helping an adult with ADHD.

Coaching is a new and exciting approach to help some adults with ADHD. Some professionals who were special education tutors, helping children and adolescents with learning disabilities, have retrained to help adults with ADHD. They call themselves coaches rather than tutors. Coaches work closely with the adult, identifying the area(s) of difficulty. The themes picked to work on often are those causing the greatest difficulty for the adult. The coach then works with the adult, analyzing the reasons for the problem(s). Compensatory strategies are developed and tried. With practice, these strategies are modified until they seem to be helpful and then practiced until they are used routinely. Alternatively, the conclusion might be reached that the specific tasks in a given area are such a problem that it would be best to have others help the adult do a particular task or to find someone else to do it.

Tasks might involve anything from managing one's finances to organizing one's life or day. They might involve getting rid of piles of things and learning how to compartmentalize and file materials, or they might be specific work-related tasks that cause difficulty (e.g., helping an attorney handle the task of monitoring billable hours or helping a plant supervisor to keep an inventory list). Whether the adult with ADHD is a disorganized individual who cannot manage the home and children or an individual who cannot handle the demands of a job, a creative coach can help this adult develop strategies for being more successful.

Summary

ADHD is a reality for many adults. The clues for recognizing that an adult might have ADHD and the process for diagnosing ADHD in an adult are the same as for children and adolescents. The treatment approaches are also the same except for the need to address the special issues faced by adults compared with those of youths.

This book focuses primarily on families with children and adolescents. This chapter identifies areas of difficulty for adults with ADHD but does not describe the models available for helping these adults. I encourage clinicians to read or refer their adult patients to read some of the excellent books available for adults.

Chapter 18

Relevant Educational and Civil Laws

Current laws require school systems to provide services for children and adolescents with disabilities. This was not always the case. Before 1975, about half of the children with disabilities in the United States could not get an appropriate education. About 1 million were excluded entirely from the public school system. The situation with children and adolescents who have attention-deficit/hyperactivity disorder (ADHD) is still not ideal. As I explain later in this chapter, this disorder is formally recognized only in civil law, not in education law.

These laws, however, do not automatically assure that the child or adolescent will receive the appropriate programs and services he or she needs. This reality is even more true now because of the decrease in federal and state funding for education. To be effective advocates for parents, clinicians must be fully informed on ADHD and on the legal issues of importance in getting the necessary services within the school system.

In this chapter, I discuss an education law that requires school systems to provide services to children and adolescents with learning disabilities. In addition, I discuss a civil law requiring schools and employers to provide appropriate accommodations for individuals with disabilities. Each is relevant for children and adolescents. The civil law is relevant for adults.

What are these laws? What do they mean for the individuals you see clinically? What must you know and do to ensure that the help needed will be in place? What can you do if you are not pleased with the way the school system is addressing the needs of the child or adolescent you are trying to help? In this chapter, I attempt to answer these questions.

History of Relevant Legislation

The major force behind today's legislation was a consumer movement led by organizations of parents of children with disabilities. Later, the individuals with the disabilities themselves joined in this effort. They focused on the lack of an appropriate public education and on the exclusion of children and adolescents from programs provided by the public education system.

In the 1960s, various groups of parents whose children had different disabilities used publicity, mass mailings, public meetings, and other well-organized, opinion-molding techniques to put pressure on state legislatures. They wanted laws making educational opportunities for persons with disabilities not simply available but mandatory. Most states responded with legislation, some more than others.

A few states did nothing. Most of the more progressive state governments passed the laws but provided no enabling funds for facilities or trained professionals to carry out their intent. The focus of these pressure groups then shifted toward enactment of a federal law that could have an effect on all states.

In 1971, the Pennsylvania Association for Retarded Citizens filed a lawsuit in that state, directly involving the federal government in these issues for the first time. Citing constitutional guarantees of due process and equal protection under the law, the association argued that the access of children with mental retardation to public education should be equal to that afforded other children. The court agreed. One year later, the federal court in the District of Columbia made a similar ruling involving not only persons with mental retardation but also those with a wide range of disabilities. This 1972 decision established two major precedents critical to future progress: 1) children with disabilities have the right to a "suitable publicly supported education, regardless of the degree of the child's mental, physical, or emotional disability or impairment"; and 2) concerning financing, "if sufficient funds are not available to finance all of the services and programs that are needed and desirable . . . the available funds must be expended equitably in such a manner that no child is entirely excluded from a publicly supported education." More than 40 such cases were won throughout the United States after these two landmark decisions.

These court actions also had a profound influence on federal legislation. The *Rehabilitation Act of 1973,* referred to as the *Civil Rights Act for the Handicapped,* prohibits discrimination on the basis of physical or mental handicaps in every federally assisted program in the country. Public education, of course, accepts federal assistance. Section 504 of this law focuses on the rights of the individuals in these programs, and it has been the keystone of parents' demands and of numerous successful court actions. The most critical issues in Section 504 are listed here:

1. As disabled job applicants or employees, handicapped people have the same rights and must be guaranteed the same benefits as non-handicapped applicants and employees.
2. Handicapped people are entitled to all of the medical services and medically related instruction that is available to the general public.
3. Handicapped people are entitled to participate, on an equal basis with the nonhandicapped, in vocational rehabilitation, day care, or any other social service program receiving federal assistance.
4. Handicapped people have equal rights to go to college or to enroll in job-training or adult postsecondary basic education programs. Selection must be based on academic or other school records, and the disability cannot be a factor. (If a person has learning disabilities, the standard entrance testing procedures, the Scholastic Assessment Test, for example, can be modified, and admission standards can be based on potential and on past performance.)
5. State and local school districts must provide an appropriate elementary and secondary education for all handicapped students.

In 1990, this law was expanded to all programs and not just to federally funded programs. The *Americans With Disabilities Act* ended discrimination against individuals with disabilities in the areas of employment, education, public accommodations, and licensing of professional and other activities. It extended the coverage of basic civil rights legislation to a wide range of public and private entities.

Section 504, especially the fifth point noted in the previous list, became the basis for Public Law 94-142, the *Education for All Handicapped Children Act*. It was passed overwhelmingly by the House and Senate and enacted in November 1976. It was a final victory for the parents who fought so hard for their children. This landmark legislation capped a heroic effort begun by a few parents who joined with others to form organizations, which then worked together to lobby successfully for the needs of all children with disabilities. This law is unique in several ways. It has no expiration date; it is regarded as permanent law. It does more than just express a concern for children with disabilities; it requires a specific commitment. The law sets forth as national policy the proposition that education, as a fundamental right, must be extended to persons with disabilities.

Thanks to these parents, education law now guarantees the person with learning disabilities the right to a good education. This assurance, as I discuss later, is not yet as clear for individuals with ADHD. The challenge for today's parents is to insist on the transformation of this promise into reality.

With federal, state, and county budget cuts, services to persons with disabilities have been cut significantly. Because of these budget cuts and loss of personnel, some school systems lead parents to believe that their child is not entitled to services or that the minimal services offered are adequate. This crisis in services is compounded by another problem. The initial law, Public Law 94-142, provided services for parent education. There was an understood need to inform parents of their rights under the law. This knowledge helped parents enter and function within the system. These parents have children who have graduated from high school. After the initial funding for parent education ended, most school systems stopped providing such education. None of the parents of current public school students benefited from this initial educational process. As I lecture around the country, I am distressed by the frequency with which I meet parents who do not know of their rights or how to fight for the services their children need.

Public Law 94-142: Education for All Handicapped Children Act

Because Public Law 94-142 is so important to understand when working with children and adolescents who have disabilities, I review it here in detail, starting with the contents of the original law and then explaining the many amendments enacted since 1976. I suggest ways you can work within this law to be an advocate for the children and adolescents with whom you work. This law is the only hope parents have for fighting for services.

The original law listed 11 categories of children with disabilities: mentally retarded, hard-of-hearing, deaf, deaf-blind, speech-impaired, visually handicapped, seriously emotionally disturbed, orthopedically impaired, other health-impaired, specific learning disabilities, and multihandicapped. In a 1986 amendment (discussed later in this chapter), two new groups were added: autism and traumatic brain injury. Despite the efforts of parent groups, ADHD was not added to this list when the revisions were made.

Learning disabilities are defined in the law as applying to those children

who have a disorder in one or more of the basic psychological processes involved in understanding or in using language, spoken or written, which disorder may manifest itself in imperfect ability to listen, think, speak, read, write, spell, or do mathematical calculations. Such disorders include such conditions as perceptual handicaps, brain injury, minimal brain dysfunction, dyslexia, and developmental aphasia. Such term does not include children who have learning problems, which are primarily the result of visual, hearing, or motor handicaps, or mental retardation, of emotional disturbance, or of environmental, cultural, or economic disadvantage.

This law makes the following guarantees for children and adolescents who have a handicapping condition:

1. A free public education is guaranteed to all between ages 3 and 21. [The term *free and appropriate public education,* or FAPE, is often referred to in school procedures.]

2. Each handicapped person is guaranteed an *Individualized Education Program,* or IEP. This IEP must be in the form of a written statement, jointly developed by the school officials, the child's teacher, the parent or guardian, and if possible by the child himself or herself. It must include an analysis of the child's present achievement level, a list of both short-range and annual goals, an identification of the specific services that will be provided toward meeting these goals, and an indication of the extent to which the child will be able to participate in regular school programs. The IEP must also be clear about when these services will be provided and how long they will last, and it provides a schedule for checking on the progress achieved under the plan and for making any necessary revisions in it.

3. Handicapped and nonhandicapped children must be educated together to the fullest extent that is appropriate. A child can be placed in special classes or separate schools only when the nature and severity of his or her handicap prevents satisfactory achievement in a regular education program. This concept of placement is referred to as being in the least restrictive environment possible.

4. Tests and other evaluation materials used in placing handicapped children must be prepared and administered in such a way as not to be racially or culturally discriminatory. They must also be presented in the child's native tongue.

5. An intensive and ongoing effort must be made to locate and identify children with handicaps, to evaluate their educational needs, and to determine whether these needs are being met.

6. In all efforts, priority must be given to those children who are not receiving an education and to those severely handicapped children who are receiving an inadequate education.

7. In all decisions, a prior consultation with the child's parents or guardians must be held. No policies, programs, or procedures affecting the education of handicapped children may be adopted without a public notice.

8. These rights and guarantees apply to handicapped children in private and public schools. Any special education provided to any child shall be provided at no cost to the parents if state or local education agency officials placed the child in such schools or referred the child to them.

9. States and localities must develop comprehensive personnel development programs, including in-service training for regular teachers, special education teachers, and support personnel.
10. In implementing the law, special effort shall be made to employ qualified handicapped persons.
11. All architectural barriers must be removed.
12. The state education agency has jurisdiction over all educational programs for handicapped children offered within a given state, including those administered by noneducational agencies.
13. An advisory panel must exist to advise the state education agency of unmet needs. Membership must include handicapped children and parents or guardians of those children.

This law guarantees *procedural safeguards.* Parents or guardians have an opportunity to examine any records that bear on the identification of a child as being disabled, on the defined nature and severity of his or her disability, and on the kind of educational setting in which he or she is placed. Schools must provide written notice before changing a child's placement. If a parent or guardian objects to a school's decision, a process must be in place through which complaints can be registered. This process must include an opportunity for an impartial hearing that offers parents rights similar to those involved in a court case, that is, the right to be advised by counsel (and by special education experts if they wish), the right to present evidence, the right to cross-examine witnesses, the right to compel the presence of any witnesses who do not voluntarily appear, the right to be provided a verbatim report of the proceedings, and the right to receive the decision and findings in written form.

The rights and safeguards of Public Law 94-142 are critical. Take the time to reread the points listed above. Each school system is required to provide parents with written guidelines explaining their rights of appeal.

Revisions to Public Law 94-142

In September 1986, Congress passed Public Law 99-457. This law, titled the *Education of the Handicapped Act Amendments of 1986,* included provisions for children of all ages with disabilities. The upper age limit remained at 21. The original starting age of 3 years, however, was lowered to include "handicapped and 'at risk' children between birth and age 6 years and their families." This law has two major components.

First, the law created a new mandate for state education agencies to serve all 3-, 4-, and 5-year-old children with disabilities by 1991. All of the rights to an education in the original law (for ages 6–21) are now required down to age 3. As in the original law, services for children in the 3–6 age group are mandated, not simply encouraged. If a state does not comply, it can lose federal funds.

Second, the law established an early intervention program, the *Handicapped Infants and Toddlers Program.* This provision of the law created a new federal program for children with disabilities and who are at risk, from birth to age 3 years and for their families. The infant and toddler program is voluntary for states, that is, they may elect not to participate; however, if a state chooses to participate or to apply for funding under this law, it must meet the requirements of the law and ensure that services are available for all eligible children.

Public Law 99-457 stresses the importance of a coordinated and multiagency approach to the planning and dialogue that is necessary to implement the new early childhood initiatives. A variety of local providers, public and private, must work together to provide the services.

In 1988, Congress approved a change in the name of Public Law 94-142 to the *Individuals With Disabilities Education Act,* or IDEA. This change was in keeping with the increased concept of political correctness. One does not speak of disabled children but of children with disabilities.

Changes never cease. IDEA was considered for revision in 1997. Many of the proposed changes would have weakened the law significantly. Through constant efforts by parent volunteers, the law was saved in a strong form. In April 1997, the latest amendments were passed by Congress and signed by the president. (The federal guidelines for implementing these changes in the law were not complete at the time this book was completed.) These amendments provide the following changes:

1. Schools must obtain informed consent from parents prior to a child's initial evaluation to determine the presence of a disability and prior to any reevaluation.
2. Parents are now members of their child's eligibility, IEP, and placement teams.

3. The 3-year reevaluation no longer automatically requires extensive or prescribed testing. The IEP team (including parents and other professionals) will determine what reevaluation information and testing is necessary based on the needs of the individual child.
4. Children with disabilities must be included in all general and district-wide assessment programs. Appropriate accommodations will be provided when necessary.
5. Alternative assessments must be developed by July 1, 2000, for those children who cannot participate in state- or district-wide assessment programs.
6. To resolve disputes about a child's special education, all state and local education agencies must make available a mediation process. Participation in mediation, however, is voluntary.
7. All children with disabilities, even if expelled or placed on long-term suspension, are entitled to educational services that meet the standards of a free and appropriate public education.

Local Implementation of IDEA

Each state developed its own laws, rules, and regulations for carrying out the intentions of IDEA. Clinicians must become familiar with the guidelines used in their state, county, and specific school systems. Although ADHD is not listed as a handicapping condition, knowledge of the law is essential to understand what can be done. Because many children with ADHD also have learning disabilities, clinicians also should know how to get help for these disabilities. Let's look at the several steps in the process established by this law:

1. *Search.* Each school system must have a system for seeking out students who might have a disability.
2. *Data collection.* Once a student with a potential problem is identified, a system should be in place for collecting information and designing an evaluation process.
3. *Evaluation.* A comprehensive, multidisciplinary evaluation should be conducted.
4. *Conference.* Parents or guardians should meet with school personnel and evaluation professionals to review the evaluation conclusions,

any labels or diagnoses established, and any proposed placement and IEP. Details should be presented in writing.

5. *Parent's decision process.* Parents or guardians, in consultation with educational or other professionals and lawyers when needed, decide to accept, request clarification of, request changes to, or reject the proposed placement and IEP.

6. *Appeals process.* If parents reject the label, placement recommendation, or IEP, an appeals process should be available that starts with the local school system and can go to the county or state level.

7. *Follow-up progress reports.* Progress reports should be provided to the family. As the end of the school year approaches, a reassessment is done. A conference should be held to plan for the next school year. Steps 5 and 6 are repeated before implementing the next year's plans.

Search.   A parent may contact a clinician because someone from their school system suggested that their child be evaluated. Alternatively, if a child who is seeing a psychiatrist shows clinical evidence of a problem, the psychiatrist can instruct the parents to initiate the search process. The contact is the principal of the neighborhood school the child would or does go to. A letter from a professional, including a description of any testing already done, helps parents in their effort to initiate this step. The parents should include a formal note requesting an evaluation.

Under federal guidelines, if a written request is made to the principal, he or she must call a meeting of essential people within 30 working days to consider this request. Usually the school psychologist, special education teacher, and classroom teacher attend this meeting, which the principal chairs. This meeting usually is called an Education Management Team (EMT) meeting, although terms vary around the country.

At this meeting, the request will be reviewed. If the team agrees to do the evaluation, parents will be asked to sign a release for such testing. If the team does not agree to do an evaluation or suggests observing the child for several months first, parents can accept this decision or can appeal it to a higher level.

Data collection.   Once school personnel agree to conduct an evaluation, specific observations and studies are made. It is helpful for the clinician to communicate with the school professionals, clarifying concerns and suggesting areas to be assessed.

Evaluation. School systems are required to have a multidisciplinary team available to evaluate preschoolers who need assessment. In most school systems, this program is called *Child Find.*

Conference. School personnel and special educators will meet with the parents. Parents may also bring professional consultants to review the results and recommendations and to advise them. Parents are entitled to receive written copies of each evaluation before the meeting so that they can have their consultants review them and advise them.

Clinicians should advise parents that angry, defensive, or demanding behavior will not facilitate the process. They need to assume that everyone there has the best interest of their child at heart. In reality, this is true of more than most school conferences. These school personnel want to do what is best for the child or adolescent.

Remember, ADHD is not listed in IDEA. Later in this chapter, I discuss other ways by which the child with ADHD can be included under IDEA. Parents whose children also have a learning disability must consider special issues when trying to obtain services. For school professionals, the question is not whether the child has a learning disability. The question is whether he or she is eligible for services. Each school system has a definition of eligibility based on a *discrepancy formula,* that is, a way to determine how far behind the child or adolescent has to be in what areas to qualify for services.

Parents have to consent to several processes. First, they will have to agree to the diagnosis or label (code) that the professionals recommend. Second, they will have to agree to the level and type of services to be provided and to the placement recommendations. These recommendations will be written in the proposed IEP. Only when the parents agree to and sign the IEP can actions be taken. No school system can act without a parent's consent.

Clinicians can help parents make a decision about coding when more than one diagnostic code is used. I find it helpful to clarify the difference between an emotional problem that causes academic difficulties and an emotional problem that is caused by academic difficulties. If the child or adolescent with whom the clinician is working has behavior problems that are caused by the frustrations and failures experienced because of ADHD and/or a learning disability, the clinician should not be too quick to agree to having him or her labeled only as *emotionally disturbed.* If school personnel insist that the individual has ADHD, a learning disability, and/or an emotional disorder, they may be correct. In advising the parents on a decision, the clinician should consider this possibility. If the individual is coded as having a learning disability as the primary diagnosis and as being emotionally disturbed as the secondary diagnosis, the placement will be in a program for students with learning disabilities with supportive psychological help. If he or she is coded as being emotionally disturbed as the primary diagnosis and as having a learning disability as the secondary diagnosis, the placement will be in a program for students with emotional disorders with supportive special education help for the learning disabilities. Which approach do you believe would be best for this child or adolescent? The primary label is critical.

School systems are responsible for placing a child in an appropriate program within their system. Only if this is not possible will the system consider an out-of-system or private placement. Parents may prefer that their child go into a particular private program; however, the school does not have to concur if an appropriate placement is available within its own system. Parents might argue that the private placement is better, and this might be true. But even if it were, the law states only that each child must receive an appropriate education, not necessarily the best education possible.

Several program levels of service are available. The task is to find the least restrictive program that still provides the most effective educational support for the child. This does not always mean being in a regular class program. The least restrictive environment for some children might be the most restrictive environment available. A child may need the security and support of a small, separate, self-contained classroom in order to feel safe enough to relax, take risks again, and become available for learning.

What about the IEP? This is the written plan identifying the instruction designed especially for a child, listing reasonable expectations for the child's achievement. A specific system should be in place for monitoring progress. At a minimum, each IEP must cover the following points:

1. A statement of the child's levels of educational performance
2. A statement of annual goals or achievements expected for each area of identified weakness by the end of the school year
3. Short-term objectives stated in instructional terms that are the steps leading to mastery of these annual goals
4. A statement of the specific special education and support services to be provided to the child
5. A statement of the extent to which a child will be able to participate in regular education programs and justification for any special placement recommendations
6. Projected dates for initiation of services and the anticipated duration of the services
7. A statement of the criteria and evaluation procedures to be used in determining, on at least an annual basis, whether short-term objectives are being achieved

In addition to an appropriate placement and IEP, the child or adolescent may need other services, called *related services*. They are to be provided to the family at no expense; they are usually provided through the school system by school professionals. Related services are defined as

> transportation and such developmental, corrective, and other supportive services (including speech pathology and audiology, psychological services, physical and occupational therapy, recreation, and medical counseling services, except that such medical services shall be for diagnostic and evaluation purposes only) as may be required to assist a handicapped child to benefit from special education, . . . [including] the early identification and assessment of handicapping conditions in children.

Parents' decision process. After the conference, parents are entitled to a full transcript of the meeting. They can also get copies of all tests that were done. The placement and the IEP recommendations also must be provided in writing. Parents can agree to the recommendations and sign the IEP, or they can initiate an appeals process.

Appeals process. The appeals process differs in each state and local school system. Each school system is to provide parents with written step-by-step guidelines for the appeals process. Many school systems require a mediation process first. Here, parents and appropriate school personnel meet with a competent and neutral person who tries to resolve the differences. Only if this mediation process fails may a parent start the formal appeals process.

The final step in the appeals process is a meeting between parents and their school system before a hearing officer, a professional knowledgeable about school law and school procedures. The hearing officer is not employed by the school system; he or she acts independently. Both sides present their arguments. Often the decisions are based on the needs of the child and on procedures of law. The officer's decision is binding. If a parent loses at this level, the only other option is to appeal under civil law (i.e., under the Americans With Disabilities Act). This process involves the court system and might take years.

The appeals process may go quickly, or it may take months. In most school systems, the child or adolescent is placed in the program proposed by the school system until the appeals process is complete.

Implementation of the IEP. Clinicians should advise parents to monitor the program when implemented. They should be sure the placement, the teacher, the related services, the composition of the class, and the implementation steps for the IEP are correct and in operation. They should ask about any apparent departures from the approved plan.

Parents need to be sure that the regular classroom teachers are aware of any special needs or programs and accommodations. They should check to determine whether the regular and special education personnel are interacting with one another.

Programs begun in September may get changed or diluted as the year progresses and the caseload increases for each professional involved. Parents should ask their child to keep them informed, or they should check for themselves. Does each professional see the child for the amount of time specified in the IEP? Are more children being added to the program time during which this youngster receives services? One hour of one-to-one support twice a week might become 30 minutes twice a week in a group of three to five other children. Parents must know their child's IEP and insist that he or she gets what is promised. No changes can be made without written notification and parent concurrence.

Services for Students With ADHD

Unfortunately, ADHD is not listed as a handicapping condition under education law, that is, under IDEA (see Chapter 13 for more on this issue). The student with ADHD can be classified under IDEA if he or she is found to have a learning disability or to be seriously emotionally disturbed. The third option is to code the student under the category, "other health impaired." The advantage of getting the student coded under IDEA is that the school system must provide services and accommodations.

The other option, as discussed in Chapter 13, is to use civil law (i.e., Section 504). Most school systems have *504 Plans* for students with ADHD. The problem is that civil law requires that the school system provide only accommodations. Services are not required. For this reason, parent organizations continue to fight to have ADHD listed under IDEA.

Summary

Clinicians working with children and adolescents who have ADHD must understand the laws that determine whether these individuals receive needed services. Parents must be active as advocates to get the care their children need. The clinician must educate parents and must be available to assist them in their interactions with the school system.

Part 6

Conclusions

Chapter 19

Conclusions

Attention-deficit/hyperactivity disorder (ADHD) is a life disability, affecting all aspects of an individual's life. For many individuals, it is also a lifetime disability. As with other chronic developmental disorders, the consequences of not recognizing, diagnosing, and fully treating ADHD can be extensive. Each stage of psychological and social development can be affected, as can academic success, self-esteem, and positive peer interactions. The resulting emotional, social, and family problems can become as great a disability for the adult as is the primary disability of ADHD. The secondary academic underachievement can affect the individual's career choice and his or her future success with work. Such an effect influences both work happiness and future income.

The early recognition, diagnosis, and start of treatment interventions is essential. Missing the diagnosis or not properly treating ADHD can result in a lifetime of difficulties. Parents need to understand ADHD and to be alert to the needs of their child. Health and mental health professionals must be aware of ADHD and their essential role in recognizing, diagnosing, and treating the disorder.

It is equally important to recognize the related emotional and neurologically based disorders so that these problems can be addressed. The secondary social and peer problems must be addressed. If having a family member with ADHD has resulted in family problems, these problems must be handled.

Unless the total individual is understood and helped, progress might be limited. A complete evaluation should be done. Looking only for ADHD might result in a missed learning disability or other related disorder. Seeing the surface emotional problems as the diagnosis will result in minimal success in treating these problems.

Treatment must be multimodal. The first step involves parent and individual education and counseling. Then, specific behavioral management or social skills help might be needed. The use of appropriate medications, managed correctly, is essential. Additional individual, behavioral, group, and/or family therapy might be necessary. Throughout all of these efforts, clinicians and parents must work closely with the school system.

It is hoped that the information in this book helps you to be effective in working with individuals who have ADHD.

Appendix: Resources

Organizations Related to Attention-Deficit/Hyperactivity Disorder

Children and Adults With Attention Deficit Disorder (CHADD)
499 N.W. 70th Avenue
Suite 101
Plantation, Florida 33317
Voice: (800) 223-4050
Fax: (954) 587-4599
Web site: http://www.chadd.org

CHADD is a national alliance of parent organizations that provides information and support to parents of individuals with this disorder.

National Attention Deficit Disorder Association (ADDA)
9930 Johnnycake Ridge Road
Suite 3E
Mentor, Ohio 44060
Voice: (440) 350-9595
Web site: http://www.add.org

ADDA is a national alliance of support groups that provides referrals and information to parents and to support groups.

Organizations Related to Learning Disabilities

Learning Disabilities Association of America, Inc. (LDA)
4156 Library Road
Pittsburgh, Pennsylvania 15234
Voice: (412) 341-1515
Fax: (412) 344-0224
Web site: http://www.ldanatl.org

LDA, formerly called the Association for Children With Learning Disabilities, is a national parent association with state and local chapters. Membership is open to parents and professionals. Through a network of national, state, and local programs, parents receive educational programs, parent advocacy advice, and support systems for individuals with learning disabilities throughout the life span.

International Dyslexia Association (IDA)
8600 LaSalle Road
Suite 382
Baltimore, Maryland 21286
Voice: (410) 296-0232 or (800) 222-3123
Fax: (410) 321-5069
Web site: http://www.interdys.org

IDA, formerly called the Orton Dyslexia Society, is for parents and professionals. The primary focus is on individuals with dyslexia, also called a language-based learning disability.

Council for Exceptional Children
1920 Association Drive
Reston, Virginia 20191
Voice: (703) 620-3660 or (800) 845-6232
Fax: (703) 264-9494
Web site: http://www.cec.sped.org

The Council for Exceptional Children is a branch of the National Education Association for educators in special education. The Division on Learning Disabilities is the specific group within the council concerned with learning disabilities.

National Center for Learning Disabilities
381 Park Avenue South
Suite 1401
New York, New York 10016
Voice: (212) 545-7510
Fax: (212) 545-9665
Web site: http://www.ncld.org

The National Center for Learning Disabilities is a foundation-like organization with extensive fundraising efforts. This money is used to further public education on learning disabilities and for specific areas of research. Information is provided to parents and professionals.

Professional Organizations

American Academy of Child and Adolescent Psychiatry
3615 Wisconsin Avenue, N.W.
Washington, DC 20016
(202) 966-7300
Web site: http://www.aacap.org

American Academy of Ophthalmology
P.O. Box 7424
San Francisco, California 94120
(415) 561-8500
Web site: http://www.eyenet.org

American Academy of Optometry
6110 Executive Boulevard
Suite 506
Rockville, Maryland 20852
(301) 984-1441
Web site: http://www.aaopt.org

American Academy of Pediatrics
P.O. Box 927
141 Northwest Point Boulevard
Elk Grove Village, Illinois 60007
(847) 228-5005
Web site: http://www.aap.org

American Medical Association
515 N. State Street
Chicago, Illinois 60610
(312) 464-5000
Web site: http://www.ama-assn.org

American Occupational Therapy Association
4720 Montgomery Lane
Bethesda, Maryland 20814
(301) 652-2682
Web site: http://www.aota.org

American Psychiatric Association
1400 K Street, N.W.
Washington, DC 20005
(202) 682-6000
Web site: http://www.psych.org

American Psychological Association
750 First Street, N.E.
Washington, DC 20002
(202) 336-5500
Web site: http://www.apa.org

American Speech-Language-Hearing Association
10801 Rockville Pike
Rockville, Maryland 20852
(301) 897-5700 or (800) 498-2071
Web site: http://www.asha.org

National Association of School Psychologists
4340 East West Highway
Suite 402
Bethesda, Maryland 20814
Web site: http://www.naspweb.org

National Association of Social Workers
750 First Street, N.E.
Suite 700
Washington, DC 20002
(202) 408-8600
Web site: http://www.naswdc.org

Sensory Integration International
1402 Cravens Avenue
Torrance, California 90501

Legal Organizations

Children's Defense Fund
25 E Street, N.W.
Washington, DC 20001
(202) 628-8787
Web site: http://www.childrensdefense.org

Many law schools have special units or programs offering reference materials or counsel on children with disabilities. If parents or their attorney need such help, they should contact their nearest law school and find out what assistance they offer. The following national programs may be of help or may provide a local resource.

Disability Legal Support Center
American Bar Association
1800 M Street, N.W.
Washington, DC 20036
(202) 662-1570
Web site: http://www.abanet.org

| Other Organizations

The National Information Center for Children and Youth With Disabilities (NICHCY)

P.O. Box 1492
Washington, DC 20013
Voice: (202) 884-8200 or (800) 695-0285
Fax: (202) 884-8441
Web site: http://www.nichcy.org

NICHCY provides extensive information and literature on all areas of disability.

Index

*Page numbers printed in **boldface** type refer to tables or figures.*